Kaj Granlund & Will Graves

The Gray Wolf Revealed

2. Edition 2019

Front cover: Photo by Kaj Granlund

Back cover: Photo by Daniel Mott

Contact: Kaj Granlund

wolf@granlund.eu

ISBN 978-952-94-1352-2

FOREWORDS

Until the late 1960s, the wolf was regarded as an unwanted beast and was killed on sight. However, a decade later, the pro-wolf movement initiated a global campaign to get wolf conservation on the agenda—a process where it was necessary to plug a new illusion into people's minds, play with emotions, grab the public's attention, and put pressure on governments. This process was, in the pro-wolf movement's own words, a dramatic success.

Some thirty years later, the focus has changed from saving the wolves to reintegrating them into landscapes inhabited by humans, and the goal is to make people accept the presence of wolves as a natural and integral part of our modern landscape. A Norwegian researcher representing the pro-wolf movement wrote,

> *There is one thing that human experience has taught us and that is the need for an honest and objective view of our own history.*

> *After all—our desire to get wildness back into our landscapes is what motivates us to conserve wolves.*

This is where our book enters the scene. We don't deny anybody the right to have a desire, but when pro-wolf actions harass the life of rural people, an objective (at least another) view of our own history is needed in order to avoid repeating mistakes from past generations. The cornerstone lies in the fact that humans are potential prey to all large carnivores, and evolutionary psychologists have made a good case that we are pretty well hard-wired to identify predators, beginning at an age when we have barely learned to speak.

We have learned from history that without controls, humans and wolves cannot coexist and wolves became a problem where humans were disarmed and the wolves were free to multiply.

During past centuries, the lack of firearms is what disarmed the humans; now it is the legislation and wolves' total protection.

Kaj Granlund & Will Graves

TABLE OF CONTENTS

Forewords 3

INTRODUCTION

The Wolf—Historical View..12
   The Lucky Wolf...12
   Wolves in Russia 12
   Tsar Alexander II 14
   Fighting Wolves in Europe 14
   Exterminating Wolves in North America 15
   Russia Failed – The Wolf Survived 16
      The Second Period of Wolf Abundance 17
      The Third Period of Wolf Abundance 17
      The Fourth Period of Wolf Abundance 17
      The Fifth Period of Wolf Abundance 18
   What Should We Learn from Russia?..18
      The Growing Wolf Population 19
      Wolves in Kazakhstan 20
   Population Management Through the Ages 21
      Moraskallet 1854 23
      Wolf Hunting in Russia 23
      Professional Siberian Wolf Hunters 23
      Summary 23
The Beloved Wolf 25
   Experiencing the Thrill...25
   Humanizing Animals 26
   Sliding on the Slope 27
   Human and Animal Rights...28

THE WOLF'S RANGE AND APPEARANCE

Geographic Distribution 30
   The Wolves Out There 31
   United States and Canada...33
      Arctic Wolf 33
      Eastern Wolf...34
      Timber Wolf 35
      Mexican Gray Wolf 36
      Northern Rocky Mountain Wolf...37
   Wolves in Europe and Asia 37
      Eurasian Wolf...38

Tundra Wolf 40
Altai Gray Wolf 41
Steppe Wolf 41
Iberian Wolf 42
The Italian Wolf 43
The Pelage Structure and Color Setting 45
The Guard Hairs..45
The Undercoat...45
The Colors of Wolf..46
Regional Variations in Color Settings..48
Young Wolves..50
The Wolf's Posture and Trail 50
The Wolf on the Move 51
What Does the Trail Tell Us? 53
The Paw Print of a Wolf 54
The Wolf's Body 57
Anatomical Aspects 58
The Skeleton 59
Craniometry and the Wolf's Skull 60
The Wolf's Tail 65
The Wolf's Legs 66
Wolves' Senses...69
Eyes and Vision...70
Ears and Hearing..71
Sense of Smell 73
The Wolf's Age 74
The Wolf's Cognitive Capabilities 74
The Wolf and the Dog...74
Intelligence, Causality, Or Conditioned Behavior...76

WOLF'S BEHAVIOR

The Wolf Pack...78
The Pack and Its Organization...78
Who Is the Leader? 78
Life Within a Pack...79
The Composition of a Wolf Pack 80
Communication Between Wolves 82
Dominance and Submission...82
Scent Marking and Urination 83
The Wolf's Tail 85
Wolf Vocalizations..85

The Territory 86
    The Size of the Territory 87
The wolf's Hunting 89
  Introduction 89
  Hunting 90
    Learning How to Hunt 90
    Hunting Strategies 91
    Surplus Killing 96
    Discovering New Prey Animals 97
  The Impact of Wolves on Nature 98
  Wolves, Livestock, and Coexistence 101
    We Should Have Known Better 104
  Wolves Hunting Wolves 107
  Summary 108
The Wolves' Four Seasons 109
  Wolf Wedding 109
    The Alpha Pair 110
  The Pack's Spring 111
  The Wolves' Summer 112
    Feeding the Litter 112
    Howling with Wolves 114
    Caring for Their Cubs 114
    Summary 115
  Wolf's Life in Autumn 115
    The Pack's Autumn Hunting 116
    Wolves' Pelage Changes 116
    Wolves Attacking Hunting Dogs 117
    Summary 119
  Winter and Starvation 119
    Feeding on Carrion 121
    The Pack Dissolves 121

HUMAN AND WOLF

A History of Attacks 124
  Attacks on Facts 124
  What Do We Know About Wolf Attacks On Humans 125
    Digging into History 125
    France 126
    Italy 129
    Germany 132
    Finland 133

Russia in the Nineteenth Century 135
Research by Sergei Korytin 136
Russia in the Twentieth Century 140
The World in the Twenty First Century 141
About Attacks on Humans 144
Mature Age and General Aggression 144
The Ring Game 146
Don't Show Debility 147
Don't Show Fear 148
It Was a Rabid Wolf 148
The Lore of The Harmless Wolf 148
Wolves Continue Attacking Humans 149
Wolves in Iran 150
Child Lifting and Wolves in India 151
What We Learned from History 151
Habituated Wolves 153
The Kenton Carnegie Case 154
The Myth Must Survive 158
Wolves Don't Kill Humans 158
The Verdict 159
The United States Against Europe and Asia 160
Countering An Attack 161
Fast as a Lightning 161
The 92–lb. Concrete Bag 161
Neophobia 162
The Wolf Is a Coward 163
What If? 163
On the Horseback 165
Protecting Livestock 166
Livestock Protection 166
Traditional Fences 166
Concrete Walls and Nets of Steel 167
Electric Fences 168
Confining Livestock Every Night 169
Livestock Guard Dogs 170
Fladry–A Proposed Solution 171
The Ultimate Solution – Culling Wolves 171
The Habitats Directive and Wolf–Livestock Conflict 172
Conservation And Wolf Management 175
Wolves and Conservation 176
The Sandpit 176

Information About Wolves is Classified 177
And the Final Confession 178
Rewilding The Western World 180
The Urban Solution 181
The New Nature Is on the Way 181
Serengeti 181
An Open–Air Zoo 182
When Extreme Religion Turns into Terror 184
We Communicate with Wolves 185
Wolves Habituate to Humans 186
Summary 188
Yellowstone Exposed 189
Introduction 190
A Basket of Wishes and Clashes 191
The Reintroduction 192
With the Wolves Comes the Diseases 193
Wolf Reintroduction Changes Ecosystem 194
Summary 195

WOLVES AND MONGRELS

Is The Wolf An Extinct Species 198
Wolf–Dog Crossbreeds 198
Evolution Through Hybridization 199
Introgression 199
How They Interbreed 201
Male Wolf and Female Dog 201
Female Wolf and Male Dog 201
Humans in the Middle 201
My Wolf Genetics Explained 203
Species ID 203
Color Locus E 203
Color Locus K 203
Color Locus A 204
Color Locus S 204
Curly 204
Ears 206
Summary 207
How Do We Know These are Wolves? 207
Challenges in Wolf Identification with DNA 207
Humans Altering Evolution 209
The Red Wolf 209

The Eastern Wolf 210
Does Protection Work Against Nature? 211
Siberian Wolves 212
Summary 212
Variations In Phenotype 213
Genotype vs. Phenotype 214
How to Recognize Introgression 214
The Tail 214
The Head 215
Paw Prints Reveal Ancestry 217
New Species Showing Up 219
The Jackal 219
The Coywolf 219
Federal Border Guards 220
Summary 221

DISEASES AND PARASITES

Wolves, Dogs, And Diseases 224
Canine Parvovirus 224
Canine Distemper 224
Sarcoptic Mange 225
Threats to Humans 226
Rabies 227
Wolves and Rabies 227
Other Sources of Transmission 229
Post-Exposure Actions 229
Why the Wolf? 230
Echinococcus 231
Echinococcus Granulosus 232
Echinococcus Granulosus Life Cycle 233
Echinococcus Granulosus Eggs in Nature 235
Echinococcus Granulosus and Human Welfare 236
Treatment of Echinococcosis 236
Physical and Medical Impacts 237
Prevention—Know the Disease 237
Prevalence of Echinococcus Among Wolves 238
Cystic Echinococcosis and Livestock 239
Economic Losses Related to Wolves 240
Summary 242
Taenia 243
Taeniasis 243

Definitive Host..245
Intermediate Host 245
Cysticerosis 245
    Wolves and Taenia 246
    Infection 246
Prevention 248
Neospora Caninum...249
    Zoonotic Aspects of N. caninum 249
Host Range 249
Life Cycle and Transmission...249
    It Starts with the Wolf, Coyote, or Dog 249
    Oocysts 250
Bovine and N. caninum 250
    Diagnosis of Bovine Abortion 251
    Treatment and control 251

HUNTING WOLVES

Introduction 254
Battue–Drive Hunting with Fladry 254
Winter Hunting with Pskovites 256
    Preparing for the Hunt 256
    The Beaters 257
    The Shooters 258
Hunting with Nets 258
Hunting With Carrion..259
Hunting with Eagles and Falcons 261
Trapping Wolves 262
    The Collarum™ Trap...264
Hunting with Wolfhounds 265
Hunting with Pigs...266
Scouting for Wolves and Finding Dens 267
Hunting with Wolf Pits 269
Hunting with Poison...269
Hunting Wolves from Light Aircraft 271
    The Hunt..272
Summary...273

BEHIND THE BOOK

Section I – Scholars Behind the Curtain...276
Section II – References 278
Section III – Internet links 287
Section IV – Obsolete Russian Units of Measurement...288

INTRODUCTION

Lev Tolstoi wrote in 1864. A Wolf wanted to pick a sheep out of a flock, and stepped into the wind, so that the dust of the flock might blow on him.

The Sheep Dog saw him, and said: "There is no sense, Wolf, in your walking in the dust: it will make your eyes ache." But the Wolf said: "The trouble is, Doggy, that my eyes have been aching for quite awhile, and I have been told that the dust from a flock of sheep will cure the eyes."

THE WOLF—HISTORICAL VIEW

Ever since I wrote my first paper about the gray wolf (*The Grey Wolf Preserved to Extinction*) I have been criticized for relying on Russian science rather than relying on all the state-of-the-art research produced during this century. Now with genetics brought into the wolf debate, the average man has no means to present an opinion in this debate. Further, as science dives deeper into itself, scientific reports are written to be understood by scientists, not by the public urgently needing facts and not scientific rhetorics.

The Lucky Wolf

Approximately 11,000 years ago, a variety of animals went extinct across North America. These were mostly large mammals, and some of these animals are well known to us as, for instance, the saber-toothed cats. Scientists studying the extinction have identified three major mechanisms that may have caused the extinction.

- Over-hunting by the Clovis people—the original immigrants.

- Climate change such as the one we are experiencing right now.

- A highly infectious hyper-disease.

Until the late Pleistocene wolves were just one of many large predators, but they were lucky. The late Pleistocene Extinction killed off the wolves' natural enemies, the great cats and predacious bears. The wolf was now freed from predation by the large cats and predacious bears. Thus, it was free to multiply and disperse (Geist 2016b).

Neanderthal people did kill wolves (Klein 1973), but wolves in central and northern Eurasia did not decline dramatically until the arrival of modern humans there some 40,000 years ago (Fan et al. 2016).

It appears that the conflict with gray wolves began right there, and has continued ever since (Graves 2007; Moriceau 2014).

Wolves in Russia

In order to describe the wolf and its behavior, we need to go back to Russia and its long history in fighting against wolves. The advantage of research and reports written by Russian researchers is that they have their origin in actual statistics, real events, and a huge amount of work in the field. This is far more than any researcher can present in our world.

Today, we use GPS-based tracking devices while we sit in front of our screens and watch the small dots, each representing one wolf moving around on the map in front of us. So-called authentic wolf experiences are available at commercial hides, where it is possible to photograph the spectacular wildlife show of (excessively fed) bears and domesticated wolves playing with each other in front of the cameras.

An old Russian proverb says: "A wolf sheds its coat every year, but its nature never changes."

Russia is the world's largest nation, with borders reaching from European and Asian countries to the Pacific and Arctic oceans. The country covers more than one-eighth of the Earth's inhabited land area, and its landscape ranges from tundra and forests to subtropical beaches. The ancestors of modern Russians were the Slavic tribes, whose original home is thought by some scholars to have been the wooded areas of the Pinsk Marshes. From the seventh century onwards, the East Slavs constituted the bulk of the population in Western Russia.

In 1547, Grand Duke Ivan IV was officially crowned the first Tsar of Russia. Under Peter the Great, Russia was proclaimed an Empire in 1721 and became recognized as a world power. Three years later, on 8 February 1724, the Russian Academy of Sciences was established, and since 1904, nineteen Nobel Prize laureates have been affiliated with the Academy.

In that era, when wolf killed livestock, domestic fowl, and dogs, they deprived peasants of the main achievements of their poor and difficult lives. The loss of a milk cow or a few sheep meant hardship for entire families, even starvation (Hoensbroech 1952). Yet in Czarist Russia, the peasants were almost defenseless against the wolves, lacking effective weapons such as, for instance, firearms.

The Russians have experienced wolves in almost every conceivable combination of climate and habitat and in combinations with numerous wild game species and domestic animals. Wolves have met people in towns, villages, farms, forests, semi-deserts, mountains, tundra, taiga, steppes, and in areas with few human inhabitants.

The Russian literature is filled with stories of wolves attacking and killing peasants and their livestock. Tolstoy, Chekhov, Nerkrasov, Vavilov, Bunin, Lazarevskij, Sabaneev, Stolpyanskij, and others wrote of these events. This, in turn, is the main reason why

Russians during the past centuries have conducted countless research projects about the impact of wolves on livestock and game populations.

Tsar Alexander II

Alexander II (1818–1881) was the Emperor of Russia from 2 March 1855 until his assassination on 13 March 1881. He was also the King of Poland and the Grand Duke of Finland. Alexander II was responsible for several large reforms, including reorganizing the judicial system, setting up elected local judges, abolishing corporal punishment, promoting local self-government through the Zemstvo system, imposing universal military service, ending some privileges of the nobility, and promoting research and university education.

Initiated by the Tsar, the Russian Government began to collect information about wolf depredation on livestock in Russia. In 1873, the Ministry of Interior reported that in forty-five of the Russian Provinces wolves killed 179,000 head of cattle and 562,000 head of small livestock; in the Ostzejskij Region, 1,011 cattle and 3,440 small livestock; in the ten provinces of Czarist Poland 2,700 large and 8,635 small livestock (Lazarevski 1876). This corresponds to an estimated loss of seven and a half million rubles, and yet the reported losses were thought to be much lower than actual losses, which did not include losses of domestic fowl and dogs.

Much additional information was collected and published by Lazarevski. His publication was the first attempt to systematically describe the wolf problem and propose solutions to it. At the same time, Leonid P. Sabaneev published his book, containing detailed information about wolves and their damage to the Russian economy. This book is considered to be the first scientific book about wolves in Russia (Sabaneev 1876).

Both Sabaneev and Lazarevski supported a total extermination of the wolves in Russia by the use of poison.

Fighting Wolves in Europe

As early as 46 to 120 AD, the first wolf bounty was reportedly opened when Solon of Athens offered five silver drachmas to a hunter for killing any male wolf, and one drachma was offered for every female (Mech & Boitani 2001).

The extermination of Northern Europe's wolves became an organized effort during the Middle Ages and continued until the nineteenth century. Large-scale wolf hunting became successful after strychnine was discovered in 1818 and firearms became widespread weapons in wolf hunting (Granlund 2016).

From the bounties in escalins paid in Flanders and Brabant since 1397, and possibly before, to the rewards in maravedís paid in the Region of Murcia starting in the fourteenth century, bounty was paid based upon the size of the animal (tallas de fieras). In many villages in the Principality of Asturias in the eighteenth century, the bounty was what encouraged people to hunt wolves.

In Sweden and Finland, a wolf bounty was introduced in 1647 after wolves had exterminated moose and reindeer populations and were forced to feed on livestock.

In the beginning of the nineteenth century, bounties of fifteen florins for a wolf cub and twenty florins for an adult wolf were paid in Austria. The Swiss canton of Tessin paid forty francs for a wolf. In 1818, France paid eighteen francs for a pregnant female wolf, fifteen francs for a male, and six francs for a cub (Lazarevski 1876).

Wolf hunting in France was institutionalized by Charlemagne between 800 and 813, when he established a special corps of wolf hunters called *louveterie*, whose purpose was to control wolf populations in France during the Middle Ages. In the beginning of the nineteenth century, there were still more than 10,000 wolves in France, and the wolf hunt continued. In 1883, up to 1,386 wolves were shot and many more poisoned by the special corps. This office is known today as the Royal Wolfcatcher (*louvetier royal*).

In France, wolves were wiped out between 1882 and 1930. The last reward for killing a wolf that had attacked a human was granted in 1896, and the last reported attack on a human took place in 1918. The last time a bounty was placed on a wolf was in 1927, in the French department of Cantal.

At the beginning of the twentieth century, the wolf was successfully exterminated from most of the northern European countries. In the Mediterranean area, wolves were found in Italy and Spain, and in the Eastern-European countries, stable populations survived.

Exterminating Wolves in North America

On the state of Montana's official website (Montana 2018), there is a short historical review about wolves in Montana in the nineteenth century. Between 1871 and 1875, an estimated 34,000 wolves were killed in northern Montana and southern Alberta, Canada. As the cattle industry rose in prominence, the territorial government began paying bounties for wolves, coyotes, and other predators. By the end of the 1880s, the total extermination of wolves became a goal of ranchers—one that was finally achieved by government-salaried hunters in the 1920s.

Below are some key dates from the above source.

1883 – Territorial legislature offers a $1 bounty for a full wolf skin. At the end of 1884, the treasury reports paying bounties for 5,540 wolves, 1,774 coyotes, 568 bears, and 146 mountain lions.

1887 – Bounty claims are so numerous, the territory can no longer afford to pay them, and bounty laws are repealed.

1899 – Under pressure from stock growers, bounties on cattle predators are reinstated, funded by a new tax on livestock.

1905 – The latest bounty pays $10 per full-grown wolf scalp. Because an immature animal cannot kill cattle as efficiently as an adult, the bounty per pup is only $3.

The wolf was persecuted in most of the states where they came in conflict with human activities.

Ironically, the pro wolf movement that initiated the reintroduction of wolves into Yellowstone did not care for nature but, rather, cared for the possibility to listen to the wolves' howling in the Park. They reintroduced the Canadian gray timber wolf, *Canis lupus occidentalis*, also known as the Alaskan tundra wolf. The original wolf inhabiting the geography of the Park was a much smaller animal, called the Rocky Mountain wolf or *Canis lupus irremotus*. From Yellowstone and Northern Idaho, the invasive timber wolf has spread to many US States.

Russia Failed – The Wolf Survived

While Western Europe and the United States succeeded in exterminating most of their local wolf populations, Russia failed. During the first period of wolf eruption in the 1870s, the number of wolves had risen to cause significant damage to the national economy. Wolves were destroying about six million rubles' worth of domestic cattle annually.

The Czarist government organized a number of programs, which in time, lowered the number of wolves to an acceptable number, and losses of domestic livestock, game animals, and attacks on humans declined. Then the Czarist government relaxed its wolf control programs because the country was moving toward revolution and civil war, and the wolf population shot upward (Graves 2007).

The Second Period of Wolf Abundance

The second period of a large increase in wolf numbers was during World War I, 1914—1918, and the years shortly thereafter. During these years, the government paid little attention to the wolf population. The wolf population was increasing, and in just one year, from 1924 to 1925, wolves killed about one million head of cattle which was about 0.5% of all the cattle in the entire USSR. The losses to wolves were especially heavy in the Volga area, where 2.2% of all cattle were destroyed by wolves (Graves 2007).

The Third Period of Wolf Abundance

The third period of high wolf abundance was during World War II. The wolf dominance in the war years was exceptionally threatening and created a dangerous situation in Soviet Russia as it was costing precious agricultural losses. The government had to once again take steps to reduce the wolf population. Following the war, there were 200,000 or more wolves inhabiting almost every region in the USSR. Some estimates put the wolf numbers as high as 240,000. These wolves caused large losses to the stressed economy, and as in previous periods of wolf abundance in numerous areas of the USSR, the wolves also attacked humans. There were documented cases of wolves eating humans. The fight to control wolf numbers started in 1945, immediately after the end of World War II. Wolf hunting brigades were formed and began to hunt and trap wolves. In 1946, they culled 62,600 wolves, and the Russians also started to use aircraft to hunt wolves in 1946. More about this in Chapter 7.

However, it was only at the beginning of the 1960s that their relentless fight against wolves started to have an effect, and the number of wolves decreased significantly (Graves 2007).

The Fourth Period of Wolf Abundance

The fourth period of excessive wolf abundance began about 1978, following relaxation of efforts to cull wolves. In just five years, the numbers of wolves doubled in the Ukraine, Belarus, and central areas of the RSFSR. After reading Mowat's *Never Cry Wolf*, some Russians began thinking that wolves were the sanitarians of nature, and the public started to believe that wolves should not be culled, but protected. Mowat wrote that wolves never kill for fun and that he knew of no valid evidence that wolves kill more than they can use, even when the rare opportunity to do so arises. Ignored were the countless documented accounts in Czarist and Soviet literature about wanton killing by wolves—surplus killing (Graves 2007)!

The Fifth Period of Wolf Abundance

The fifth period began in 1992 after the collapse of the USSR. There was an obvious change and disruption in the infrastructure of the entire country. Many wolf control programs were dropped, and often, bounties were stopped or reduced. It is certainly understandable that during this period of upheaval, there was a lack of attention to the wolf population. The numbers of wolves started to increase rapidly in many parts of the newly recognized Russian Federation and in some of the newly established republics, all of which had been part of the former USSR.

Figure 1.1. The Zemstvo dines (Painting by Grigoriy Myasoyedov).

The wolf population in the Russian Federation increased from 29,000 in 1987 to 42,000 in 1997, in just ten years. This increase is contributing to a substantial decline in moose numbers throughout the Russian Federation. Moose, other domestic hoofed animals, and hares make up about 76% of the wolf diet. Data shows that the significant reduction in the number of moose corresponds with the increase in wolf numbers. The moose population decreased by 33%, from 904,000 to 604,000 from 1988 and 1997. As result, the number of moose available to hunt and the numbers bagged by hunters is down by 33%—from 66,000 in 1991 to only 22,000 harvested in 1996 (Graves 2007).

What Should We Learn from Russia?

During five periods in the history of Czarist Russia, the former USSR, the Russian Federation, and the new republics of the former USSR, when governments reduced support for wolf culling, the wolf populations expanded rapidly. In each case, the result was an overpopulation of wolves, with serious predation on game and domestic animals.

Also, when wolves were not hunted, they became bold and entered villages—even towns—searching for food. Wolves would lose their normal fear of man and kill dogs, cats, geese, sheep, goats, and large livestock right under the noses of humans.

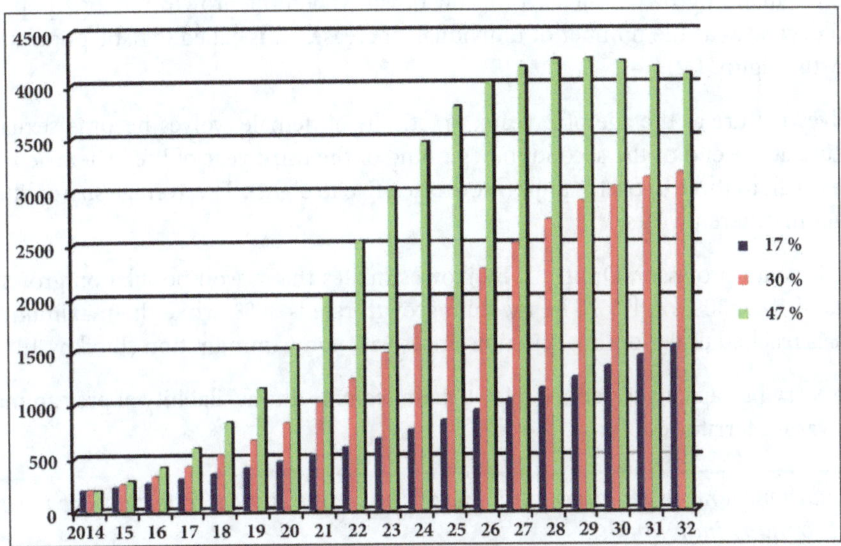

Figure 1.2. The logistic growth of a wolf population

There was also an increased risk of wolves encountering humans, some of which ended in tragedy. In Russia, the number of wolves was apparently not controlled by nature but only by human intervention. During each period, intervention had to be initiated and supported by governments in order to lower the number of wolves to a point where there would be little serious impacts on humans.

If, in the five specific periods during the history of Russia, nature did not control the number of wolves, then why should we in the West believe that nature would control the number of wolves in North America or Europe?

The Growing Wolf Population

A population is defined as a group of individuals of the same species living in the same area. The measurement of how the size of a population changes over time is called the population growth rate, and it depends upon the population size, birth rate, and death rate.

As long as there are enough resources available, there will be an increase in the number of individuals in a population over time, or what we call, a positive growth rate. However, most populations cannot continue to grow forever because they will eventually run out of water, food, space, or other resources. As these resources begin to run out, population growth will start to slow down. When the growth rate of a population decreases as the number of individuals increases, it is called logistic population growth (Figure 1.2).

Wolves mature at the age of 2 years; practically all female wolves become sexually mature at the end of the second to beginning of the third year of life. A female wolf gives birth to three to twelve pups (more often five to eight). The average size of litters varies in different years.

The Russian professor, Dmitry I. Bibikov estimates that a wolf population grows at rates of 17%, 30% or 47%. The medium growth rate is 30%, while the maximum of 47% is reached under optimal circumstances with some immigration (Bibikov 1985).

The carrying capacity is defined by two main factors—the availability of prey animals and vacant territories.

Populations tend to get larger until there is no longer enough food or space to support so many individuals.

The three growth curves in Figure 1.2 show the logistic growth where I used 4,500 as the carrying capacity. Instead of approaching the carrying capacity, the growing wolf population changes the carrying capacity as the number of prey animals starts to decline. This is why the curve does not follow the traditional S-shaped curve, but starts declining. Bernt Lindqvist describes this situation with a practical example in his report (Lindqvist 2008b).

Wolves in Kazakhstan

The rapid growth of wolves in Kazakhstan caused massive losses of the country's natural prey, the saiga antelope, and as these populations were declining, wolves started attacking farm animals such as cattle and sheep—and occasionally people. When the prey animals were gone, the wolf population started to decline, and soon, there were large areas totally emptied from both wolves and prey animals. In a conference held in Moscow on 23 February 2001, the president of Kazakhstan's wildlife management, Nicolai S. Paschinski, asked the audience

Do you really believe that true diversity in nature is a result of empty forests?

And he continued

Come and take a look how our invaluable populations of herbivores disappeared in a couple of years. After them the wolves disappeared and now we have nothing left.

Bernt Lindqvist presents similar results from Central Russia, where the moose population has declined to 0.006 individuals per 1,000 hectares (2,471 acres). This can be compared to other Northern European countries, where the moose population is between one and seven individuals per 1,000 hectares (Lindqvist 2008b).

Today, Kazakhstan is home to the world's largest population of wolves, with an estimation of 90,000 to 100,000 wolves. The source for this estimate is the Institute of Zoology of the Ministry of Science and Education of the Republic of Kazakhstan.

With its natural prey—namely as saiga antelope—in increasingly short supply, wolves are attacking more farm animals such as cattle and sheep—and occasionally, people. According to one study, wolves killed an estimated 150,000 domesticated animals in 1987 and 1988, mostly camels, cows, and sheep, and 14,000 wild animals, including bear, deer, ibexes, elk and bighorn sheep. Recently, there have been fifty attacks by rabid wolves on humans.

Population Management Through the Ages

There is a common belief that wolf populations are stable and humans are able to control the population sizes. This assumption is true up to a certain limit, but as long as there are enough prey animals, the wolf population keeps on growing at an exponential rate, after which human efforts to limit the population, by hunting, for instance, has a limited effect (Lindqvist 2008b).

David L. Mech wrote about this issue, saying (Mech 2017)

When a wolf population is low in numbers or distribution, human limitations by hunting, trapping, poaching, or livestock-depredation control can be effective. However, once a wolf population becomes well established and widely distributed, such techniques have limited impact.

Wolves are by far the most difficult mammals to hunt and to be successful, a well-organized hunt is time-consuming and may require up to one hundred hunters. This should not be compared to current wolf hunts in Western Europe and North America, as the wolves are habituated and less afraid of humans. As hunting pressure increases with growing wolf populations, the wolf becomes cautious and much more difficult to hunt. Below, some specific experiences are recounted.

The author and a professional wolf hunter in Yakutsk, Siberia.

100+ wolf hides waiting for documentation at the Sachabult factory in Yakutsk.

Wolves piled on the floor of the laboratory.

Figure 1.3 Wolf research in Siberia

Moraskallet 1854

An example of difficulties in hunting wolves comes from the city of Mora in Sweden, where a large wolf hunt was carried out in 1854. The intention was to eradicate the local wolf population. This massive event had participation from 4,000 beaters and 500 shooters. The beaters walked in a chain, pushing the animals toward the shooters. The hunt took three days, and the result was that twenty-three bears and two wolves were killed.

Wolf Hunting in Russia

Leonid Pavlovich Sabaneev was the first wolf researcher to compose a scientific book about wolves and wolf hunting in Russia. In the book, the author describes different methods for hunting wolves, the efficiency of each method, and practical experiences. One important observation noticed by Sabaneev was that successful hunting was possible only in snow. Another observation was that it was not possible to catch the whole pack regardless of the number of hunters. Usually the hunters were able to catch one wolf at a time.

Do we have snow all the time in Europe and North America?

Professional Siberian Wolf Hunters

In January 2016, the University of Oslo, Norway, signed an agreement with the Yakut State Academy of Agriculture. Their intention was to study Siberian wolves and obtain measurements as well as genetic material from Siberian wolves.

The project needed twenty wolves from different parts of Yakutsk, and for this purpose, we hired several Siberian wolf hunters. The hunters had fourteen weeks to catch twenty wolves and they caught nineteen wolves of the required twenty, the last of which was shot on the day of our arrival.

Yakutian hunters catch wolves either with traps or by chasing them with snowmobiles. According to local hunters in Yakutsk, the only effective method to control the wolf population would be using poison. However, the use of poison is prohibited in Russia.

Summary

The uncontrolled growth of wolf populations in Europe as well as in North America is the beginning of a game of Russian roulette with rural populations, and the entire food production industry is at stake. We know from experience that declines in prey populations forces wolves to look for alternate prey. This has happened before and will probably happen once again.

Professor Jean-Marc Moriceau from the University of Caen in France is a French historian and specialist in rural history. To date he has documented 9,031 cases where wolves have attacked and killed humans. The text below is from one of his publications (Moriceau 2014).

Marie, aged approximately 7 years, daughter of Jacques Prudent and his first wife, Tiennette Maroyer, was snatched from her doorway by a wolf and devoured in a field. Only her head, one arm and her stomach were found, and nothing besides. These pitiful remains were buried in the cemetery of this church the following day, fifth October, before my entire parish, who had gathered for Sunday Mass.

Source: Parish registers of La Chapelle-Thècle (Saône-et-Loire), 8 October 1749. (Archives of the French administrative department of the Saône-et-Loire, online civil registry, La Chapelle-Thècle, Baptisms, Marriages and Burials, 1743-1752, image 66).

In the nineteenth century the wolf population in France had grown to 10,000 to 15,000 wolves (Moriceau 2014).

This gives us another view of one of the parameters of carrying capacity. In Scandinavia and Finland, the size of the local wolf population is estimated based upon an average territory size of 30×30 kilometers, or 900 km^2. France has an area of 640,679 km^2 (247,368 square miles), and assuming an average pack size six wolves and the number of lone wolves 20%, then the size of the average wolf territory is 17.8×17.8 km or 320 km^2.

Nature did not control the number of wolves in France during the nineteenth century, so why should we believe that nature will control the number of wolves today?

THE BELOVED WOLF

Until the 1960s, the wolf remained a pest and parasite that should be exterminated, but in Europe and the United States, new urban generations had grown up in prosperity and welfare after World War II. Little was known about the rural population's fight against wolves and nothing about the predator named wolf.

Animal welfare organizations grew up in all parts, and the wilderness became a resort and a source of experiences rather than a part of nature. We can read about an organization named Rewilding Europe wanting more space for wild nature and wildlife across Europe. They write on their website at https://rewildingeurope.com/:

Rewilding is about reconnecting a modern society – both rural and urban – with wilder nature. We invite people to experience and live in these new, rewilded landscapes.

Experiencing the thrill of wild nature reconnects people with our living planet. This improves health and wellbeing and builds a shared sense of humanity and pride, both on the countryside and in cities.

Experiencing the Thrill

Life in Western civilizations gets easier and more boring. In the 1950s, there was a shortage of food throughout most of Europe. People lived in small apartments, with several persons sharing one bedroom. All money had to be earned, and nothing was given for free. My mother, as most women did, sewed almost all my clothes, often refurbishing old secondhand clothes.

We were forced to experience the thrill of survival!

Those days are gone, and today, everything is served on golden plates. Just raise your hand and you get whatever you may need. No fighting for survival; just remember to push the right button or write the right number next time you choose between candidates in an election.

Social security and welfare are surrounded by a network of legislation. Everything is regulated by law, and we don't even know what is right or wrong because the law no longer correlates with common sense. The strictly protected gray wolf is defined by its genotype rather than its appearance, while we learned in school how to identify animals by their appearance and expressed traits.

Now the modern man experiences the thrill of interpreting a mesh of regulations.

It seems as if wolves are calling urban people to live their lives as they desire, free and uninhibited by the various restrictions that society and the people they are surrounded by, are imposing on them. Above all, loving wolves could reveal the uncivilized and wild part of the wolf lovers' nature.

Howling wolves brings my thoughts to the sirens of Greek mythology, whose enchanting music and signing lured nearby sailors into shipwrecks on the rocky coasts of their island.

Humanizing Animals

Pets have always been treated as family members by urban people. Most pet owners buy birthday presents like fancy grooming services or other unnecessary indulgences for their pets. According to *National Geographic*, more than 80% of pet owners would risk their lives for their fluffy family members—but they would not lift a finger to save someone from being killed on the street.

Our society seems to humanize animals and dehumanize ourselves.

Most cartoons for kids present humanized animals. We know them from the 1960s: Donald Duck, Mickey Mouse, Tom and Jerry, Roadrunner, and more. In these cartoons animal societies act and talk as humans do. They enter into the child's daily life as pals.

Later in life, the same youngsters watch lions in Africa, tigers in India, and wolves in Alaska. The narrator's monotone voice explains how mom Sissy and dad Pete take their five children on a walk to the nearby lake, where they all howl while the sun slowly sinks in the west. Later, in the dusk, the happy family returns to their lair, and mom Sissy puts the pups to sleep. Dad Pete takes a short sleep, too, and at early dawn he disappears into the dark forest, looking for a piece of flesh for the family.

The hypnotic and monotone voice pushes the impression deep into the minds of the young ones.

At the University of Tampere, Finland, we found a master's thesis about humanizing wild animals (Laitinen 2012). The following observation was found in the thesis:

Children are often disappointed when they watch animals in a zoo, simply be-cause reality does not match with what they have learned from so called animal documents. The spectator (in this case the child) believes that a document, be-cause of its name and type, exhibits the reality better than any ordinary movie or zoo.

This gets even worse, when adults want to experience a chilling night at a predator observation hide in Kuhmo, Finland. From the hide, the visitor is able to photograph and observe bears, wolves, wolverines, eagles, and black kites.

Many exciting photos have been taken from these hides, but the visitors do not know that these bears and wolves are fully habituated to humans and human odor. They visit the area in front of the hide simply because there is a huge pile of carrion hidden behind a big log.

Simply watch the overweight brown bears and how their stomach is reaching all the way to the ground, and you understand that all this is far from real nature.

If you disregard these facts, the website www.wildfinland.org gives you an opportunity to experience semi-wild nature in an open-air zoo.

Sliding on the Slope

The discussion about nature has come to a point where an increasing number of peo-ple participate in it without having the slightest knowledge about either the animals in question or nature. Most of these individuals have received their information from TV programs, visits to animal parks, or by spending one night in a hide, just beside carrion, watching the life of habituated wild animals.

The situation becomes even worse when so-called professionals and bureaucrats get their knowledge about nature from dissertations, theoretical studies, and politically influenced surveys, thus causing environmental protection to depart from practical knowledge and experience, and accurate information disappears into cyberspace.

The wolf has been upgraded from a bloodthirsty, powerful predator and surplus killer to a lovable, furry agent promoting the balance of nature. Thus, it is hardly surprising that the wolf has the role of hero and/or villain in this contest.

Our ability to interact with dogs, and the ability of both parties to interpret emotions, gestures, and facial expressions have suddenly been extrapolated to include the wolf.

The wolf is seen as a symbol of the big fierce forests, and wolf enthusiasts attempt, through these "cousins" of the family dog, to experience the unbounded freedom that urban people lost long ago.

Lines have been drawn, and a countdown has begun. One of the first victims of this contest will be the authentic gray wolf.

Human and Animal Rights

A natural step from humanizing animals is the animal rights movement. This is a social movement which seeks an end to the rigid moral and legal distinction drawn between human and nonhuman animals, an end to the status of animals as property, and an end to their use in the research, food, clothing, and entertainment industries.

Critics argue that nonhuman animals are unable to enter into a social contract, and they cannot have duties and thus, they cannot be possessors of rights.

Most of all, this is more evidence of human domination and how we want to impose our ethics upon nature. However, nature does not recognize rights to any species, but every living organism is a part of a huge entity with its only purpose to survive and develop. What happens in nature is a process known as evolution.

Evolution is the only mechanism able to produce sustainable diversity in our nature.

Sharks and crocodiles have survived in nature for millions of years although the average time for a species to survive is 2 million years. Both humans and wolves passed this milestone long ago, and now it is up to nature how long we will remain on the earth—probably less than a tiny fraction of a galactic year.

The more we fight against evolution, the shorter our stay on this earth will be.

Charles Darwin wrote the following to Emma Darwin on 5 July 1844:

> *If, as I believe that my theory is true and if it be accepted even by one competent judge, it will be a considerable step in science.*

THE WOLF'S RANGE AND APPEARANCE

Everyone knows that before starting a fight with an enemy, one must know his weaknesses, learn his habits—in short, find out with whom he is dealing. Therefore, this chapter aims to describe the gray wolf's geographical distribution, its physical traits, and appearance in detail.

This chapter also presents some of the most common subspecies of Canis lupus, but the description focuses on the Eurasian wolf (Canis lupus lupus) as originally described by Carl von Linné in 1758.

GEOGRAPHIC DISTRIBUTION

Wolf ancestors began to develop in the Paleocene, about sixty million years ago. By the Miocene, about twenty million years ago, canines and felines had branched into two separate families. The wolf developed from primitive carnivores known as miacids that appeared in the Lower Tertiary about fifty-two million years ago.

The earliest *Canis lupus* specimen found was a fossil tooth discovered at Old Crow, in Yukon, Canada. The specimen was found in sediment dated at one million years before present (YBP), however, the geological attribution of this sediment is questioned.

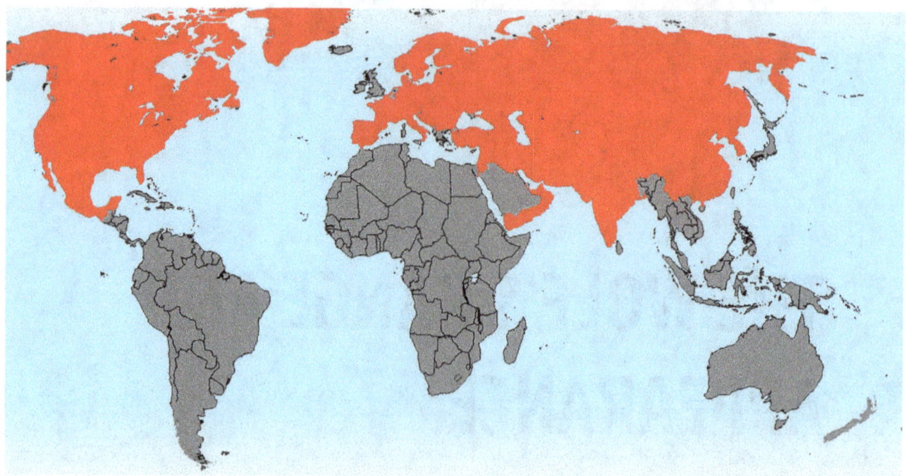

Figure 2.1. The Gray Wolf distribution map.

Slightly younger specimens were discovered at Cripple Creek Sump, in Fairbanks, Alaska, that dated 810,000 YBP. Both discoveries point to an origin of these wolves in east Beringia during the Middle Pleistocene (Wikipedia).

It is believed that canids originated in North America and then spread to Asia and South America, while others claim that a small type of wolf crossed into Siberia from Alaska, where it eventually developed into the larger, present-day gray wolf. The gray wolf then migrated to North America, where it populated what are now Canada and the United States, except for the southeastern section of the United States.

Originally, the gray wolf was the world's most widely distributed mammal, but as mentioned in the previous chapter, it became extinct in many Western European countries, Mexico, and the lower forty-eight states of the United States. Although the gray wolf still faces some threats, its population is relatively widespread and stable at the global level.

According to The International Union for Conservation of Nature (IUCN), the gray wolf does not meet, or nearly meet, any of the criteria for the threatened categories and is therefore assessed as least concern (LC).

However, at regional levels, several wolf populations are seriously threatened. In North America, some of the reintroduced populations are still threatened, and in Europe, the wolf is classified as endangered in several regions.

This reasoning leads to logical contradictions. The wolf is endangered outside its normal distribution area and abundant within its distribution area.

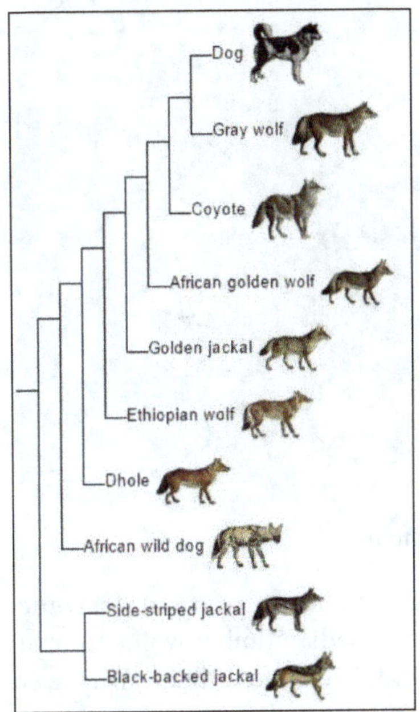

Figure 2.2. The wolf's family tree (Wikipedia Commons).

The Wolves Out There

The taxonomic authority, **Mammal Species of the World**, lists thirty-eight of *Canis lupus* subspecies. The first and nominate subspecies is *Canis lupus lupus* or the *Eurasian wolf,* named by Carl von Linné in 1758. The last *Canis lupus* subspecies was described in 2002 when the noted paleontologist R. M. Nowak reaffirmed the morphological distinctiveness of the Italian wolf and recommended the recognition of *Canis lupus italicus*.

Genetic research is able to produce a computerized analysis (a phylogenetic tree) as a sort of a wolf family tree. Splits far to the left means that the groups separated long ago. Splits to the right mean that the groups separated recently. Figure 2.2 shows such a tree with dog and wolf ancestors. A similar chart can be created including wolves from different parts of the world.

For everyone having studied wolf morphology, it is obvious that in places where the wolves are returned, there is nothing like a distinct subspecies but, rather, a mongrel having inherited its traits from a bunch of different canines. We have several interesting examples of this.

BBC News reported on September 6, 2011, how wolves have returned to France after having been extinct for some sixty years. The French wolves are said to have their roots in Italy and thus belong to the subspecies ***Canis lupus italicus***. After having roamed through highly industrialized northern Italy (the valley of river Po) and crossed over the French Alps, they appeared in a department called Hautes-Alpes in southeastern France.

At the same time, they switched from Canis lupus italicus *to* Canis lupus lupus.

The German wolf population roamed from Poland to Germany and switched from purebred Eurasian wolves to mongrels with morphological and genetic traits putatively inherited from German Shepherds.

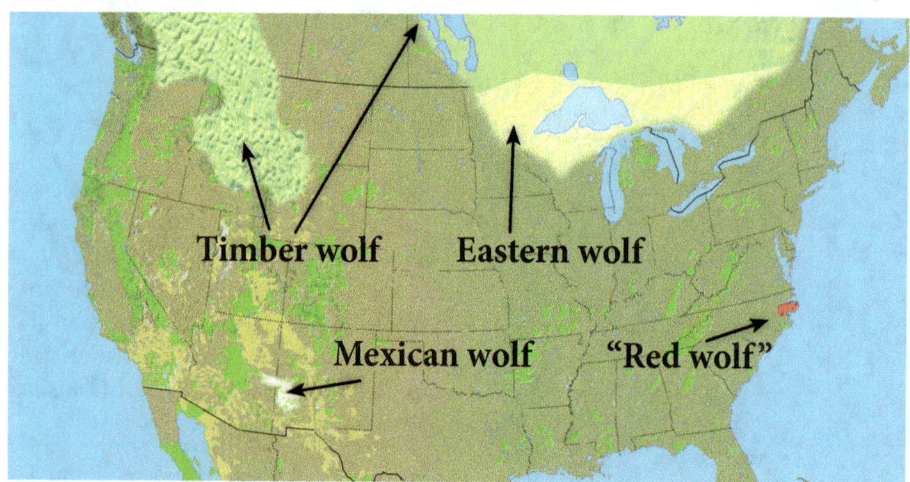

Figure 2.3. The wolves' range in the United States and Canada.

The timber wolf having inhabited Yellowstone, seems to be a mixture of dogs, the Arctic wolf, the northern Rocky Mountain wolf, the Canadian timber wolf and–you name it. Also, the impact of coyotes on wolves in the United States is huge (Wayne et al 2016). The following is taken from Wayne et al.'s (2016) paper.

We found that all North American wolves and coyotes have significant amounts of coyote ancestry. In addition, we detect a strong geographic cline in the proportion of coyote ancestry across North American canids. Alaskan and Yellowstone wolves have 8 to 8.5% coyote ancestry, Great Lakes wolves have 21.7 to 23.9% coyote ancestry, Algonquin wolves have at least 32.5 to 35.5% coyote ancestry, and Quebec sequences have more than 50% coyote ancestry. As expected, Eurasian wolves and dogs, which are allopatric to coyotes, do not have coyote ancestry.

Consistent with the above results, Great Lakes region wolves and red wolves are admixed populations composed of various proportions of gray wolf and coyote ancestry.

Because the development goes toward a gray wolf whatever that means, I limit this study to the most significant subspecies and their distribution.

Figure 2.4. Arctic wolf (photo by Jim Cumming).

United States and Canada

Despite old science recognizing up to twenty-four different *Canis lupus* subspecies in the United States and Canada, Ronald Nowak's consolidated list from 1992 gives a good picture of today's wolves.

Arctic Wolf

Canis lupus arctos, or the Arctic wolf, was first described as a distinct *Canis lupus* subspecies by British zoologist R. I. Pocock in 1935, after he had examined a single skull from Melville Island. The wolf is almost completely white with a black snout and small spot of black guard hairs on the tail at the height of the anal glands and it also has some black-tipped guard hairs on its back (Figure 2.4).

The white color is a result of what we call adaptation. Adaptation is a process by which an animal or plant species becomes fitted to its environment, and it is the result of natural selection's action upon heritable variation. Every organism must be adapted in a variety of ways in order to survive in its environment.

The Arctic wolf is an excellent example of how evolution optimizes species in nature. A black timber wolf would not survive in the Arctic landscape simply because of its color.

Figure 2.5. The Eastern wolf (photo by Michael Runtz).

Eastern Wolf

Canis lupus lycaon, or the eastern wolf, is a canid native to the northeastern side of North America's Great Lakes region as well as southeastern Canada. It is of intermediate size, somewhere between the coyote and gray wolf. The average weight of males is 30 kg (66 pounds), and females weight around 23 kg (50.7 pounds). Its average life span in nature is three to four years, but some may live up to twelve to fifteen years (Theberge 2004).

The eastern wolf primarily preys on white-tailed deer but may occasionally attack moose, beavers, muskrats, and mice.

The eastern wolf is particularly susceptible to hybridization due to its close relationship to the coyote and its ability to bridge gene flow between coyotes and gray wolves. Furthermore, human persecution over a period of 400 years caused a population decline, which reduced the number of suitable mates, and thus facilitating coyote gene swapping into the eastern wolf population.

The main population of pure eastern wolves is currently concentrated within Algonquin Provincial Park eastern Ontario and south-central Quebec. However, a study from 2016 concluded that even the eastern wolf has about 32% coyote ancestry (Wayne et al. 2016).

Figure 2.6. The timber wolf (photo by James Cumming).

Timber Wolf

Canis lupus occidentalis is recognized as a subspecies of *Canis lupus* in the taxonomic authority *Mammal Species of the World* (2005). The timber wolf is known by several different synonyms: the Mackenzie Valley wolf, Alaskan timber wolf, Canadian timber wolf, or northern timber wolf. It ranges from Alaska and the upper Mackenzie River Valley southward to the Canadian provinces of British Columbia, Alberta, and Saskatchewan as well as the Northwestern United States (Wikipedia).

The timber wolf is probably the largest of the *Canis lupus* subspecies. Below are some facts about the timber wolf provided by Yellowstone Park Service, found under "Yellowstone wolf facts" (Internet A16):

- Average life span: 4–5 years (maximum 12.5 years), 18% >5 years old.

- Pelage: gray or black (ratio 50:50), rarely white.

- Black coat color: caused by K-locus gene thought to have originated from historic hybridization with domestic dogs 500–14,000 years ago.

- Average body mass: males 50 kg (110 pounds) females 41 kg (90.3 pounds).

- Height at shoulder: males 81 cm (31.9 inches) females 77 cm (30.3 inches).

In 1991 Congress directed the US Fish and Wildlife Service to develop an environmental impact statement for the purpose of reintroducing wolves into Yellowstone National Park (Yellowstone Science, volume 13, number 1, Winter 2005). In January 1995, fourteen wolves were captured from east of Jasper National Park, Alberta, Canada, and the wolves arrived in Yellowstone in January 1995. Seventeen additional wolves captured in Canada were released into the park in April 1996.

One could ask, if this really was a reintroduction or if the timber reintroduction wolf an invasive species as far as Yellowstone is concerned. There is no reintroduction because the wolf introduced into Yellowstone Park is not native to this geography and had never naturally been there to begin with. The gray wolf is, ironically enough, a human introduced invasive species (Fanning 2007).

The only thing we know for sure: Despite all protests, the timber wolf is here to stay, and over a short period of time, expanded its territory into many US States.

Mexican Gray Wolf

Canis lupus baileyi, or the Mexican wolf, was commonly known as "lobo." The wolf once inhabited Mexico and southwestern United States. Today, the Mexican wolf is the most endangered of the *Canis lupus* subspecies and may be one of the rarest land mammals on earth. Most of these wolves live in captive facilities around the United States and Mexico, but since 1998, when thirty-five Mexican wolves were released in Apache National Forest in Arizona, the population has grown to over one hundred individuals.

A typical Mexican wolf weighs between 22 and 35 kg (50 and 80 pounds), it is about 165 cm (5 ½ feet) in length including the tail, and at withers is about 70 cm (28 inches) tall. It has a richly colored coat of buff, gray, rust, and black, often with distinguishing facial "masks." Solid black or white variations do not exist as with other North American gray wolves. Known prey for Mexican wolves include elk, mule deer, and white-tailed deer, but wolves can and do occasionally kill livestock, especially young calves.

Northern Rocky Mountain Wolf

Canis lupus irremotus, or the northern Rocky Mountain wolf, is a subspecies of gray wolf native to the northern Rocky Mountains. It is a light-colored, medium-to large-sized subspecies with a narrow, flattened frontal bone. The subspecies was initially listed as endangered on March 9, 1978, but had the classification removed in the year 2000 due to the effects of the northern Rocky Mountain Wolf Recovery Plan. On August 6, 2010, the northern Rocky Mountain wolf was ordered to be returned under Endangered Species Act protections by US District Judge Donald Molloy in a decision overturning a previous ruling by the US Fish and Wildlife Service. The subspecies was later removed from the endangered list on August 31, 2012, because Idaho, Montana, and Wyoming were meeting the population quotas for the species to be considered stable. This wolf is recognized as a subspecies of *Canis lupus* in the taxonomic authority *Mammal Species of the World 2005* (Wikipedia).

Figure 2.7. The Mexican wolf (photo by Jim Clark, USFWS).

Wolves in Europe and Asia

The color setting of wolves varies depending on their environment. Through natural selection, evolution gradually causes adaptations of camouflaging colors until the perfect shape and color is obtained. A perfect camouflage enables wolves to sneak up on their prey—and the perfect camouflage of a prey animal keeps it hidden from wolves.

Wolves usually exhibit two types of camouflage. A concealing coloration when the wolf's fur has the same color as his background, and a disruptive coloration when stripes, spots, or patterns create a visual disruption that makes it difficult to see the animal's outline.

As the main color of a landscape goes from light towards dark, the color of a wolf's pelt follows the same scheme. In the north, we have lighter wolves, while the southern wolves exhibit a darker overall setting, usually reddish-brown with gray and black-tipped guard hairs on the back.

Eurasian Wolf

The Eurasian wolf (*Canis lupus lupus*) was described in 1758 by Carl von Linné, a Swedish botanist, physician, and zoologist who formalized the modern system of naming organisms. He is also known as the creator of modern taxonomy.

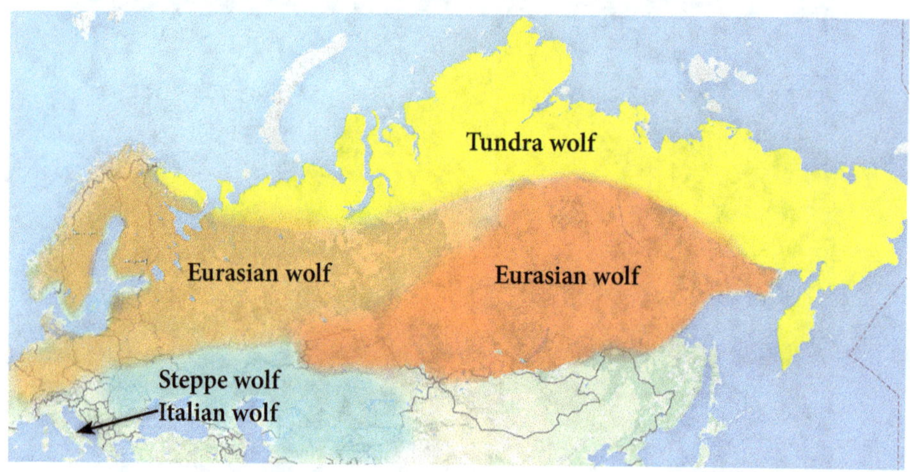

Figure 2.8. The wolves' range in the Europe and Asia.

The Eurasian wolf is, by mass and size, among the largest wolves. The average weight of an adult male is 45–50 kg (99–110 pounds), and weights up to 80 kg (176 pounds) are not unusual. A yearling may reach up to 35 kg (77 pounds) and a juvenile up to 25 kg (55 pounds).

The wolf's coat consists of two layers: a soft, gray, dense underfur and the long guard hairs over the underfur. The guard hairs shed moisture and keep the underfur dry.

Much of the underfur and some of the guard hairs are shed in the spring and grow back in the fall. The coat is thick across the shoulders, where guard hairs may be 10–13 centimeters (4–5 inches) long, and thins out on the muzzle and legs.

Figure 2.9. The Eurasian wolf (photo by Daniel Mott).

The long, dark-tipped guard hairs are primarily found on the shoulders and along the back, down the spine. The underside of the tail, insides of the legs, belly, and underside of the muzzle are usually light. The tip of the tail is dark, and there is always a dark spot on the tail marking the location of a scent gland.

The color of the coat range from shades of cream, and ocher to gray, brown and black.

Figure 2.10. The pelt of a young tundra wolf in Sachabult fur shop, Yakutsk (photo by Kaarlo Nygren).

Officially, the Eurasian wolf's range covers the whole area between Western Europe and the Russian cost at the Pacific Ocean. Within Russia and Siberia, the appearance is stable, but within Europe, there are a great number of the variations in appearance.

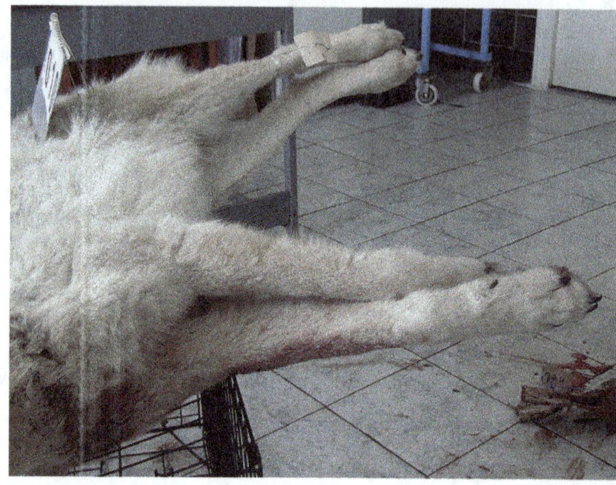

Figure 2.11. An adult Tundra wolf under investigation in Yakutsk 2016 (photo by the author).

Tundra Wolf

The tundra wolf (**Canis lupus albus**) is a subspecies of gray wolf native to Eurasia's tundra and forest-tundra zones from the Kola Peninsula to the Kamchatka Peninsula. There is one documented observation of the tundra wolf in Finland made by Dr. Erik S. Nyholm. The tundra wolf was first described in 1792 by Robert Kerr, who described it as living around the Yenisei and as having a highly valued pelt.

The tundra wolf is large. The body length of males is 118–137 cm (46–53 inches), with a tail length 42–52 cm (16–20 inches) and an average weight 40 kg (88 pounds), up to a, maximum of 49 kg (108 pounds). Females have a body length of 112–136 cm (44–53 inches), tail length of 41–49 cm (16–19 inches) and an average weight of 36 kg (79 pounds), up to a maximum of 41 kg (90 pounds).

The longest skull length for males is 248–270 mm (9.7–10.6 inches) and for females, 237–256 mm (9.3–10 inches).

The pelage is very long, dense, fluffy, and soft. The length of guard hairs is 150–160 mm (5.9–6.2 inches), and the underfur is about 70 mm (2.7 inches). The usual color is light and gray, with underfur that has two zones of color: the lower is lead-gray and the upper is reddish-gray (Heptner & Naumov 1967). In winter, the tundra wolf feeds almost exclusively on wild and domestic reindeer. The stomach contents of 74 wolves caught in the Nenets Autonomous Okrug in the 1950s were found to consist of 93.1% reindeer remains (Heptner & Naumov 1967).

Research that I concluded in Yakutsk in 2016 suggests that the difference between the Eurasian wolf and the tundra wolf is minimal. Of the more than one hundred pelts we investigated, color setting and the structure exhibited the same features in both wolves. Figure 2.10 shows the pelt of a young tundra wolf, and Figure 2.11 shows the almost white belly of an adult tundra wolf.

Figure 2.12. The Steppe wolf (photo by Sergei Zalinyan).

Altai Gray Wolf

The Altai gray wolf (***Canis lupus altaicus***) was described by the German biologist Theophil Noack. The range of this wolf is not clearly documented but the Russian scientist Flerov suggested in 1935 that this wolf lives between the Ural Mountains and the Lake of Baikal. Another Russian scientist, Kuznetsovin, proposed in 1952 that *Canis lupus altaicus's* range extends from the Ural Mountains to the Pacific, while *Canis lupus lupus* lives west of the Ural Mountains (Heptner & Naumov 1967).

The taxonomic positions, origin, and kinship of various forms of the Altai gray wolf remain debatable. The results of a phylogenetic study confirm that the forest–steppe Altai gray wolf population is a part of the mountain–taiga population.

Steppe Wolf

The steppe wolf (***Canis lupus campestris***) is a subspecies of gray wolf native to the Caspian steppes, the steppe regions of the Caucasus, the lower Volga region, southern Kazakhstan, the northern Urals, and the steppe regions of the lower European part of the former Soviet Union. It was first described by the Russian scientist Dwigubski in 1804.

The steppe wolf is a medium-sized wolf whose average dimensions are somewhat smaller than the Eurasian wolf. Pelage is shorter, coarser, and sparser. Color on the sides is relatively light and gray, and the back is rusty-gray or brownish with quite a strong admixture of black hairs. The differences between the steppe wolf and the Eurasian wolf have been mentioned and are accepted by all authors, although there has been no study of this question based upon reliable material. At the present time, the wolf is absent or very rare in a considerable range of the European steppes (Heptner & Naumov 1967).

In the population of steppe wolves, particularly in the Ukraine, few very large individuals are encountered. They are mainly found in the northern part of the steppe zone, and apparently, these individuals intrude from the north.

Figure 2.13. The Iberian wolf (photo by Arturo de Frias Marques).

Iberian Wolf

The Iberian wolf (*Canis lupus signatus*) is a subspecies of the Eurasian wolf, with smaller dimensions and weight. Maximum height at the withers is 70 cm (27.5 inches), and weight ranges from 25 to 40 kg (55–88 pounds). Its body coat is yellowish-brown, and the muzzle has ocher or brown tones. A black stripe is present on its back from neck to tail. In addition, there is a well-defined black stripe on the front legs, which is more visible in the winter.

The species was first described by Ángel Cabrera in 1908.

The Iberian wolf inhabits the forests and plains of northern Portugal and northwestern Spain, and the population is estimated to be around 2,000 wolves. Some consider it to be beneficial because it keeps the population of wild boars stable, while sheep farming suffers from this predator. On the other hand, Raúl Rejón, a journalist from Madrid, reports that these wolves kill sheep, goats, horses, and cows. To compensate farmers for their losses, the government spends more than 1.5 million euros per year (Rejón 2016).

Today, the hunting of Iberian wolves is banned in Portugal, but it is allowed in some parts of Spain. The European Union has placed parts of the Iberian wolf under Annex IV of the Habitats Directive (i.e. wolves living south of the 39th parallel), while the populations north of the Duera and Greek (the 39th parallel) are placed under Annex V. Wolves under Annex IV are strictly protected, while wolves under Annex V can be culled.

Although hunting the Iberian wolf is strictly protected in Portugal, about 45% of wolf deaths are caused by human activities, including poaching.

Figure 2.14. The Italian wolf (photo by Gilles Pretet, Wikipedia Commons).

The Italian Wolf

The Italian wolf (*Canis lupus italicus*), also known as the Apennine wolf, is a subspecies of the gray wolf found in the Apennine Mountains in Italy. The Italian wolf was first described in 1921 by zoologist Giuseppe Altobello but officially recognized as a subspecies in 2002, when R. M. Nowak reaffirmed the morphological distinctiveness of the Italian wolf in a study of gray wolf skulls from Italy.

The Italian wolf is a medium-size wolf. Males have an average weight of 24 to 40 kg (52–88 pounds). The body length of the Italian wolf is usually 100 to 140 cm (39–55 inches).

Between 1960 and 1970, the population was almost exterminated from Italy, reaching an all-time low in the early 1970s. In 1971, the Italian wolf was protected. Research revealed that the Italian wolf population consisted of some 100 wolves distributed throughout a fragmented range in the main mountainous areas of south-central Italy (Wikipedia). From Italy, the population is said to have roamed into southern France, particularly in the Parc National du Mercantour.

Genetic research carried out by the Italian professor Ettore Randi's research team reveals extensive introgression of dog genes among the Italian wolves. Their report suggests that 87 % of the Italian wolf population carries genes inherited from dogs (Randi et al. 2014). Hybridization, as we have seen in the United States, is the only reason why black wolves have been reported in the north-central Apennines.

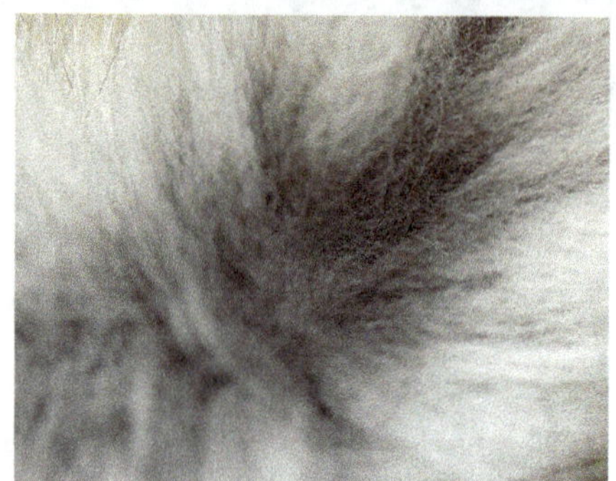

Figure 2.15. The wolf's pelage (photo by the author).

The upper left photo shows the long black-tipped guard hairs. The upper right photo shows the same guard hairs from another direction. The lower right photo shows the lead-grey underfur close to the skin. This pelt structure is common to all wolves.

THE GRAY WOLF IN DETAIL

Earlier in this chapter, we presented some subspecies of the gray wolf (*Canis lupus*). This part of the chapter describes the gray wolf in detail. We assume, that most of the different *Canis lupus* subspecies share the same expressed traits despite some variations caused by adaptation to their local ecosystem.

The Pelage Structure and Color Setting

We start by analyzing the gray wolf's pelt. To most of us, it might seem as if the pelt separates different subspecies from each other. However, that is only true to a point. The Russian scientist Dmitry I. Bibikov wrote in his book about wolves (Bibikov 1985) as follows:

Despite differences in hue all Canis lupus subspecies exhibit the same basic color scheme.

The wolf's pelage consists of guard hairs and underfur, as shown in Figure 2.15.

The Guard Hairs

The first layer is made up of tough guard hairs that repel water and dirt. The longest guard hairs are found on the wolf's neck, where they can reach up to a length up to 150 mm (5.9 inches). The long guard hairs continue down the spine toward the root of the tail. These guard hairs measure from 100 to 145 mm (3.9 to 5.7 inches). On the flanks, the guard hairs can grow up to 100 mm (3.9 inches).

The Undercoat

Under the guard hair is a layer called the undercoat. This layer is dense and keeps the wolf warm in the winter. As with dogs, the undercoat is shed in late spring or early summer. In the autumn, when the weather gets colder, the undercoat grows to its ordinary thickness. With this annual cycle, the wolf's appearance changes. The thick and dense underfur makes the wolf appear larger, with most change observed on the head, where thick whiskers grow and create the impression of a huge head.

The Colors of Wolf

With the exception of black timber wolves in the United States and Canada, the wolf's color setting is based upon white or black and hues of yellow, ocher, brown, or gray. The wolfs back can be white, but it is definitely not ocher or brown. Usually, it varies from light to dark gray or almost black. Areas inside of the rear legs and the belly are always white or light yellow except for on young wolves, which exhibit different shades of gray (Figure 2.21). The tail tip is always black or dark brown, and there is always a caudal mark on the tail at the height of the caudal glands.

Figure 2.16. The back of a gray wolf (photos by the author).

Figure 2.17. The belly of a Siberian gray wolf (photo by the author).

A fully black color (melanism) or red color (erythrism) is extremely rare in other parts of the world. Where this is found, it is considered evidence of hybridization with dogs. This is also true for the black timber wolves, but in this case, hybridization is assumed to go back at least 500 years.

Figure 2.18 shows the face of a Russian wolf used to analyze traits typical of all wolves. We recognize seven traits common to wolves using Bibikov's *The Wolf (1985)* as reference.

Figure 2.18. The facial marks of a Russian wolf (photo by the author).

The rhinarium is always black, and proceeding toward the eyes, the area on the upper jaws (Circle 7) is brown or dark gray. Except for the Arctic wolf, we don't find white in this area, nor do we find black. There is a genetic variant exhibiting a black melanistic mask, but this trait is putatively inherited from dogs.

Around the eyes, there is a light gray area, and the eye itself is surrounded by a black border. This black border is typical of nocturnal animals that hunt in the dark (Figure 2.18, Circles 5 and 6).

The breast and the lateral sides of the upper jaw are white or light yellow (Circle 2). A black stripe runs from the rear side of the eyes toward the whiskers (Circle 3).

The forehead is dark, usually gray (Circle 4). Some subspecies exhibit a dark brown forehead.

On both sides of the head, we find that the whiskers are visible, especially in winter (Circle 1).

A wolf should not exhibit what we call a dorsal saddle. This trait is usually inherited from dogs such as, for instance, German Shepherds. The dorsal saddle is a solid black area that covers the back and parts of the flanks.

Figure 2.19. A wolf's ear (photo by the author).

Figure 2.16 shows the typical color setting of two wolves' backs. The wolf on the left has slightly lighter grayish fur, and the wolf on the right has darker fur.

An interesting detail is the triangular area of the belly, between the hind legs, which usually consists of light underfur only.

The wolves' ears are filled with dense fur, and the small ears are triangular, with a round tip. The rear side of the ears are usually covered with ocher or red-brown fur, not black or gray. Figure 2.19 shows a wolf's ear.

Regional Variations in Color Settings

At first, we analyze the color variations of the wolf's head. We noted some traits in Figure 2.18, and now we can check how these traits match in wolves from different parts of Eurasia. Figure 2.20 shows the heads of six different wolves, three of which come from Siberia, two from Finland, and one from Sweden.

In this photo, we recognize all features mentioned above with only minor variations in hue. Despite a geographical distance of 4,747 km (2,949 miles) between the habitats of the Finnish and Siberian wolves, no significant differences are observed. The Siberian wolves are found in the left column, and the right column shows two Finnish and one Swedish wolf in the middle.

An important detail common to all wolves is the distance between the ears and their triangular shape. Wolves do not have floppy ears, nor do their ears stand upright and close to each other. Above all, they are small compared to the ears of German Shepherds and other dogs.

The dominant color of the Eurasian wolf is a mixture of different hues of ocher and gray with yellow and white dominating on the belly. The color is lighter in the northern habitats and gets darker moving towards southern areas. The Iberian wolf and the Mexican wolf are typical examples of southern subspecies.

The overall color setting varies when moving from north Siberia to the southern parts of Kazakhstan, Iran, or Afghanistan (Bibikov 1985).

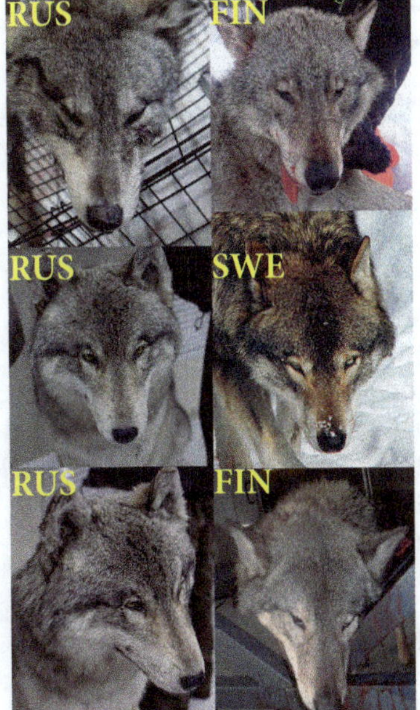

Figure 2.20. Wolves' heads (photos by the author).

The Siberian wolves are light gray with black-tipped guard hairs along the back. These wolves do not exhibit any variations of brown or ocher.

The color variations of wolves in north Kazakhstan include reddish-gray or brown-gray enhanced by the black-tipped cover hairs along their back. In south Kazakhstan, Iran, and Afghanistan the wolf exhibits a light gray or yellow-gray color with long black-tipped guard hairs forming a ridge along the spine.

When moving toward the Carpathian Mountains, the reddish-brown overall color dominates, with —again—the black-tipped guard hairs along the spine.

With this description of the gray wolf's appearance, what Dmitry Bibikov says about wolves' colors is obvious.

Yes, the gray wolf's appearance varies from place to place, but the basic scheme remains the same–except for the almost completely white Arctic wolf.

Based upon available information, it seems as if the assumptions about wolves' appearance are valid as far as the northern Rocky Mountain wolf and the Canadian timber wolf are concerned. The timber wolf described in Figure 2.6 exhibits many of the same traits as we noticed in the Eurasian wolf.

The origins of the red wolf, the eastern wolf, and the Mexican wolf remain uncertain. Both the red wolf and the eastern wolf seem to be wolf–coyote(–dog) crossbreeds. The Mexican wolf has gone through something called a bottleneck, which may affect its heritage and most probably results in wolf–dog mixtures.

Young Wolves

The young wolf sheds its fur two times. The first time, it sheds the soft, dark pup's fur, and the second time, the juvenile sheds its first winter fur and the adult wolf's color setting becomes visible.

Figure 2.21A shows a young pup probably two to three weeks old. The fur is black all over, and no white or brown spots can (or should) be found. The black color gives the pup good camouflage as long as it hides in the lair.

Figure 2.21. Young wolf (photos by Gisela Möller and the author).

As weeks pass, the ears become erect and the pup's soft fur is replaced by the adult wolf's fur although gray is the dominant color. We see a young wolf's dirty gray color in Figure 2.21B.

Toward late autumn the soft underfur starts growing, and the juvenile exhibits a dirty looking mixture of gray and ocher. This color setting remains until next spring, when the juvenile sheds its winter fur. Figure 2.21C is a juvenile euthanized in February; thus it is approximately 9 months old and does not yet exhibit an adult color setting.

The Wolf's Posture and Trail

Again, we have to stress the fact that evolution shapes all organism through natural selection, which along with mutation, migration, and genetic drift, is one of the basic mechanisms of evolution. Charles Darwin's idea of evolution is based upon the simple fact that prey animals lacking an effective camouflage tend to get eaten by wolves, and thus they reproduce less often than prey animals with good camouflage.

So an elk with an advantageous dark brown color will have more offspring with the same color than, for instance, a white elk. As this process continues, all individuals in the elk population will become brown.

The advantageous trait dominates and shapes the population.

If we have variations within a wolf population, the outcome of natural selection will, sooner or later, be a uniform population. This is exactly what we saw in the wolf population until the first human interventions in the twentieth century.

The Wolf on the Move

Most of the time, the wolf keeps its head below the horizontal line continuing from its back and over its neck. This is observed in Figures 2.9, 2.13, and 2.22. Only when the wolf's attention is attracted by something does it raise its head as shown in Figures 2.6 and 2.12.

The belly line is straight and horizontal, unlike most dogs with a belly line that twists upward. This trait is also a result of evolution. When the wild wolf catches prey, it may eat up to 10 kg or even more of meat, and it may be over a week before the wolf gets its next "dinner." A domestic dog is fed daily, and thus it does not have any need to consume more food at one time.

Photo 2.22. A gray wolf (photo by the author).

Dmitry I. Bibikov (1985) recognized three kinds of movement.

Figure 2.23A shows a trotting wolf as it moves from one place to another in its search for prey. An adult wolf trots at about 8 to 11 km/h (4–6 mph). When wolves move over long distances in their search for food, trotting consumes less energy than loping. To reduce energy consumption, the wolf pack travels in a straight line across the landscape. This behavior is important when the pack moves in deep snow, because every member of the pack steps in the footprints of the wolf ahead of it. This behavior is also observed in shallow snow less than 2.5 cm (1 inch) deep.

Figure 2.23B shows a loping wolf. This is typical of young wolves playing on solid ground without snow. If an adult wolf needs to run faster for some reason, it starts loping–and consuming more energy.

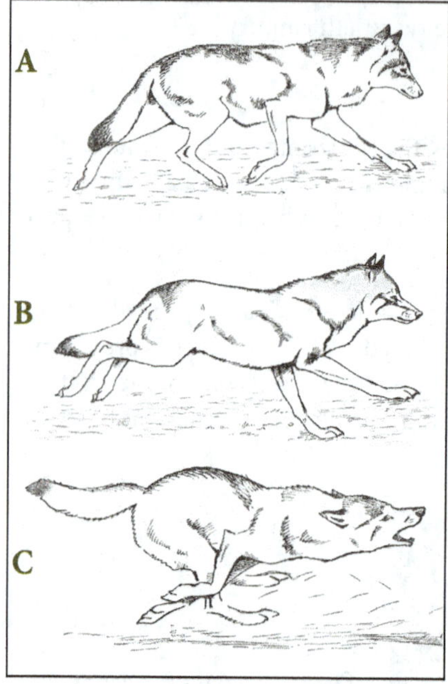

Figure 2.23. A wolf moving (Bibikov 1985).

Figure 2.23C shows an escaping or attacking wolf. This kind of movement consumes a lot of energy and wolves usually do not run at maximum speed for more than 500 to 1,000 meters (1,640–3,280 feet).

A wolf cannot consume all its energy on chasing prey because it has to retain some strength for overtaking the chased prey.

Hunting dogs may follow a prey animal for tens of kilometers, but they don't have to save energy for killing the prey.

An adult moose reaches a speed of 60 km/h (37 mph), which it can maintain for approximately 600 meters (1,968.5 feet) after which it falls back to fast loping. The wolf, in turn, reaches a maximum speed of 40 to 50 km/h (28.5–31 mph), and thus the wolf cannot overtake a moose on solid ground by chasing it (Pavlov 1982).

Wolves usually travel in a trot where the left fore and hind legs land in the same spot, and each right front and hind leg land in the same spot. The distance from where one foot lands until it lands again is the stride length, which varies from 120 to 160 cm (47–62 inches).

To understand why evolution furnished wolves with this trait, we must return to efficiency and the amount of energy consumed during movement. Figure 2.24 shows how a wolf moves its feet in a normal trot. We can observe how the hind paw moves forward and steps right where the fore paw left the ground.

This type of trotting is innate in all wolves.

When the front paw steps into the footprint of the wolf ahead, the rear pad follows into that very same footprint. Now, only the first wolf must forge a trail, and the rest of the pack follows.

Wolves also tend to follow the same trail and step into the same footprints simply in order to make it easy for themselves. Dogs love loping and side trotting. That is an easy and fast way to move on roads and solid ground. In deep snow or wet swamps any type of loping consumes energy and prevents the wolf from running long distances. The explanation for this is simple. When loping in snow, each jump causes the wolf's full weight to press its front feet into the soft snow thus causing the need for extra effort to push itself up out of the snow with the hind feet.

However, when a wolf is chased in deep snow by skis, for instance, the wolf moves slowly, trotting ahead of the hunter. As the hunter chases the wolf, it starts loping, until it simply is too tired to escape and falls down on the snow (Sabaneev 1876).

The former Finnish wolf researcher Dr, Erik S. Nyholm once told me about a hunt, where he chased a wolf by skiing. He said

When I saw that the wolf, after having been trotting for hours, switched into loping, I knew I had won the race and it was only a matter of minutes for me to overtake it.

Figure 2.24. A trotting wolf (photo by the author).

What Does the Trail Tell Us?

The wolves' trail forms a straight line through the landscape. As the wolves step into each other's footprints it makes it practically impossible to count the number of wolves. Only when the pack reaches a road or some obstacle does it disperse, and then the number of wolves may be counted. When the pack continues, the wolves merge back into the same trail.

Figure 2.25 shows a trotting wolf from behind. In this photo, we observe how the wolf's paws form a straight line. Dogs often leave a wider trail, where the left and right paw prints are separate from each other.

The difference between a wolf trail and a dog trail has been explained by several wolf researchers. In this case, I refer to Dmitry I. Bibikov's drawing shown in Figure 2.26.

Figure 2.25. A wolf from behind (photo by the author).

We can notice two tracks, the upper track from a wolf, and the lower track from a dog. The wolf places its paws in a straight line, as seen in Figure 2.25. When the dog moves from left to right, as shown in Figure 2.26, the upper paw print is from the front leg and the lower print from the hind leg.

It is obvious that this dog has a short body and long legs because it swings its hind paw ahead of the front paw. It would be impossible for a wolf pack to follow a trail if the wolves stepped like this dog does.

Sometimes, there are wolflike paw prints but the trail is still typical to dogs. This is usually the case if it is a wolf with dog ancestry.

The Paw Print of a Wolf

Not only can the trail tell us about the wolf but several details can also be observed from individual paw prints. Figure 2.27A shows two paw prints, one from a wolf, and the other from a dog. In this example, the dog's paw print is much smaller than the wolf's paw print. This is no rule because large dogs have large paw prints, and small dogs small paw prints.

However, there are three important details that separate most dogs from wolves. The left paw print in Figure 2.27A is a typical paw print of a wolf, where the paw pads are

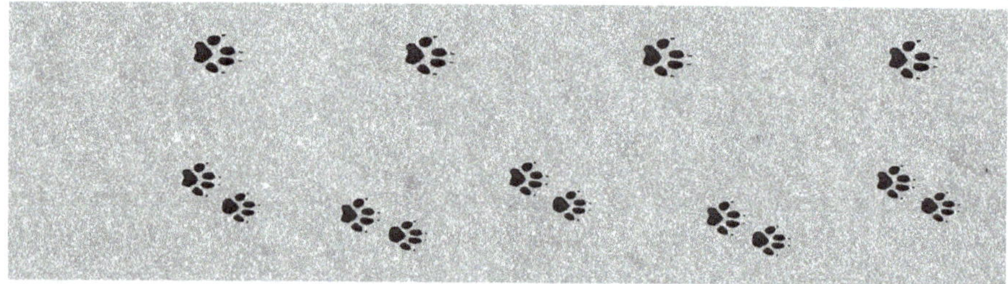

Figure 2.26. A wolf and a dog trail (Bibikov 1985)

placed such that the three lines of A to B, C to D, and E to F can all be drawn without crossing a paw pad (Bibikov 1985).

The lower photo (Figure 2.27B) is front paw of a Eurasian wolf, confirming what was said earlier about the paw prints.

Evolution has developed the wolf's paw to prevent the wolf from sinking deep into snow or soft swamps. There is a rule saying that the pressure under a wolf's pad is usually is less than 140 gr/cm^2 (1.84 psi) (communication with Dr. Erik S. Nyholm).

The length of a male wolf's paw print is approximately 1.3 times the width, while the length of a female wolf's paw print is 1.5 times the width.

The fore leg's rear pad is concave (toward the front), and the hind leg's rear pad is convex.

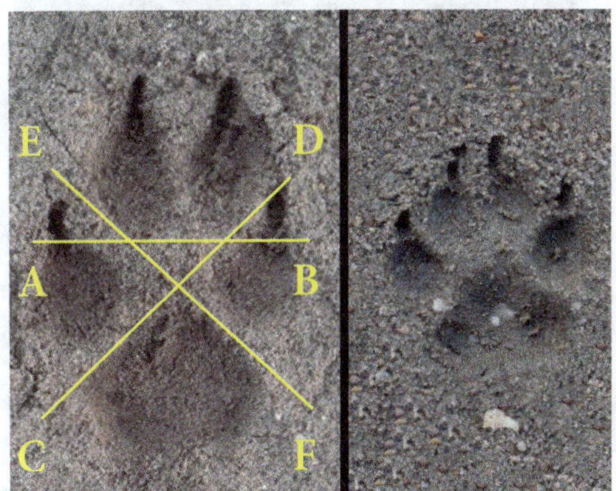

Figure 2.27.A. Wolves' paw prints (photo by Wernher Gerhards).

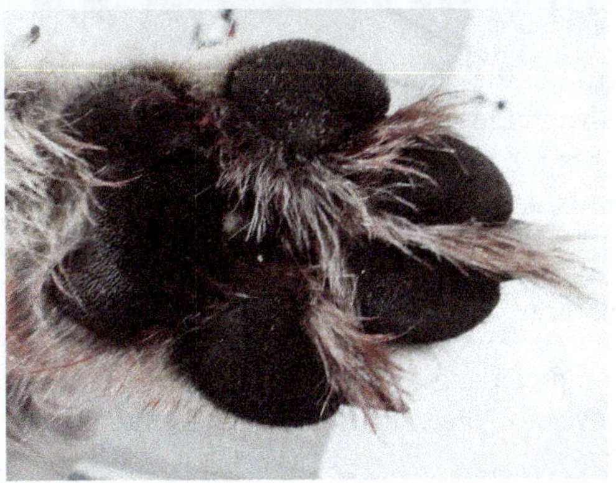

Figure 2.27.B. Wolf's fore foot paw (photo by Wernher Gerhards).

In snow, there are two methods for determining the age of a wolf track. One is to analyze the friability of the trail. On an old trail, both the depressions and the edges are hard. If the snow is powdery, it is found in the paw prints. Drag marks between tracks are typical of hind foot dragging, but they disappear after some hours.

The wolf is less likely to walk; that is, it prefers a slow trot, and when trotting, its paw prints are more correct than with a quiet pace, which most often is noticed in deep snow.

Figure 2.28. The trail of two wolf–dog hybrids (photo by Vadim Sidorovich).

Figure 2.29. A wolf pack's trail (photo by the author).

When escaping dogs, the wolf relies on its strength and flies into snowdrifts, spreading the toes of the forepaws wide, while the toes of the hind legs are pressed together. The wolf never makes loops and gaits, nor does it jump to the side trying to confuse its chaser (Sabaneev 1876).

Dr. Vadim Sidorovich from Belarus sent me the photo in Figure 2.28 showing the tracks of two wolf–dog hybrids. Notice that in the left track, the paw prints are placed in an almost straight line. This hybrid has the right physical dimensions. The right track is typical of dogs or wolf–dog hybrids, and follows exactly the drawing made by Dmitry I. Bibikov.

In Figure 2.29 we see a wolf pack's regular trail in a deep snowdrift.

A wolf tries to avoid deep and soft snow, preferring to follow roads or frozen riverbanks. Russian hunters observed that wolves also prefer to use trails left by the runners of a sleigh or snowmobile (Sabaneev 1876).

Further, old wolves in particular follow the trail rather than their old paths. Using this habit, some trappers use sleighs with particularly wide runners and place wolf traps under the trail (Sabaneev 1876).

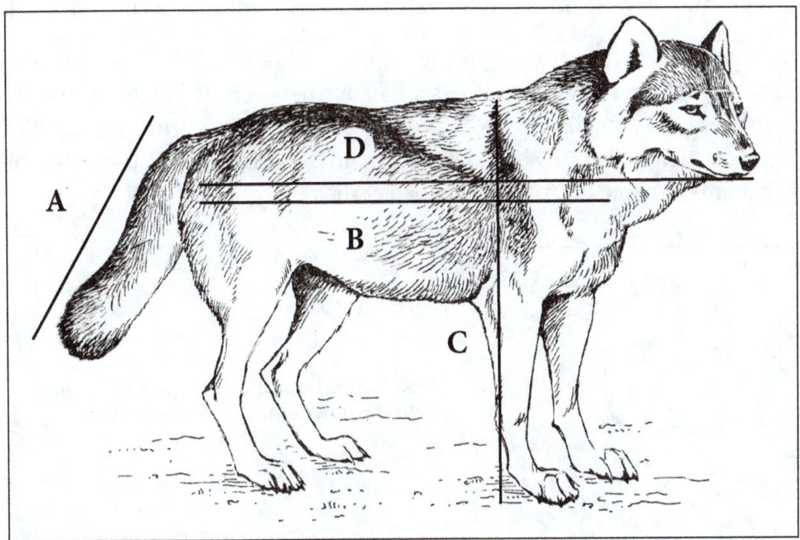

Figure 2.30. A wolf's dimensions (Bibikov 1985).

The Wolf's Body

Although the wolf may resemble a large mongrel, this similarity is superficial. It differs from any dog breed, with a high scruff, thick neck, some swagger depending on the habit of bending the hind legs, and a fluffy tail, which never bends upward.

The cheeks and lower part of the neck of males are often bordered by a thicker and longer coat, the so-called whiskers, which give the ferocious appearance to the wolf. The width of the forehead and, generally, the posterior part of the skull are determined by the size of the cervical muscles. Their thickness and strength causes inflexibility of the neck, which distinguishes the wolf from the dog.

The forehead reaches extraordinary widths, especially in old males, which is unthinkable in dogs of equal heights. The eyes are rather large and oval. Compared to dogs of the same size, the wolf's head is 30% larger.

A strong, almost straight and inflexible spine, turns slightly down, which makes it seem as if the butt is weak, but in strength of the hind legs, the wolf has no competitors.

Anatomical Aspects

Earlier, in Figure 2.24, we observed how the wolf puts its hind paw in the same paw print from which the fore paw has been lifted. This habit is innate regardless of the type of environment, time of year, or number of wolves trotting on the same trail.

However, to be able to trot this way, the length of the body and the height of the wolf are crucial. A well-constructed wolf has a balance between its height at the withers and length from the hip joint to the shoulder. Using variables from Figure 2.30, we say that the quotient C over B should be less than 1. If this quotient is greater than 1, the wolf becomes unable to trot as described earlier.

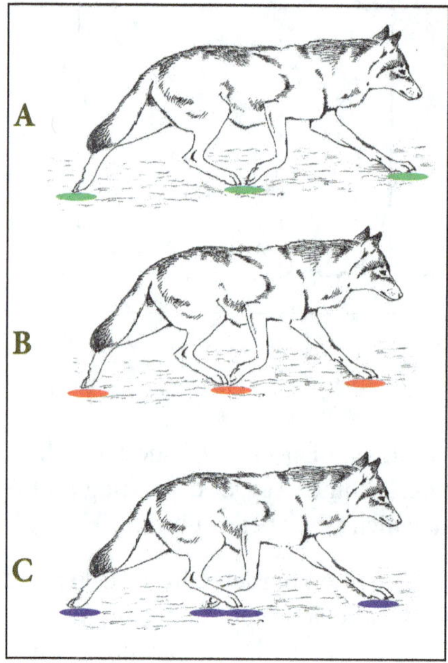

Figure 2.31.

A. Normal trotting. Hind paws are placed in the paw print of the fore paws.

B. Short body. Hind paws are placed in the paw print of the fore paws. Speed is reduced, and there are problems in synchronizing trotting with other pack members.

C. Short body. Hind foot passes the fore foot. This wolf cannot follow the other pack members in certain terrain such as deep snow.

We note the following measurements of an adult wolf in Figure 2.30. The torso plus the head is 105 to 160 cm (41.3–62.9 inces), length of the tail (A) is 30 to 50 cm (11.8–19.6 inches), and the height at the withers is 70 to 85 cm (27.5–33.4 inches) (Heptner & Naumov 1967).

To be able to move their legs this way, there are some anatomical requirements, which we will study next.

Figure 2.31A shows a trotting wolf with the right dimensions. It moves quickly and the hind pad hits the ground where the fore pad left.

Now, suppose the torso is shorter, as shown in Figure 2.31B and 2.31C. In that case, either, the step is shorter, making it stumble and move slower, as shown in B, or it is unable to follow the pack in the same trail because its hind paw has to pass its front paw, as shown in C.

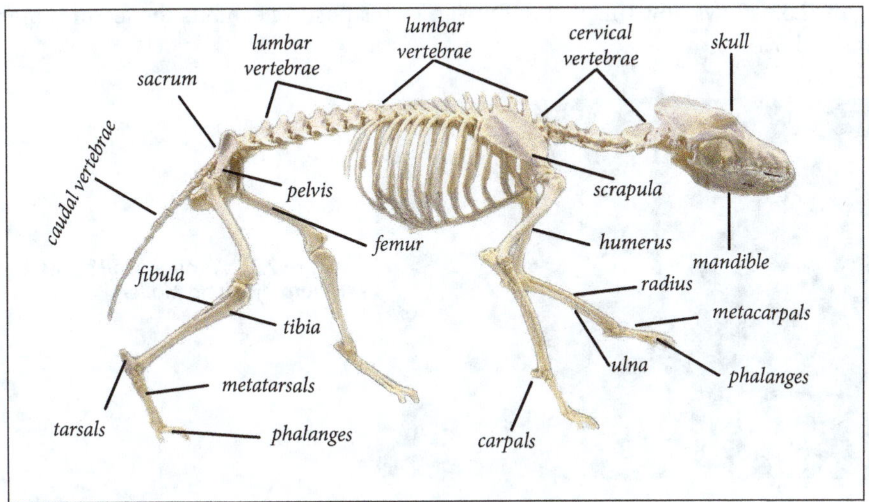

Figure 2.32. A wolf's skeleton (Wikipedia Commons/Guy Bar-Oz).

The latter trot makes the canine move sideways, as many dogs do, thus consuming much extra energy when swinging the hind paw around the front paw. Examples of wolves with the wrong physical dimensions are found in several places throughout Europe.

If a wolf has the wrong dimensions, it is practically unable to move in a line with other wolves through deep snow.

The Skeleton

The wolf's skeleton reveals a number of details we need to know. (Figure 2.32).

The angle between the femur and tibia is usually smaller than a dog's. One reason is that the spine at the lumbar vertebrae and the sacrum are bent downward. This gives an impression of a strong thigh. Additionally the knee hides a male wolf's penis.

The upper arm angles backward from the point of the shoulder to the elbow and is never perpendicular to the ground. The angle between the humerus and the radius varies from 90 to 120 degrees.

The metacarpals–radius and metatarsals–tibia angles should be less than approximately 160 degrees. Correct angles and well-developed metatarsals and metacarpals enable a long stride and fast movement in snow as well as in the forest.

Figure 2.33 shows how this young Russian wolf's posture exhibits the features mentioned above.

Figure 2.33. A young wolf's posture (photo by Gisela Möller).

Craniometry and the Wolf's Skull

Craniometry is measurement of the cranium, and it is used to study morphological variations in the skull. Within wolf craniometry, a number of standardized variables are defined, some introduced by professor Henryk Okarma from Poland and others (Okarma and Buchalczyk 1993). In this chapter, we cover some of the most important variables, although some scientists consider craniometry obsolete.

For instance, when studying differences in local wolf populations, the resolution obtained by craniometry is not enough to allow separation between populations. One observation supporting this was reported by a research team in Iran (Khosravi el al. 2012).

Craniometry

The dorsal view of a wolf's skull in Figure 2.34 presents a number of variables used in wolf craniometry (Okarma & Buchalczyk 1993).

- ZyB – zygomatic breadth (Zygion–Zygion).

- C^{1}B – breadth of alveolus of the upper canine C 1 (measurement taken between exterior edges of canines).

- MB – maximum mastoid breadth (Othion–Othion).

- LB – minimum breadth of skull (minimum aboral breadth of the supraorbital processes.

- NaL – nasal length (length of joint between os nasale).

- MNaL – maximum nasal length (from anterior edge of os nasale to its posterior edge).

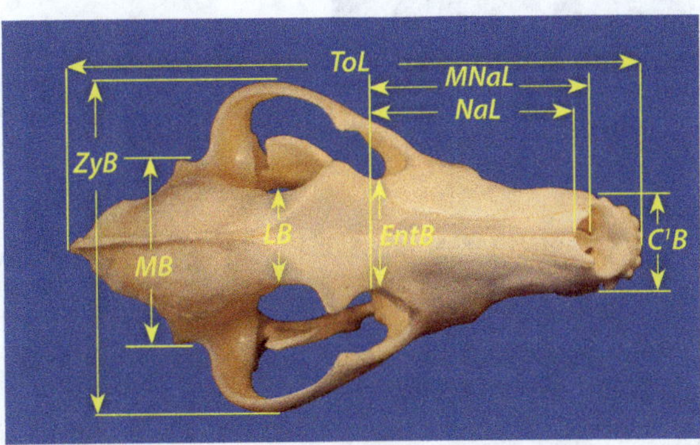

Figure 2.34. Dorsal view of a wolf's skull (photo by the author).

- EntB – minimum breadth between the orbits (entorbitale–entorbitale).

- ToL – total length (prosthion - sagittal crest).

The ventral view in Figure 2.35 presents another sets of variables from the same source (Okarma & Buchalczyk 1993) as follows.

- CbL – condylobasal length (aboral border of the occipital condyles–prosthion).

- BaL – basal length (from posterior edge of alveolus of I$_1$ to foramen supramastoideum).

- FaL – facial length (frontal midpoint–prosthion).

- NeL – upper neurocranium length (frontal midpoint–opisthion).

- PaL – palate length (from posterior edge of alveolus of I^1 to anterior edge of incisura palatina).

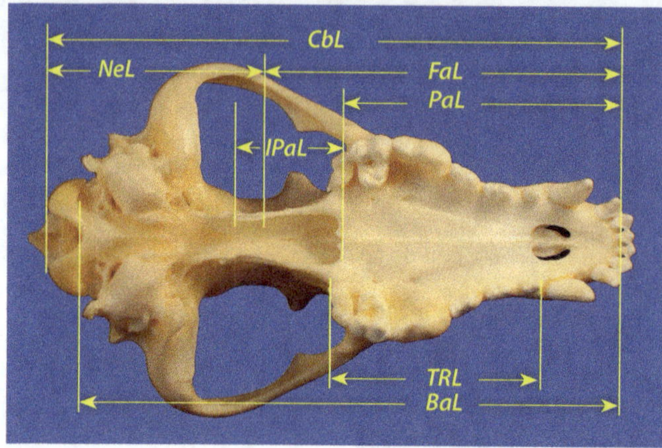

Figure 2.35. Ventral view of a wolf's skull (photo by the author).

- IPaL – length of incisura palatina (from its anterior edge to the posterior edge of hamulus pterigoideus).

- TRL – length of upper tooth row (from anterior edge of P^1 to posterior edge of alveola of M^2).

The lateral view of the same skull, including mandible (lower jaws), shows three variables (MdL and SH, from Okarma and Buchalczyk 1993).

- MdL – total length of mandible (infradentale - condyle process).

- SH – skull height,

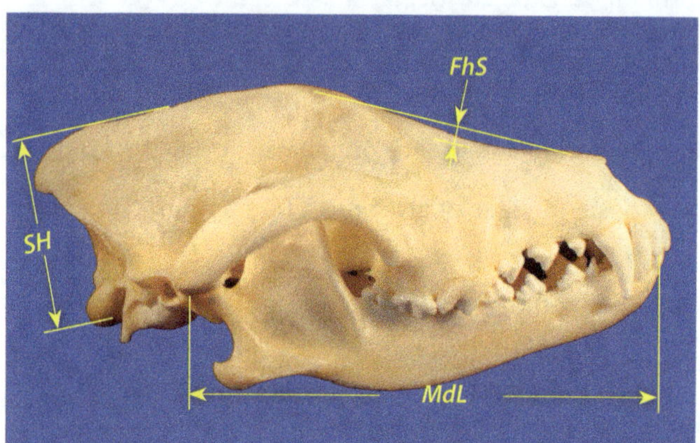

Figure 2.36. Lateral view of a wolf's skull (photo by the author).

- FhS – forehead slope. This parameter is widely used in human craniometry and is used in this context to measure the height of the forehead (Granlund 2015). The mean FhS value measured from 25 Finnish wolves was 5.76 mm. Maximum was 12 mm, and the variance was 5.96. I would not expect pure wolves to exhibit values greater than 6 to 7 mm.

The last variable in Figure 2.36, the orbital angle (OA), describes the width of the forehead. This angle should not be greater than 46 degrees. There are studies claiming that a maximum value of 52 degrees have been observed (Janssens et al. 2016). In my studies, I have observed angles up to 53 degrees which overlap the values for dogs.

The *sagittal crest* is a ridge on the top of the brain case. The bone serves as attachment for the *temporalis* muscle, which is one of the main chewing muscles. This bone develops during the juvenile stage, in conjunction with the growth of the *temporalis* muscle. The size of this ridge is directly proportional to the biting force, and thus it is a feature that distinguishes dogs from wolves.

As with the sagittal crest, the *zygomatic arches* are attachment points, in this case for the jaw muscles, and their robustness also correlates with the bite force.

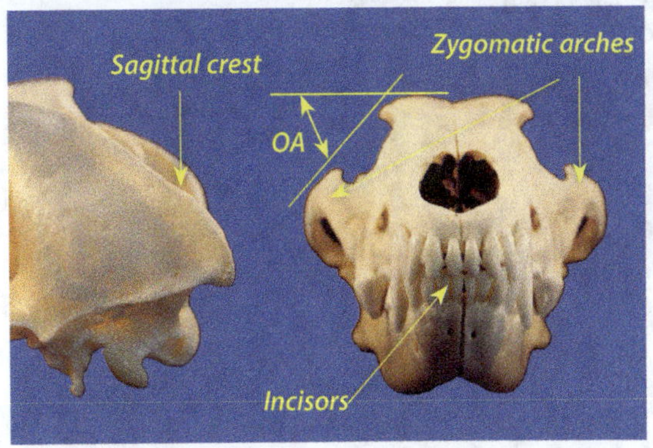

Figure 2.37. Orbital angle and the sagittal crest (photo by the author).

The Wolf's Teeth

The wolf's teeth are described in Figure 2.38.

- The incisors are marked with I(1-3); they are mainly used to cut meat. Wolves' incisors differ from many dogs in that they are evenly spread and symmetrical.

- The canines (C) are remarkably sharp and reach a tremendous size. In this respect, no other species from the *Canis* family can compare to a wolf (Sabaneev 1876). The wolf uses the canines to hold its prey. The length of the canine teeth varies from 27 to 32 mm (maximum 40) on the upper jaw and 25 to 30 mm (maximum 33) on the lower jaw.

- The premolars, or *carnassials* P(1-4) are used to shear and slice meat.

- The molars lie behind the premolars and are used to crush bones.

The wolf's bite force is estimated to be 493.5 N (363.9 ft.-lbs.) at the canine tip and 773.9 N (570.7 ft.-lbs.) at the carnassials (Christiansen and Wroe 2007).

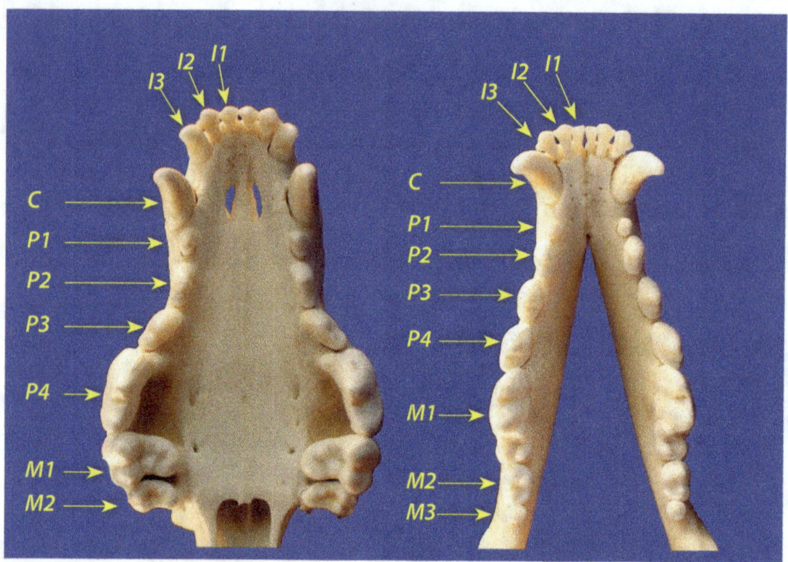

Figure 2.38. A wolf's teeth (photo by the author).

How the Skull Develops

The shape of the skull changes with age. Figure 2.39 shows the head of a young wolf, which resembles a dog's head. The snout is short and the forehead high. During its first year, the snout grows but the skull retains many features typical of dogs. The head is narrow because the *zygomatic arches* are not fully developed, and the *sagittal crest* is just starting to grow. The milk teeth that appeared at the age of 3 weeks begin slowly being replaced at the age of 4 months, starting from the lower jaw.

The skull grows most rapidly during the early postnatal period. A growth model applied to Arctic wolves estimates that 97% of the asymptotic *condylobasal* length is reached by the age of 10 months (Larter, Nagy, and Bartareau 2012). The report also propose that there is a linear relation between the growth of the zygomatic width and the condylobasal length.

Summary

The different craniometric variables described in this chapter are largely used in science. However, there are several other features of craniometry that are used to identify dog heritage in wolves. We will not discuss these features here as these methods have been replaced by population genetics, and at the moment it seems as if population genetics is pushing the wolf's morphological traits toward dogs.

Figure 2.39. A young wolf's head (photo by Gisela Möller).

The Wolf's Tail

If someone is lucky enough to see a wolf in the wild, there are three details that catch his or her attention. At first, there is the silhouette of the wolf carrying its head lower than or at the same level as its back. The second detail noticed is the way wolves move across the terrain, with their back remaining at the same level while their legs do all the work. The third detail is the tail. The wolf's tail points down, while the dog's tail, when relaxed, has a minor upward curve at the tip. When the wolf is running, its tail may have a doggish curvature right above the tip, which is seen in Figures 2.30 and 2.31, but when the wolf slows down or stops, the tail turns downward and may even drop between the hind legs. The tail reaches the wolf's heels but never goes below it (personal communications with Dr. Erik S. Nyholm). A closer look at a wolf's tail reveals a **supracaudal gland** (also called violet gland) marked with black-tipped cover hairs located about one-third of the way down the tail from the root, approximately above the 9th caudal vertebra. The supracaudal gland is an important gland found on the upper surface of the tail of wolves and other mammals. The secretion from this gland is used for intra-species signalling and scent marking, and it contributes to a strong odor that can be quite unpleasant. The gland's secretions are fluorescent in ultraviolet light.

The gray wolf's tail tip is always black or dark brown.

The wolf's tail is almost completely straight and devoid of the mobility and flexibility that we notice in hunting dogs. Except for the breeding pair, wolves never lift their tails above their backs but, rather, mostly keep it low; nor are they able to curl their tail as some dog breeds do. We will discuss wolves' use of their tails later in this book.

Figure 2.40. The wolf's posture and its tail (photo by the author).

There is some evidence that a long tail with a slight curvature is inherited from dogs. The four canines in Figure 2.42 exhibit different tail shapes. The canine in photo A is an almost pure male wolf, and in genetic population analysis is found among Siberian wolves. The one in photo B is a low content female wolf–dog and the hybrids in C and D are their offspring (A + B). The wolf in A has a tail typical of wolves while the hybrid in B has a long tail with minor curvature. Their offspring have a doggish tail with curvature close to the tail tip.

The Wolf's Legs

When it comes to the strength of hind legs, the wolf has no rivals. An old Russian proverb says "The wolf is fed by its legs," and indeed, the strength and width of the cervical and spinal muscles prove the remarkable physical strength of the wolf. The wolf relies most of all on the strength of its teeth and legs.

Figure 2.43 reveals the main differences between wolves' legs and dogs' legs, although all dogs do not look like this one.

Figure 2.41. The tail of a wild Russian wolf (photo by Gisela Möller).

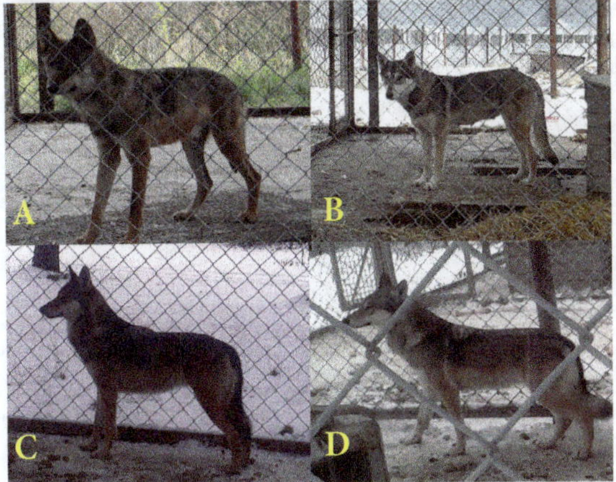

Figure 2.42. Wolves and hybrids behind bars (photo by the author.

The hind legs are heavily muscled through the thighs. When viewed from the rear, the wolf's hind legs are cow-hooked. The wolf's feet act as shock absorbers when its body interacts with a surface, and they help the body adapt to the terrain. The toes adapt further to the terrain and give extra propulsion during gait. The wolf's stifles are bent forward, as shown in Figure 2.43B and its elbows and hock joints are bent backward as shown in Figure 2.43A and D. The angle from the shoulder tie via A to C is almost 90 degrees, while in most dogs, it is an almost straight line.

The anterior (front) side of western European wolves' front legs are dominated by a dark or black strip. As populations move eastward, the strip diminishes (Pulliainen 1965). This strip is visible in the Iberian wolf, which is one the reasons why this subspecies is named *Canis lupus signatus*. Material collected from Siberian wolves suggests that this strip is also found on most Siberian wolves. However, a master's thesis accepted at the University of Oslo shows that this strip is diminishing when comparing extinct wolves to the extant ones.

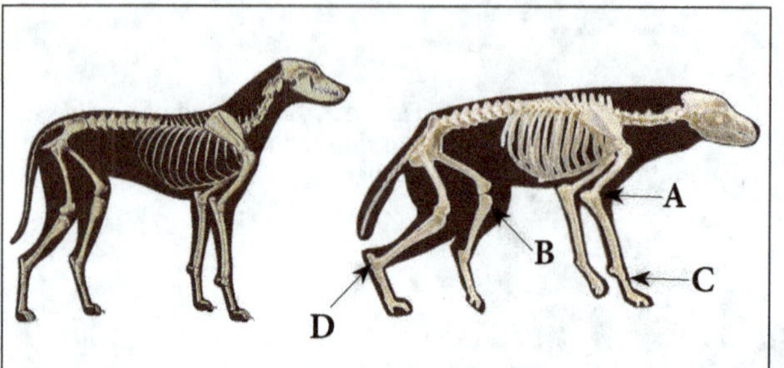

Figure 2.43. Dog and wolf skeletons.

Wolves are digitigrade animals, which means that their digits are the weight-bearing surface of their body. Thus the phalanges (finger bones) form an important part of the wolf's foot. The names of the bones, following the numbers in Figure 2.44 are as follows:

1. Carpals.

2. Metacarpals or metatarsals.

3. Proximal phalanges.

4. Intermediate phalanges.

5. Distal phalanges.

Figure 2.44 shows the phalanges and how they are positioned on the wolf's foot.

The wolf's claws are always black. This is an observation documented by Bibikov, Hepner and Naumov, Pulliainen, and Sabanneev. It is one of the traits that identifies the wolf. Among the more than one hundred wolves I have studied some have had yellow stripes on their claws (Figure 2.45B) or completely yellow claws (Figure 2.45A). However, these dog-like traits are not observed alone but are usually exhibited along with other unusual traits in the same wolf.

It is worth noting that eumelanin is responsible not only for the black color but also makes the claws more durable than white claws.

The black claws shown in Figure 2.45C are from a Russian wolf shot by Bernt Lindqvist in Russia in the 1990s.

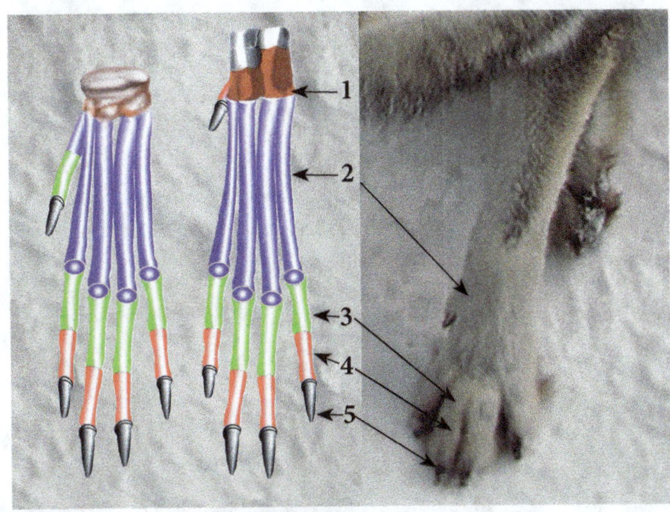

Figure 2.44. A wolf's phalanges.

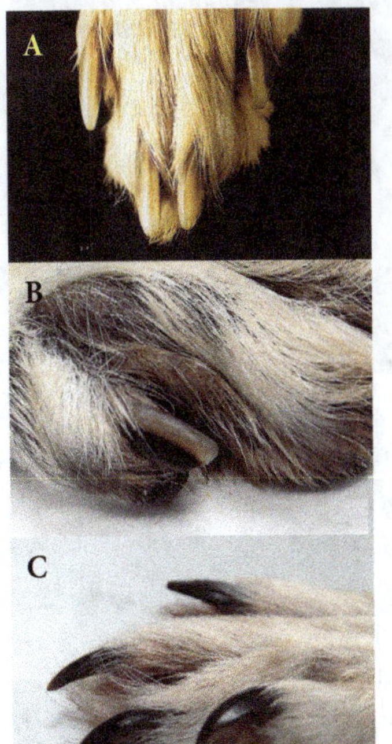

Another observation claims that the wolf's claws are vertically flattened, while most dogs have triangular claws.

Some scientists suggest that if a canine is positioned within a genetic population, then the color of the claws do not matter. However, the relationship between genotype and phenotype follows a symmetrically equivalent relationship such that

If a wolf looks like a wolf, then the genotype should prove it is a wolf, and if the genotype proves it is a wolf, then it should look like a wolf.

If the above conditions are not satisfied, then science has to re-evaluate their genetic methods, because the wolf's appearance has not changed due to genetics analysis.

Wolves' Senses

The wolf's most important senses are taste, sight, hearing, and smell. Investigation of taste is difficult

Figure 2.45. Wolves' claws (photos by the author).

due to the fact that the influence of smell often plays a major role in how food tastes. Sabaneev wrote in his book ***Predatory Animals (1876)***,

> *The taste of the wolf is weakly developed. This is proved by wolves' extreme indiscrimination in food and the fact that it prefers already rotten, even decaying carrion before fresh, and mainly because it does not feel bitter taste. No matter how meat is stuffed with strychnine, and therefore extremely bitter, the wolf will still eat it and only stops when it is about vomiting.*

This weak development of taste and indiscrimination in choice of food is explained by the wolf's gluttony.

Figure 2.46. The development of a wolf pup's eyes (photo by Gisela Möller).

Eyes and Vision

Wolves are usually born with blue eyes, which lighten and then gradually fade into the adult wolf's eye color over the first six to ten weeks. Figure 2.46 shows a wolf pup on June 17 with blue eyes (on the left) and the same pup on July 2 (on the right). We can see the change in eye color that occurred during those two weeks.

Due to the shape of a pup's head, with a short snout and a high forehead, the eyes point forward. As the pup grows and the skull's shape changes toward an adult wolf's skull, the color of the eyes turn to amber, yellow, light brown, or gold. Wolves with blue eyes have inherited this color from dogs such as Huskies.

The adult wolves' eyes are almond shaped and slanted, with the corners of the eyes lining up with the outer base of the ears. The almond shape is also observed when studying wolf skulls. In Figure 2.34, we notice how the orbitals (the cavities in which the eyes are situated) are elongated. Figures 2.47 and 2.48 show the facial expression of wolves and how their eyes are situated in the head.

A wolf's eyesight is just about as good as that of a human being. However, there is some uncertainty as to whether or not a wolf is nearsighted. According to Sabaneev, the

Figure 2.47. Two adult Russian wolves captured at the border to Finland. Both wolves exhibit the slanted eyes typical of wolves (photo by the author).

wolf's vision in daylight is no better than a domestic dog's. He claims that the wolf's vision, in general, develops more in steppes, where the eye adapts to longer viewing distances than in forested areas (Sabaneev 1876).

Although a wolf is not a fully nocturnal animal, its night vision is superior than the dog's. Self-preservation has long encouraged wolves to look for food primarily at night, which has affected their night vision. This also explains why the wolf 's eyes have a completely different expression, and like many nocturnal animals, they shine in the dark with phosphorescent light.

Figure 2.48. Six wolves shot in Finland in 1965. All exhibit typical wedge-shaped large heads with slanted eyes typical of wolves.

Another detail is how wolves see objects in the wild. Figure 2.49 shows that wolves' (and dogs') ability to distinguish colors is quite different from human vision. The wolf's weak ability to distinguish yellow from green or orange from red makes the environment look quite different through a wolf's eyes than it does through human eyes.

Ears and Hearing

A wolf's ears are triangular rounded across the top, and shorter than coyote or fox ears.

The two wolves shown in Figure 2.50, as well as the wolves in Figures 2.47 and 2.48, show how the wolves' ears are placed far apart. This, in turn, depends on the width of the wolf's skull and the thickness of the temporalis muscle. As mentioned earlier, the ears are filled with fluffy fur, and the rear (posterior) side of the ears are ocher or brown with some short, dark gray hair between the ears.

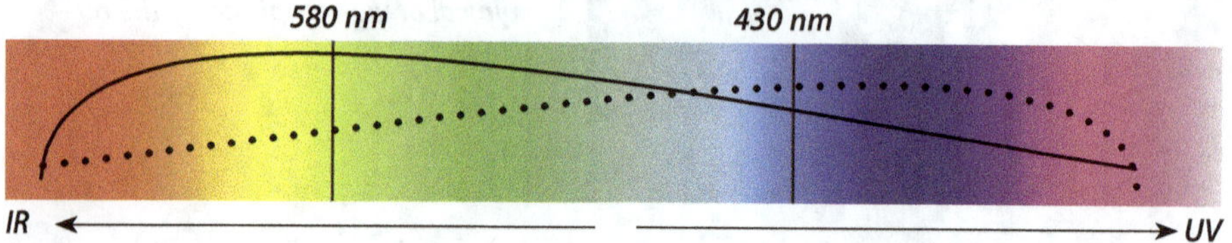

Figure 2.49. Human color vision (solid line) and wolf color vision (dotted line).

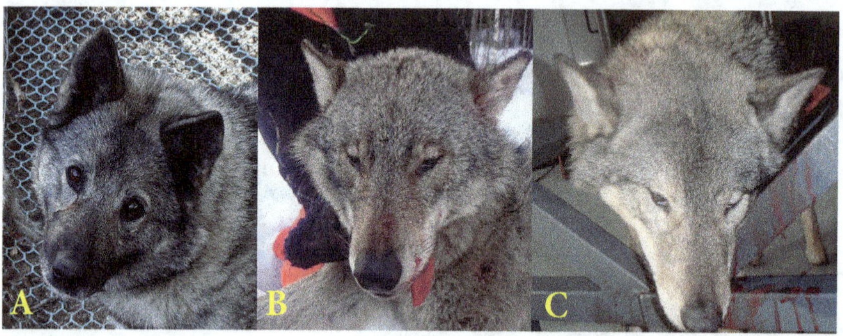

Figure 2.50. The front view of a hunting dog (A) and two wolves (B, C) (photos by the author).

The wolf uses its ears independently of each other. This is observed in Figure 2.9, where one ear is listening to sounds coming from the rear, while the other ear is listening to sounds coming from the front.

The wolf hears much farther away than it can smell scents with nose–a fact known by all wolf hunters. A successful wolf hunt requires complete silence, and the direction of the wind is important because, like all of us, the wolf hears better against the wind. Here, again, it should be noted that sensitivity to various kinds of sounds is determined by the terrain. In forested areas, sounds are not only more diverse than in open fields but they are audible with a wind of moderate strength at greater distances. In the forest or in the bush, it is difficult to approach a wolf, because the wolf relies more heavily on hearing than on the sense of smell. Even when sleeping, the wolf reacts to every suspicious sound, which may spur him into flight (Sabaneev 1876).

Wolves are able to hear frequencies far above the limits of human beings. The limits of a dog's hearing has been found to be from 67 Hz to 45,000 Hz (Warfield 1973). Thus we can safely suppose that range of frequencies a wolf hears is approximately the same. Wolves have been known to react to imitated howls from a distance of five kilometers, but they may, under optimal circumstances, recognize sounds at distances up to 15 kilometers.

The problem with measuring hearing is that sound is dependent on the direction of the wind, as well as the density of trees and other obstacles between the wolves and the source of a sound. In addition, the temperature may affect the propagation of sound as temperature inversion can cause distant sources of noise to sound much closer than they actually are.

Sense of Smell

The wolf's sense of smell is highly developed, as can be expected with an animal possessing numerous scent glands. The distance at which any scent can be detected depends on atmospheric conditions, but under the most favorable conditions, a wolf can smell its prey from about 2.5 km miles away, and wolves usually travel until they encounter the scent of a prey species ahead of them.

It is not clear how much a wolf (or dog) relies on its sense of smell, but it is obvious that the way these animals use their sense of smell is comparable to the way humans rely on vision. In the same way as a human's vision is able to extract small details of the landscape, a wolf can separate and identify every weak odor from a large number of different scents. Sniffing dogs are good examples. It is practically impossible to conceal drugs from well-trained sniffer dogs. Trying to mask the smell of a drug by surrounding it with something exuding a stronger smell is doomed to fail and simply shows a profound lack of understanding of how a dog's sense of smell works.

When a dog or wolf sniffs a tree, it is in essence "checking a pee mailbox." The smell left by another canine is much more than just a bunch of water, urea, chloride, sodium, potassium, and creatinine. A scent mark left in the wild probably contains dozens or hundreds of different odors, each carrying specific information about the canine leaving the mark.

The wolf has several specialized scent glands, including one around the anus and another on its back. The scent from these glands is as individually identifying for a wolf as a fingerprint is for a human, and scent marks left in the wild serve as the wolf's business card. The scent marks are also used to delineate the boundaries of wolves' territories.

The Wolf's Age

The wolf's life differs from the dog's in several aspects. First, a wolf cub is able to take care of itself at the age of 6 months, but it is unlikely that a young dog of this age would be able to live and fend for itself. However, the wolf reaches maturity much later than a dog does, with females maturing no earlier than two years and males during their third year.

Wolves are generally strongest at 5 to 7 years of age, but at an age of ten, teeth, especially the long canines wear off and turn yellow. They slowly become blunt or even invisible so that old wolves are no longer able to cause serious damage to their prey.

These old wolves live alone, their eyes sunken and their pelage getting almost gray. Such old individuals are very rare for understandable reasons and are encountered among males more often than among females. In the difficult struggle for their existence, few wolves survive and live ten years.

The Wolf's Cognitive Capabilities

Many anecdotes are told about the wolf's mental abilities. Some authors claim that the wolf's mental abilities surpass all other animals and are not inferior to human' abilities. Either these writers' fantasies or their credulity are rich.

There is no doubt that wolves use some tricks to get their food, but the same or similar tricks are used by many other animals, and they are solely at the level of attacks on a herd of prey animals from two or three different directions. However, it is worth comparing the wolf to the dog to understand what domestication has done to the wolf during the past 10,000 to 20,000 years.

The Wolf and the Dog

The domestication of dogs has brought about changes in their behavior, so wolves differ significantly from domestic dogs in behavior as well as appearance. Dogs and wolves have different lifestyles that require different abilities and skills. The skills and behaviors a wolf needs to find food, breed, and survive differ from those a pet dog needs when living in a human home. As a result, dogs have learned to depend on humans, while wolves are on their own. This means, in part, that dogs are more predisposed than wolves to form social attachments to people.

Dogs are sometimes labeled as less intelligent than wolves, but for everything that wolves do better than dogs, there are other things that dogs do better than wolves. Their differences don't make dogs and wolves more or less intelligent than each other, but, rather, they simply reflect the fact that they have followed different evolutionary paths.

We also require different things of dogs than what nature demands of wolves. Through domestication, we have selected dogs to be attuned to our behavior and to work with us. As a result, dogs are much less neophobic, meaning that they are not afraid of new or unfamiliar things and people they encounter. Dogs are much more tractable than tame wolves, and in general, they are much more responsive than wolves to coercive training techniques involving fear, aversive stimuli, and force. Dogs also tend to be poorer than wolves at observational learning, while they are more responsive to instrumental conditioning.

An interesting study was carried out by a Hungarian research team who compared communicative abilities of dogs and wolves that were socialized to humans at comparable levels. The study was divided into two parts.

The first part demonstrated that socialized wolves were able to locate hidden food indicated by touching and, to some extent, pointing cues provided by a familiar human supervisor, but their performance remained inferior to that of dogs. However, in the case of touching all individuals performed significantly better than chance.

Although these results indicate that dog-like rearing of young wolves teaches them to interpret some human gestures, their performance was generally worse than that of the dogs.

The second part found that after undergoing training to solve a simple task of manipulation, dogs faced with an insoluble version of the problem from part 1 looked to a human, while socialized wolves did not. Based on these observations, researchers suggested that a key difference between dog and wolf behavior is dogs' ability to "ask for help." Because looking has an important function in human interaction, dogs have adopted parts of this mechanism, which has led to a complex form of dog-human interaction that cannot be achieved with wolves.

The observations in both parts suggest that after facing difficulty in getting food, dogs initiated face or eye contact with the human earlier and maintained it for longer periods of time than did the socialized wolves (Miklósi et al. 2003).

Summary

On the other hand, there is research proving the opposite. Researchers at the Max Planck Institute claim in an article (https://www.shh.mpg.de/625264/wolf-cognition) that both dogs and wolves were able to follow communicative cues to find hidden food. However, the problem with communicative cues is that all tests have been carried out with socialized wolves, which undermines the value of these research results.

Intelligence, Causality, Or Conditioned Behavior

Causality connects the cause with the effect, where both parts are dependent on each other. So far, there is no difference in conditioned behavior and causality. To understand where intelligence enters the scene, consider the following:

> *A wolf senses the smell of sheep, and excited by the possibility of killing a couple, it rushes toward the flock, but runs into an electric fence. An electric chock of 5,000 volts strikes the wolf, and it backs a couple of meters. However, the wolf is smart enough to follow the fence for another mile and decides to make a new trial. Fortunately, someone has forgotten a mat of isolating rubber on the ground under the fence, close to an old oak, and the wolf is lucky to step on the mat as it crawls under the electric wires. Because the wolf's pads are isolated from the ground, the electric circuit from the wire to the ground is not closed by the wolf, and it can pass under the fence without problems.*

What did the wolf learn?

1. It is safe to crawl under the fence at the old oak!

2. The mat protects the wolf as long as it does not touch the ground with its pads.

3. The mat may be moved to another fence or place. In other words, it can be used as a tool to crawl under any electric fence.

A wolf's capabilities are probably limited to number 1, while a chimp might understand the implications of 2 and 3.

Intelligence is using the mat as a tool, causality is understanding that "I am safe as long as I stand on the mat," and conditioned behavior is understanding it is safe to cross the fence at the old oak.

WOLF'S BEHAVIOR

The theory of evolution is the overall central theory for all biological sciences, including genetics, biochemistry, physiology, and behavior. Behavior is the trait by which an animal adapts to its environment, and ethology is the science studying animal behavior with a focus on behavior under natural conditions.

Behavioral isolation is one of the prezygotic barriers that prevent reproduction between similar species because each group possesses its own characteristic courtship behaviors.

In order to understand and recognize the wolf, we must understand its behavior.

THE WOLF PACK

As evolutionary processes shape an organism's physical traits to adapt to its environment, genes also capture the evolutionary responses of prior populations' behavior. Acclimatization is the process through which an animal adjusts to a change in its environment, thus allowing it to live in a wide range of environmental conditions. With this environmental flexibility, animals have the opportunity to adjust to changes in behavior during their own lifetime.

Adaptation is the long-term evolutionary process that fits organisms to their environment, enhancing their evolutionary fitness.

This is how genes and the environment come together to shape animal behavior.

The Pack and Its Organization

Different terms are used for groups formed by animals of the same species. The term herd is generally applied to grazing ungulates. The word flock is used in conjunction with birds, sheep, or goats. Large groups of carnivores are usually called packs. In nature, a herd or a flock is classically subject to predation by a pack.

Social interaction is the cornerstone when forming a herd, flock or pack. Simply clumping animals together is not a requirement for social behavior, but it increases the opportunities for interaction to occur between two or more individuals of the same species. Interaction happens when animals form simple aggregations, cooperate in sexual or parental behavior, engage in disputes over territory and access to mates, or simply communicate across space.

Social behavior is defined by interaction, not by how animals are geographically distributed.

When a female wolf emits pheromones to attract potential mates, she is engaging in social behavior.

Who Is the Leader?

Social animals live in a hierarchical community. In packs with developed social behavior, the highest ranking individual is sometimes referred to as alpha. In cases where one male and one female fulfill the role of pack leaders, they are referred to as the alpha pair. Other animals in the same social group exhibit subordinate behaviors toward the alpha(s).

Every leader needs followers, something that is true for wolves as well as humans. In nature, the leader's position has to be earned. Each member of a pack tries to increase its status within the pack, sometimes by fighting, and sometimes without. For instance, yearlings are more obstreperous when challenging other wolves within a pack because such behavior uncovers any debility in its object. Wolves are likely to respond to signs of debility with testing and possibly attack, even if they have a long history of friendly interactions with their victim (Frank 1987).

Thus we strongly recommend that even familiar people, if they are debilitated in some way, should not handle wolves (Frank 1987).

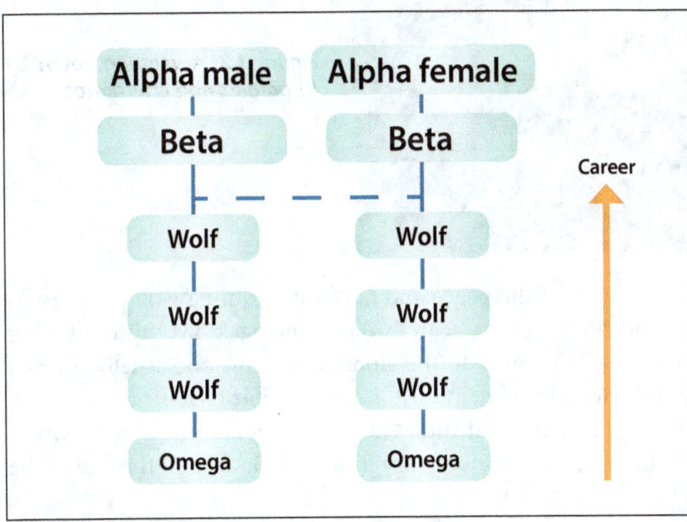

Figure 3.1. The social hierarchy within a wolf pack

Life Within a Pack

Within a wolf pack, there are different ranks. We commonly distinguish between the alpha pair and the rest of the pack, where the alpha pair is the mating pair that gains preferred access to food and other desirable items. Thus, they are dominant over the rest of the pack.

However, the "ordinary wolves" form their own hierarchy below the leaders, the highest of which are the beta wolves. Below the beta wolves are ordinary wolves, and at the bottom, we find what are called the omega wolves.

Beta animals act as second-in-command and will take on the alpha role if an alpha dies or if an alpha (usually the female) is dismissed from the pack.

Omegas are at the bottom of the pack's hierarchy. They are inferior to all others in the community, and are expected to be submissive to the other wolves. However, the omegas play an important role in the pack, allowing frustration to be vented among the wolves without fights. Being the scapegoat for the other wolves in the pack, they are the last to feed at the site of a pack's kill—if they are allowed to feed.

It is interesting to note that packs that loose their omega(s) enter into a period of mourning, where the entire pack stops hunting and just lies around looking miserable.

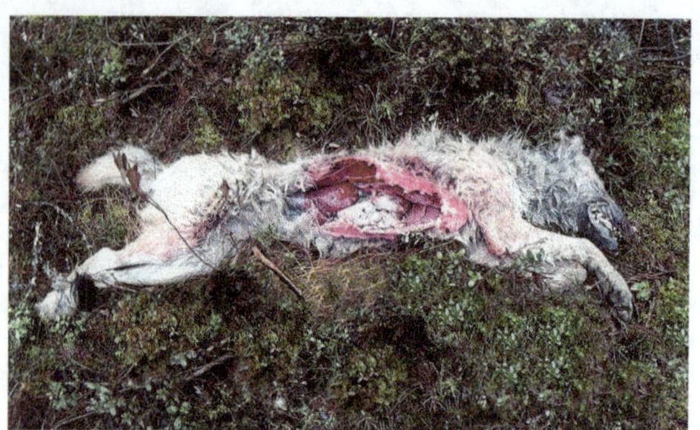

Figure 3.2. A yearling eaten by its parents and littermates.

Sabaneev presents another view of the peace and harmony within a wolf pack, especially in winter when food resources are scarce. When the pack has captured a big prey animal, the lion's share always goes to the alpha male. This one cruelly offends the young wolves and alpha female, who, in turn, raise a terrible bickering when they share the leftovers. Often it happens that the weakest individuals are torn to shreds by their more powerful littermates. It is necessary to show blood—and the fate of the unfortunate is solved (Sabaneev 1876).

The yearling in Figure 3.2 was killed and partially eaten when a wolf pack tried to share a killed hunting dog.

The Composition of a Wolf Pack

Most wild wolves live in packs. However, an estimated 15% to 25% of the Finnish wolves roam alone, while the rest live in couples or packs (Internet A25). In the autumn we find wolf packs consist of an alpha pair, a number of yearlings (cubs from the previous year), youngsters (cubs from the current year), males from earlier litters, and immature females. Mature females are always expelled from the pack unless the male dismisses the old female instead.

Average litter sizes										
Number of cubs	1	2	3	4	5	6	7	8	9	10
Observations	5	3	4	**10**	**14**	**13**	6	7	-	1

Table 3.1. Litter sizes (Marvin 1959).

Table 3.1 shows results from a study carried out in Karelia examining the average litter size of Russian wolves (Marvin 1959). According to this study, the average litter size is between four and six cubs. However, the number of offspring is almost entirely dependent on the availability of prey animals (food)–a fact known by dog breeders.

The composition of the pack varies within the year.

The number of prey animals is a factor that regulates the size of a wolf pack. When there is a shortage of food, some wolves (usually males) leave the pack and others (usually females) are expelled (Zimen 1976). Kudaktin suggests that these expelled wolves attack and kill livestock (Kudaktin 1977). As food becomes scarce, wolves start to die of starvation, and the first casualties are youngsters and wolves of lower rank (inferior wolves).

When food is scarce, the next step is to expand the territory, but this most often ends in fights with other packs–fights that result in several casualties. (Mech 1977).

Figure 3.3. A wolf demonstrates its dominance with its posture (modified from Bibikov 1985).

Communication Between Wolves

Dominance and Submission

The order of dominance and submission is displayed in a wolf pack through a complex mix of sounds and physical gestures. Wolves use a variety of methods to express their status in the pack, including posture, ear and tail positioning, and facial expression, accompanied by vocalizations to exhibit their dominance over subordinate wolves.

Figure 3.4. A wolf demonstrates its dominance with its teeth (modified from Bibikov 1985).

The position of a wolf's tail tells much about its rank. When the tail is straight out and slightly up, the wolf indicates dominance, while the inferior wolf tucks its tail between the hind legs. The superior wolf's ears point up or forward, while the inferior wolf's ears are held close to the head. Figure 3.3 shows how two wolves sort out their relationship within a pack. The left wolf is a subordinate, and the wolf on the right is exhibiting its dominance.

Sometimes, posture is not enough, and the wolf expresses dominance by revealing its teeth, which may be enough to sort out misinterpretations. The typical postures of two wolves exchanging opinions about dominance are seen in Figure 3.4.

Too often, a bold youngster decides to challenge an older wolf in order to advance in the pack's hierarchy, which frequently results in the cub ending up on the pack's dinner table.

Internal fights are the main reason for the high mortality of cubs during their first year.

When an inferior wolf challenges a superior wolf, the former puts its jaws near the neck of the latter. The inferior wolf shows a strong intention to bite, but being inferior, it does not dare. Most often, the posture of the superior puts forward a challenge that the inferior is unable to face. On occasion, the inferior actually grips the head or muzzle of the superior, but because the latter maintains his proud, challenging posture, the former does not dare to bite with strength (Schenkel 1967).

Inferiority among wolves is often combined with an antagonistic or hostile attitude. The inferior tends to avoid the superior's vicinity by means of flight, or it shows defensive aggression (Schenkel 1947). A combination of avoidance and defense can frequently be observed when the superior points at the inferior's hindquarters. If the inferior has no chance to escape, he shows symptoms of social stress, such as diarrheic defecation, and his tail is bent downward between the hind legs (Schenkel 1967).

Active Submission

Active submission is an activity in which the signs of inferiority are evident. The posture is slightly crouched, the tail is low, and the ears are directed backward, lying close to the head. There is no hostility in this attitude. Active submission occurs frequently as a group ceremony, where the alpha male is surrounded by all other pack members who nose-push, lick, or tenderly seize his muzzle or face.

Figure 3.5. An inferior wolf challenges a superior wolf (modified from Bibikov 1985).

Passive Submission

In passive submission, the signs of inferiority are clear. The inferior lies on its side, exposing the ventral side of its chest and sometimes the abdomen. This occurs as a reaction to olfactory investigation in the genital region. The ears are directed backwards and lie close to the head. The tail is bent ventrally between the thighs.

Scent Marking and Urination

The wolf's sense of smell is another important aspect of the way wolves communicate. Wolf scent glands produce a personal signature in the form of pheromones. These glands exist all over the wolf's body, leaving a personal stamp of odor whenever they move. The pack's territorial boundaries are marked with scat and urine to keep other packs away; however, the smell from the scat or urine is not the primary mechanism that keeps neighbors from the territory.

When a wolf pack finds scent marks from other wolves, they intensify marking their own territory while one wolf tracks the newcomers on the demilitarized zone between two territories, to see if they simply passed by. There are no observations indicating that wolves turn around as soon as they encounter odors from unknown wolves.

When two wolves meet, they analyze the scent from the different glands to see if they have met a wolf from their own pack or a stranger. If a stranger enters a wolf pack's territory, the wolves attack it without any rituals, and if the alien cannot escape, it risks being seriously injured or even killed and eaten (Pålsson 1984). However, there are cases where a stranger has been accepted by the pack when the foreign wolf enters the pack's territory.

Figure 3.6. A wolf's scat, typically tapered on one or both ends. The scats are often composed of fur, bones, and meat. This scat was used to mark the wolf's territory (photo by the author).

When scent marking, males urinate from different positions (Bibikov 1985).

1. The wolf marks (urinates) standing on four legs, with its back slightly bent in the sacrum area–this posture is typical for young males.

2. When marking small objects, sexually mature males wolves raise their hind leg under the body.

3. When marking high objects, the male urinates with the hind leg raised.

Females sit down on all four legs, holding the tail parallel to the ground. Less often, the female marks with a hid leg raised. This is characteristic only for high-ranking females and females in estrus.

The posture for defecation does not differ between males and females.

The Wolf's Tail

The wolf never curls its tail like some dogs do. If the wolf rises its tail above the back, it is signaling its superiority. If the tail is kept below the back, then the wolf is relaxed or indicating submission. The direction of the tail is sometimes seen as a gauge for indicating a wolf's status in the hierarchy. A slowly wagging tail pointing backward is often an indication of a coming attack.

Within the pack, a wagging tail is a sign of friendship or passive submission.

Wolf Vocalizations

The wolf uses four vocalization methods to communicate with other wolves.

1. Wolves bark as a warning, the way dogs do, to warn their pack of an approaching stranger. The alpha male may bark to his pups because he senses danger. Barking together with howling is used to show aggression when protecting the territory.

2. Wolves use growling to signal their aggression—again, as dogs do. Most fights, such as with intruders, are met by growling when the wolf needs or tries to show domination.

3. Whimpering is primarily used in two situations, when the alpha male needs to nurse the pups or when an inferior wolf backs out of a situation, where it has challenged a superior wolf.

These three vocalizations are local, meaning wolves use them to communicate with each other over a short distance.

4. Howling is a form of communication used by wolves over long distances.

However, wolves do not use loud howling all around the year. In the beginning of summer, not earlier than end of June, the wolves begin to howl at night. As long as the cubs don't move around by themselves, which happens when they reach an age of 6-8 weeks, the wolf's howl is almost not audible. The breeding pair is afraid of revealing the location of their defenseless offspring. During daytime they do not howl, but call the pups and echo each other with a short squeal.

In July, when the cubs hear the female or male returning to the den, they raise a terrible howling and bickering, audible in the dawn for a great distance. L. P. Sabaneev described the howling of an alpha male with the following:

The sun had set. The bird choir was already silent, the sky was clear, and the silence was unperturbed. The old wolf stood up, stretched, and arched its back.

Only a barely noticeable movement of its ears showed that it was listening to something. It heard the creaking of the gates shut in the nearby village and the sound of the postal bell dying away in the distance. The wolf raised its head up and howled. The forest seemed to come alive. In different places, young wolves, males and females, responded to the old man's howl. Then all gathered and ran behind the old man to the smothered calf. Another twenty steps and dinner would be ready. In the east, the dawn flushed, and the wolves started on their return trip. Coming to the den, the adults howled again, and again, the whole brood responded to it.

Late in the autumn, wolves rarely respond to the voice of a hunter, trying to lure them by imitating their howling.

Howling is like a roll-call between members of a wolf pack.

Latitude	Region	Summer–km²	Winter–km²	Source
47.75 ° N	Minnesota, USA	110	116	Fuller 1989
52.75 ° N	South Poland	95	196	Jędrzejewski et al. 2007
54.92 ° N	NW Alberta Canada	263	502	Ballard et al. 1997
63.00 ° N	NW Alaska, USA	622	1,372	Ballard et al. 1998
64.45 ° N	NW Territories Canada	11,340	37,360	Walton et al. 2001

Table 3.2. Territory vs latitude (Jędrzejewski et al. 2007).

The Territory

A common belief is that a male wolf and a female wolf suddenly run to each other and decide to "get married" and establish their own territory. One would then ask, why has evolution developed scent marking for females that attracts males? In practice, females come into heat and start scent marking. Soon, several males are attracted by the smell, and during the forming of new pairs, a period called "wolf wedding" is manifested when a group of males gather around one female. These "weddings" are accompanied by violent struggles and hard fights between young males for the female. The fight sometimes ends with death, and the dead wolf may even be devoured. The female bonds with the strongest wolf of this gang, and thus a new pair is formed, which lasts until the death of one or both "spouses." If the female already has a mate (i.e. they are a breeding pair) the female most often selects the old male, and no fighting occurs (Sabaneev 1876; Heptner & Naumov 1967).

The new pair starts looking for a vacant area where they can establish their territory.

The main requirements are: vacancy, access to water, and stable and abundant food resources.

The Size of the Territory

The size of the territory varies depending on the number of prey animals, and it seems to increase with latitude (Jędrzejewski et al. 2007). Table 3.2 shows results from Jędrzejewski et al.'s study. A key factor determining the ability of wolves to respond to changes in prey availability and to fully exploit prey populations is their flexibility regarding territory size, which is known to vary with prey densities (Fuller et al. 2003). The wolves defend their territory, and strangers are usually met with an aggressive attack. The borders are marked with scent marks, which are supposed to keep other wolves away.

Figure 3.7. Components of wolf territory in Germany. (Source: Wernher Gerhards).

Figure 3.7 shows a typical wolf territory drawn as a hexagon. Notice the no man's land (Wolfspass) between two adjacent territories, allowing stray wolves to roam and preventing scent marks from being overwritten by neighbors. Within this territory, the dotted line represents the pack's regular route.

When the pack is looking for prey within the territory, it regularly refreshes old scent marks. Poyarkov studied scent marking in the Manturovo district and noticed that the male of the breeding pair placed scent marks at intervals of 130 m to 160 m, and the female marked at intervals of 300 m. When the wolves crossed a swamp, Poyarkov did not find any marks within a distance of 2 kilometers, but as soon as the wolves entered the forest, the male made seven scent marks and the female two scent marks within the next kilometer (Pålsson 1984).

As they continued on their way, the wolves made twenty-four scent marks within a distance of four kilometers, and on their way back they made fifteen more scent marks. They marked a total of twenty-six places, of which twenty-four were marked in both directions.

A pack marks a greater number of places than a single pair, but the number of marks is not proportional to the pack size (Pålsson 1984).

In their search for prey, wolves move around their territory along a definite route, using the same trails for extended periods, and restoring them after snowfalls. The wolves always find their old tracks and follow them exactly, track by track. Trails are laid out along the banks of rivers and shores of lakes, in places of passage between plantations, ravines overgrown with shrubs, and other such sites. They also prefer roads and paths made by humans (Semenov 1954).

THE WOLF'S HUNTING

Introduction

The mental abilities of an animal are in accordance with the development of known parts of the brain and its sense organs. Thus, the wolf's broad forehead does not tell us much about its capabilities, but does tell us about the thickness of its cranial bones.

The capacity of an animal's skull is insignificant.

There is no doubt that wolves use tricks to get their food, but these are the same tricks all predators use. They may lure stupid dogs and attack a herd from two or three different directions. They sometimes even crawl to the prey, but these tricks do not require extraordinary mental skills.

The wolf is cautious, but this caution is not reasonable self-preservation, as with the fox, which is never lost in moments of danger. Instead the wolf's cautiousness is cowardice. Only strong hunger is able to supersede the cowardice of a wolf, but then it becomes bold and reckless (Sabaneev 1876).

The adult wolf is afraid of everything, even horses, cows, and sheep in those areas where it only feeds on wild animals and has never seen domestic ones. To be able to recognize an animal as prey, it has to go through a long training program.

The cowardice has its explanations, and especially in the summer, this fear is purely instinctive. At that time of the year, the wolf does not attack dogs, foxes, or other animals that can wound him. Due to the inflexibility of the cervical and spinal vertebrae, it is unable to lick wounds on its back and sides, and in the summer, the slightest scratch in these places bleeds for a long time and easily turns into an infected sore.

A video on YouTube (https://www.youtube.com/watch?v=08cPaFJOYA0&feature=youtu.be) shows three wolves attacking a dog in Italy. As long as the dog keeps escaping, the "brave" wolves go on persecuting it, but when the dog turns around and shows some aggression, the wolves stop and back off. We see the same cowardly behavior in a wolf hunt, where a couple of barking dogs can chase the whole pack through the forest, although with minor efforts and using a combined attack, the pack would be able to kill the persecuting dogs.

The wolf's mental abilities are superseded by cowardice.

Hunting

The wolf relies on its feet and jaws, not on its brain. The wolf's brain is simply a random access memory (RAM), where its stores instructions for how to handle different situations. It lives in a cage of interlocking instincts and imprint-like learning. It will act on the dictates of those instincts and learning, and thus will not attack potential prey that does not match what it has learned.

Because of its only innate strategy, cowardice, the wolf's behavior is dominated by one rule:

Escape if there is no scheme programmed for a specific event.

We have learned that wolves are afraid of humans, but as Sabaneev wrote, it is afraid of everything new, which science calls neophobia.

Figure 3.8. A wolf pack beds down in the forest. (photo by Yellowstone National Park Service).

If, for instance, the wolf pack in Figure 3.8 were taken by surprise by, two bold barking Swedish Drevers, the pack would most probably disperse and flee in panic.

Learning How to Hunt

When the youngsters start hunting with the pack in late August, a common belief is that the leading wolves (the breeding pair) teach the youngsters how to hunt. The only thing the youngsters may learn is that it is time to earn their living by themselves and how to fight for the food. There is no school where dad says, "Now we start lesson 2 and practice killing sheep."

The youngsters have only trained using three innate behaviors:

1. Sneaking up on another pup and attacking it with a jump.

2. Chasing another pup and jumping on it.

3. Playing kind of ring game where a number of pups circle around a "prey pup" and when the "prey pup" stumbles, they all jump on it.

However, all these games have one feature in common. The hunters know the prey (a pack mate). Thus, cowardice does not take over and force the pups to retreat and hide.

Why not simply attack any animal?

Wolves cannot risk being injured when attacking an unknown prey species. The greater the discrepancy between what they learned in their youth and the new animal's appearance, sound, and smell, the greater the resistance to exploring the new animal as potential prey. And that resistance increases should the new prey act bold, assertive, and fearless (Geist 2016).

Hunting Strategies

Wolves use diverse methods when searching for prey. Russian authors claim that the hunting techniques used by wolves vary more than those of foxes and jackals. The arsenal of hunting techniques of wolves varies according to the type of prey, terrain, and other circumstances (Sabaneev 1876). In general, we recognize five stages in wolves' hunting behavior:

1. Searching and finding prey.

2. Concealment and approach.

3. Breaking up a herd or group of prey.

4. Attacking the prey.

5. Killing the prey.

Searching and Finding Prey

The route that a wolf takes to search for prey is normally developed over a period of time. It knows from earlier years where prey animals live and where they are calving. This has nothing to do with instinct or logical reasoning but is only a result of the fact that wolves and their prey are tied to old habits. This instinct is found among bears in Alaska when they catch salmon going upriver at certain time of the year.

To make it simple:

Every time animals adopt a new habit, their brains are forming new neural pathways. The more they do it, the stronger those neural pathways become and the deeper the animals become embedded in their known routines.

Upon smelling a moose, wolves stop and examine the surrounding area. This is a universal characteristic of wolves whenever they are hunting cloven-hoofed animals.

Sneaking on Their Prey

After wolves discover prey, they try to conceal themselves as they move as close as possible to the prey animals. They make every effort to approach close enough for an attack without being detected. They show great patience. Sometimes wolves crawl, keeping close to the ground as they approach their prey. When the prey raise their heads to look around, the wolves stop moving and stay frozen close to the ground. Often, the wolves wait until their prey is chewing before trying to move closer.

Figure 3.9. Wolves trying to break up a herd of bison (photo by Yellowstone National Park Service).

If the wolves are able to approach within a few meters of their prey, the attack begins. They will quickly leap the last few meters and grab the prey.

Breaking up a Herd or Group.

Russian game managers have documented extensive experience observing wolves hunting prey in a herd. The wolves try to break up the herd or separate one or two animals from the herd. The methods they use vary and include tactics, such as distracting the attention of the herd, suddenly attacking the herd, attacking from opposite sides, penetrating into the herd to create panic, and attacking animals that are a short distance from the herd.

When the wolves have separated some of the prey animals from the herd, they start chasing these to intercept one. This technique is often successful because prey animals typically run in circles when being chased.

Setting Up an Ambush

To catch their prey, wolves may set up an ambush along trails that are frequented by prey or which are likely escape routes for their prey in the case of an attack. Wolves may set up ambushes near water holes or use the same ambush site over and over again. The ambush is used for hunting various species of big game, sometimes for dogs, and occasionally even for rabbits.

Figure 3.10. An elk has been separated from its herd (photo by Yellowstone National Park Service).

Chasing Their Prey

If the wolves are not successful in grabbing their prey, the chase begins. During a chase, the pack will split into two or more groups. One group drives the prey, and the other moves into position to attack the prey when the animal is turning. It has been observed that in attacks on moose up to 400 meters, the wolves tried to grab the perineum area and, if unsuccessful, they stopped the attack. During observations of 149 hunts on cloven-hoofed animals, only twelve times did the wolves chase their prey up to four kilometers (Kudaktin 1978).

Wolves gain an advantage when chasing prey in deep or crusted snow or boggy salt marshes. They are skilled, crafty hunters who strive to put their prey at a disadvantage. Crusted snow gives the wolves an advantage because the sharp hooves of cloven-hoofed animals break through the crusted snow, which may cut their legs and cause bleeding and crippling. Wolves, however, easily run over crusted snow, saving their energy for the final kill.

Wolves have also developed an interesting method of chasing sheep down steep slopes in the French Alps (Internet A3). This kind of attack may result in the killing of up to 500 sheep at one time. Similar attacks in Russia have been reported by Dmitry Bibikov (as cited by Pålsson 2003), where the wolves killed moose by chasing them over a cliff.

Figure 3.11. Wolves playing the Ring Game with a bison (photo by Yellowstone National Park Service).

Playing the Ring Game

When the prey is exhausted after a long chase or wounded and unable to escape, wolves start circling around the prey just as they did when playing the ring game as cubs. No animal or human escapes this situation alive. We can see in Figure 3.11 how unconcerned the wolves are, as if they just are watching and waiting for the bison to fall. When the bison gets careless and wearily bends its head down a bit, a wolf makes a fast attack trying, to bite the soft tissues in the perineum area. If the bison stumbles, the whole pack attacks; otherwise, the recently attacking wolf retreats. The bison faces a brutal and painful death, and in normal wolf fashion, the pack will feed on the still alive bison, often eating out the meaty rear portions–and leaving the animal to suffer a lingering death. To bring down a sizeable animal such as this can take several days, and the hungry pack will aggressively defend their food source.

Killing Their Prey

When killing large animals, wolves try to grab their prey in the perineum area where the tissue is soft. Sometimes, they try to grab the nose of the prey, but they always avoid the hooves of large animals. Wolves try to tear large pieces of soft tissue from the victim, causing massive wounds that bleed profusely. The loss of blood soon weakens even the largest and healthiest animal. Wolves may rip open the abdominal cavity and begin feeding before the animal is dead, be it large or small prey. This is what happened with the horse in Figure 3.12. This horse was confined in the proximity of the owner's house when the wolves attacked. It was eaten alive, and it probably died from the loss of blood.

No matter if this is wolves' normal behavior. This horse was a young girl's best friend.

Figure 3.12. A horse being killed and partly eaten by wolves.

Figure 3.13. A reindeer calf seriously injured by wolves (photo by www.paliskunnat.net).

Another incident was reported to me by the reindeer herders in Northern Finland, where predators cause a lot of damage to their business. Figure 3.13 shows a reindeer in its first year, seriously bitten by wolves as they killed its mother. Here the wolves have grabbed the calf by its nose, where the tissue is soft, pulling out its tongue.

With soft tissue, wolves can tear huge chunks from the animal, causing long, wide, deep wounds, resulting in severe hemorrhaging that quickly weakens the prey. The victim may also lose coordination of movements and loss of running speed. The entire attack might take just seconds, but the wolves often leave the bleeding victim in the forest as if their intention is to keep the prey animal alive for some time (my own observations).

When wolves attack domestic sheep, they usually bite the sheep on the top of the neck or in the rear part of the sheep. While biting, the wolf pushes the sheep down to the ground and makes sure it stays down after which it proceeds to the next victim. This is what happened in Figure 3.14, when wolves killed twenty-six sheep in one night but consumed only two.

Surplus Killing

Surplus killing occurs when, in a short period of time, one or more wolves kill more prey than they can consume. The Russian wolf researcher Mikhail Pavlov wrote about this habit:

The wolf seems to collect a storage of carcasses it never intends to use.

Figure 3.14. One of twenty-six sheep killed by wolves in Kivijärvi, Finland (photo Harri Piispanen).

This is exactly what it is all about. It seems as if they are killing prey animals just for fun. However, there are two distinct forms of surplus killing:

1. Wolves chase a herd of sheep over steep slopes and down into ravines, killing 300 to 500 sheep at a time. This could be called unintentional surplus killing.

2. Wolves systematically kill sheep, reindeer, roe deer, or cows one by one. This is intentional as, at some point, the wolf should know that it is time to start eating. However, the innate instinct of killing takes over as blood flows, and the wolves seem to enjoy it all.

All over Europe and Russia, it has been well documented that when wolves enter a flock of sheep, they often wantonly kill many more than they eat. Kozlov described the consequences of some attacks on sheep (1966):

One night in November 1953, five wolves attacked a herd of sheep in the district of Krasnojarsk, killing ninety-four of ninety-nine sheep. In August 1957, two wolves killed twenty-five sheep in the same district, and later in September, they killed seventy-two sheep during one attack.

In 2015 wolves killed fifty-two sheep in Rodenbeck, Germany (Internet A4).

Figure 3.15 shows sheep (surplus) killed by wolves in Finland.

Figure 3.15. Sheep killed by wolves loaded on a truck in southwestern Finland.

Figure 3.16. 19 elk killed by wolves in Wyoming, US (photo by Wyoming Game and Fish/Jim Hageborn).

Figure 3.16 shows nineteen elk slaughtered by wolves in what a National Geographic article described as a "rare surplus killing, leaving game officials scratching their heads in Wyoming". The article completely neglects the fact that this is normal wolf behavior (Internet A5).

Why and when do wolves engage in surplus killing?

Collecting food for bad times is a normal habit among animals. The red squirrel sets up storage of cones, the mink collects fish for future use, and the wolf "collects" prey animals it never intends to use. However, there is one large carnivore, the wolverine, who collects carcasses for the winter, but in this case, the wolverine uses the cold winter and thick snow as a freezer. In the spring, when its cubs are growing and the snow starts melting, the wolverine family gnaws the carcasses revealed by the warm sunshine.

The habit of surplus killing, when combined with the fact that wolves often live in close proximity to domestic animal herds in many parts of the world, is probably the main reason why the human–wolf relationship never has and never will work (Satunin 1915).

Strict protection of wolves only makes things worse.

Discovering New Prey Animals

To discover new prey, a wolf has to start learning how to hunt that animal. The process starts by observational learning about the new prey. With regard to livestock, wolves have been observed in daylight at some distance from the pastures, simply watching the herds. They may lie on a barrow leeward from the livestock for some time after which they disappear, only to return the next day. A pack may disappear for a couple of weeks as it continues searching for prey in its territory. At some point, they may return and make false attacks on the livestock in order to evaluate their resistance, usually by biting the prey to evaluate the reaction.

When wolves explore large livestock, it ends in docked tails, slit ears, and gashed hocks. Soon, the first seriously wounded cattle are found, and they tend to have injuries to the udders, groin, and sexual organs severe enough to require putting the animals down.

Figure 3.17. The Finnish forest reindeer (photo by the author).

When the actions of wolves become more brazen, cattle or horses may be killed close to houses and barns, where the cattle or horses were trying to find sanctuary. Wolves may follow riders and surround them, or they might climb up on verandas and look into windows (Geist 2007).

As far as the observation of wild animals are concerned, it may be difficult to separate predatory attacks from the final stages of a prey discovery attack as explained above.

The Impact of Wolves on Nature

Wolf predation has a huge impact on nature. The politically correct view puts forth the "wonderful ecosystem" fallacy, according to which wolves restore an ecosystem and "a healthy ecosystem needs wolves." But nature is not a scale with an ultimate balance between species; rather, it is a continuous and everlasting war between them. Balance only exists where some species use allies for a type of close and long-term biological interaction called symbiosis. However, in symbiosis, these interactions are prerequisites for survival of both species.

One battlefront exists between predators and prey animals, and this war knows no rules. It is simply a question of killing and survival, and the fight goes on to the last man standing. Predators don't regulate prey populations, and it reaches the point where food resources become scarce, and nature then regulates the predators' populations.

The balance is reached when the forests are empty.

Bernt Lindqvist wrote in his paper (2008-2b) that the extermination of wolves in Europe became possible when wolves ran out of prey. They became bolder and approached settlements, where they were caught with snares and traps or poisoned with strychnine.

Observations and experience suggest that wolves' impact on moose populations varies from 85% to 120% of the annual reproduction. At worst, wolves can reduce a moose population to a fraction of its original size (Lindqvist 2008-2b). When the moose population deceases, the wolves switch to other prey animals, and the destruction continues.

Finally, the wolves starve, limit their reproduction, or move to another territory, leaving empty forests behind them (Lindqvist 2008-2b).

Since the reintroduction of Canadian wolves in the United States, the population of Northern Yellowstone elk is down 80% from nearly 20,000 to less than 4,000 today.

Before the Soviet Union collapsed in 1991, their moose population allowed for an annual culling of 50,000 moose. This was possible because during the Soviet regime, the wolf population was reduced to some 30,000 wolves. During the chaos in Russia during the 1990s the wolf population grew freely. Wolf predation on moose limited the annual moose hunt to 16,000 individuals on a total area of 2,300,000,000 hectares (5,683,423,773 acres).

The Finnish forest reindeer (*Rangifer tarandus fennicus*) is a rare and threatened subspecies of the reindeer native to Finland and northwestern Russia. They are found primarily in Russian Karelia and the provinces of North Karelia, Savonia, and Kainuu in Finland (Wikipedia). This forest reindeer was reintroduced into parts of Finland, where the population in Kainuu reached its maximum in 2001 (1,700 individuals), and then the wolf population started to expand in the area. The forest reindeer population was soon affected by the growing number of wolves, and in 2016, only 721 individuals were found (Internet #A6).

In Finland, the wolves have diminished moose populations on large areas, thus preventing traditional moose hunting. Another side effect has also been observed. Moose (*Alces alces*) and white-tailed deer (*Odocoileus virginianus*) flock into human settlements to escape predators and exploit rich food sources. Thus, our settlements become refuge from predation which, in turn, attracts hungry predators following the prey animals.

Figure 3.18. A white-tailed deer killed by wolves in the middle of a village in southwest Finland.

Figure 3.18 shows a White-tail deer killed by wolves in the proximity of a school close to the town of Turku, Finland. This cow tried to escape the wolves into human settlements, but the wolves followed her. The photo also reveals an interesting difference between wolves in Europe and wolves in the United States and Canada.

The European gray wolf does not eat fetuses!

Wolves change nature but maybe not in the direction some people expect.

The growing and habituated wolf population may bring back lethal diseases and parasites that had been exterminated from Western Europe and the United States. These diseases and parasites require both, herbivores and carnivores to complete their life cycles. Professor Valerius Geist asks (2007):

Is the spreading of lethal diseases with the spreading of wolves in "multi-use landscapes surrounding houses, farms, villages and cities" such a wonderful idea that one can insist on proceeding and let the affected citizen bear the cost?

Wolves, Livestock, and Coexistence

From what we have read up to now, it is obvious that coexistence is not a matter of living with wolves. It is a matter of withstanding whatever is to come. Since the 1990s, the number of wolves in Europe has steadily increased, and the total number of wolves, excluding Russia, Belarus, and Ukraine, exceeds 12,000. At the same time, conflicts between farmers, wolf protectors, and authorities are becoming more frequent.

Wolves living in Central Europe, Finland, and Scandinavia must cope with the fact that there are human settlements throughout their habitat. This results in a strong habituation to humans and a growing number of attacks against cattle and sheep under the cover of darkness as well as at dusk and dawn. The appearance of wolves in settled areas in broad daylight seems to be more and more the rule rather than the exception.

While European authorities explain this as being a part of the wolf's normal behavior, human tolerance in areas where wolves return is rapidly lowering. Wolf depredation on livestock, and especially surplus killing, has resulted in several clashes between farmers and authorities in France and Italy.

Despite all efforts, the wolf population does not grow according to common expectations. Thus, authorities announce that the wolf population is declining due to poaching.

Poaching and Coexsistence?

Is the illegal killing of wolves, or poaching, threatening the viability of the European wolf population? The question is twofold.

David Mech writes (2017):

> *When a wolf population is low in numbers or distribution, human limitations by hunting, trapping, poaching, or livestock-depredation control can be effective. However, once a wolf population becomes well established and widely distributed, such techniques have limited impact.*

This theory is supported by Bernt Lindqvist in his paper ***Varg och vargjakt*** ("Wolves and wolf hunting") (Lindqvist 2008a).

Research on wolf poaching (Liberg et al. 2012; Suutarinen & Kojola 2017) focuses on statistical methods in efforts to estimate the number of wolves killed by poachers. However, the reliability of research on poaching is complicated due to the difficulty of documenting true intentions to poach (St. John et al. 2012).

If poaching is widespread, we should ask why people living in rural areas kill wolves illegally. A notable theory is that the efforts to increase tolerance of wolves among the rural population fails as the authorities cannot understand the situation where habituated wolves dwell on suburban roads and sleep in yards. For families living among all these wolves, there is just one solution—shoot, shovel, and shut up.

The Finnish Food Safety Authority (EVIRA) investigates all wolves that have been shot or found dead. Between 2001 and 2014, they performed autopsies on eighty-one wolves, fourteen of which were killed illegally, and wounds from rounds or shotgun pellets were found in seven wolves (EVIRA 2017).

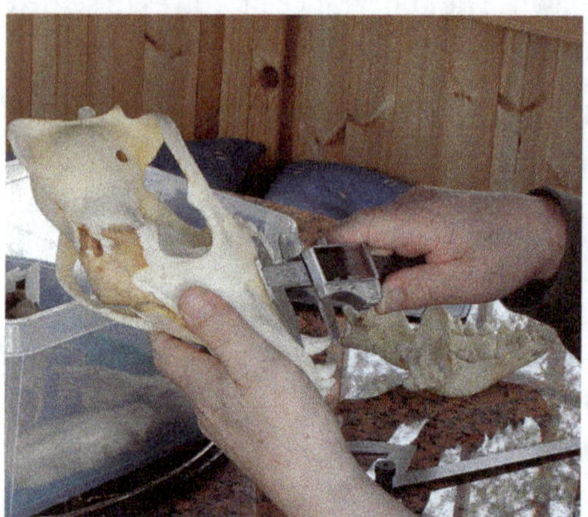

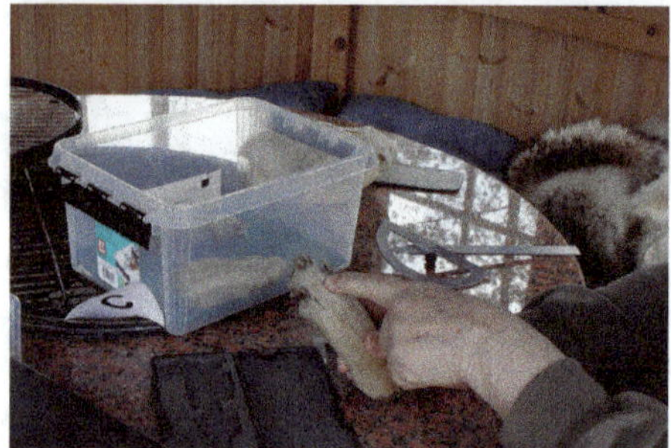

Figure 3.19. Cleansing and documenting a wolf's skeleton (photos by the author).

My own research (Figure 3.19) revealed small, capsulated shotgun pellets in two of five randomly selected wolves. One pellet was found in the intervertebral discs of one wolf, and another pellet was found in the elbow of the other. Both pellets were less than 3 mm in diameter.

Small shotgun pellets found in wolves can be the result of an effort to chase wolves out of yards rather than an actual attempt to illegally kill them. Most shotgun owners are hunters who know that small pellets may hurt wolves, but do not kill them unless shot from a distance of less than 20 meters.

Wolf Predation on Livestock

Wolves' impact on livestock varies with latitude. Due to the cold climate in northern Finland and Sweden, wolf predation on livestock is concentrated on reindeer. However, the reindeer herding area in Finland is listed under Annex V in the Habitats Directive (EU Commission 2007), making it easier to cull wolves.

Figure 3.20. Poachers on trial for illegal killing of three wolf-dog hybrids (HSS Media/Österbottens Tidning).

In Southern Finland, Sweden, and Norway, wolves usually prey on sheep and dogs.

In Central Europe and the Mediterranean area, wolf attacks on sheep cause considerable losses to sheep breeders. The worst incidents have been in France, where wolves have killed hundreds of sheep in single attacks. After such an attack in 2010, a sheep breeder found 593 of his sheep killed in one night by a wolf pack (de Menten 2010).

In France alone, wolves killed 10,234 domestic animals and livestock in 2016, 9,788 of which were sheep. The average number of sheep killed during one attack was 3.57 (Le Monde des Pyrenees 2016).

In Italy, up to 2,600 wolves roam the Alps, especially in the Apennines, which cross Italy from north to south. In the region of Maremma, nearly 300 shepherds have abandoned sheepherding due to heavy wolf predation. In 2016, there were more than

600 predatory attacks on sheep in the Maremma area alone, causing losses of up to one million euros for sheep breeders.

Wolf packs are prowling close to villages in the Republic of Sakha (Yakutia) in Siberia, where, as in much of the rural Russia, people fight with a perennial problem of excessive predation by wolves. In 2013, the regional government of Yakutia said wolves killed about 16,000 domesticated reindeer and 313 horses.

Monetary Compensation

The EU Commission has been conducting a wide range of activities to promote a dialogue among stakeholders with the hope of reducing the level of conflict around large carnivores, and to find solutions to the conflicts arising between cattle and sheep breeding and the presence of wolves.

Monetary compensation has become an increasingly common strategy all over Europe. The systems vary from country to country, with some paying more than market value and others paying less. Most countries only pay for animals that are documented as being lost (dead and wounded).

Some examples of monetary expenses include

1. In 2014, France paid approximately 325 euros per sheep in compensation for damages caused by wolves (Le Monde des Pyrenees 2016). Using this estimate, the total compensation in 2016 should have been 3,181,100 euros. This amount equals the price of 1.36 kg beef per day for each of the 400 wolves in France. This calculation uses a standard retail price of 15.93 euros/kg.

2. In Spain, wolves kill sheep, goats, horses, and cows. To compensate farmers for their losses, the government spends more than 1.5 million euros per year (Rejón 2016).

3. Finland pays a monetary compensation for purebred dogs killed by wolves. The maximum amount for a trained hunting dog is 8,200 euros (approximately $10,000). The monetary compensation paid for damages caused by wolves to dogs and livestock in Finland during 2016 was approximately 1.7 million euros.

We Should Have Known Better

The German philosopher Georg Hegel once said, "We learn from history that we do not learn from history," and, indeed, we did not learn anything from history!

Back to the 1800s

Predation on livestock is well documented in the Russian Empire. The Russian researcher V. M. Lazarevsky collected statistics kept by the Zemtzvos and his research is referred to by L. P. Sabaneev (1876).

Lazarevsky calculated that the indirect losses brought by the wolf to feathered game was 50 million rubles, which was almost fourfold the losses caused to domestic animals. Information collected in 1873 in forty-five Russian provinces show that wolf predation on livestock that year resulted in the deaths of 179,000 large animals (horses and cows) and 562,000 small animals (includes sheep, calves, and foals). In the Ostsee Territory 1,011 large and 3,440 small animals were killed, and in ten provinces of the Kingdom of Poland, 2,766 large and 8,635 small. Assuming the average value of a large animal (horses and cows) was 30 rubles, and the value of small animal was 4 rubles, the total losses incurred by the population of forty-five provinces was over seven and a half million rubles.

Figure 3.21. Wolves attacking cows. (painting from 1800s by Jacques Raymond Brascassat).

The Finnish government kept annual statistics covering wolf predation, among others. These statistics were collected by Dr. Jouko Teperi and published in 1977. Table 3.3 summarizes the annual losses over a period of twenty-two years. At the end of the 1870s an extensive wolf hunt (extermination) started due to the large number of human victims—mostly children. The impact of the declining wolf population is apparent in Table 3.3. Starting in 1878, the number of sheep killed by wolves each year was nearly 10,000, but it was reduced to one-fifth that amount before the end of the nineteenth century.

To fully understand the losses caused by wolves, the price of a horse was 250 - 400 Finnish Marks and the average wages for one days work was 1 Mark. On the contrary, in 2018 a second hand tractor was sold for $35,000 and the average daily wages were

$196,56. Thus, to buy this tractor one needs to work 178 days. The losses caused by wolves killing a horse in the middle of the nineteenth century, corresponds to the loss of a new tractor today.

Without insurances and social security, the impact was disastrous.

Year	Horses	Cows	Sheep
1878	529	1984	9,656
1879	463	1626	9,295
1880	467	1545	8,939
1881	281	1168	6,442
1882	274	864	5,246
1883	216	715	4,254
1884	138	708	4,803
1885	97	648	3,469
1886	62	506	4,594
1887	37	489	4,020
1888	55	362	3,478
1889	35	225	2,986
1890	41	307	3,187
1891	44	276	3,330
1892	46	295	3,283
1893	13	149	3,008
1894	22	214	2,503
1895	20	215	2,425
1896	14	123	1,941
1897	15	126	2,207
1898	12	112	2,090
1899	17	127	2,447
Total	2,898	12,784	93,603

Table 3.3 Livestock killed by wolves. This information was collected by Dr. Jouko Teperi. He used the Finnish Government's Annual statistics from the nineteenth century. (Teperi 1977).

A peasant might have even given his house as security on a loan to purchase a horse, and after a wolf attack, he and his family might have ended up as beggars on the road (Figure 3.25).

L. P. Sabaneev writes about the peasant's situation in Russia during the late half of the nineteenth century (1976):

It's extremely sad to admit that our peasants, who just managed to get rid of slavery, who hardly stopped paying a heavy tribute to the landlords, again fell into bondage and again bear their mites, not only to people, but to a predatory beast.

Figure 3.22. Comparing expenses of agricultural "machines" (photos by the author).

Today the average wages are US $196,56 per day and the price of this New Holland TS 100 was US $35,000 on the purchase date. Thus, an average worker needed to work 178 days to buy this tractor.

In 1880s a man's wages were 1 mark per day and to buy a horse he needed to work 240 to 400 days.

Wolves Hunting Wolves

Cannibalism is not rare among wolves. In times of hunger in winter, the pack often attacks weak or injured animals. A male struggling for a female who becomes severely wounded may be eaten. In captivity, cannibalism is noted during the transition of young wolves from meat to milk or vegetable foods. Stronger cubs have been observed attacking and eating the weak ones (Barabash-Nikiforov 1957). Hungry wolves fight fiercely for food and frequently kill the weaker ones, which are consumed later, and there have been cases described of wolves killing and eating the wounded or the dead bodies of their kin (Makridin 1959).

The two wolves in Figures 3.23 and 3.24 are typical remains of an internal fight ending in the weaker being eaten.

Wolves kill wolves for many reasons. During a study of seven killed wolves, it was determined that five were killed at the boundaries of two territories and two were killed during clashes between a resident wolf pack and another pack, when for unknown reasons, wolves headed deep into another pack's territory. Most of the victims were dominant (alpha) wolves.

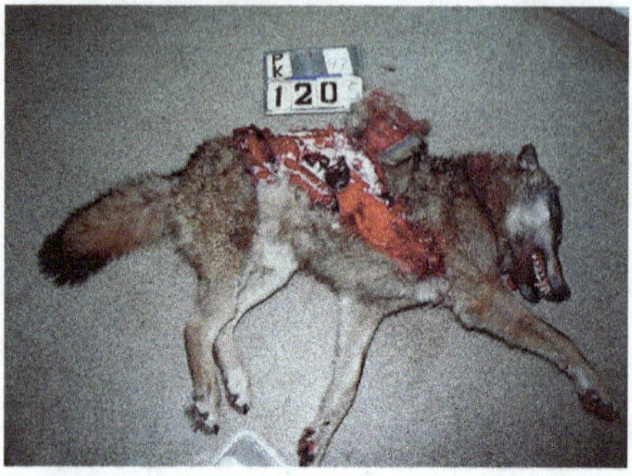

Figure 3.23. An adult wolf killed and partially eaten by its pack mates (photo Kaarlo Nygren)

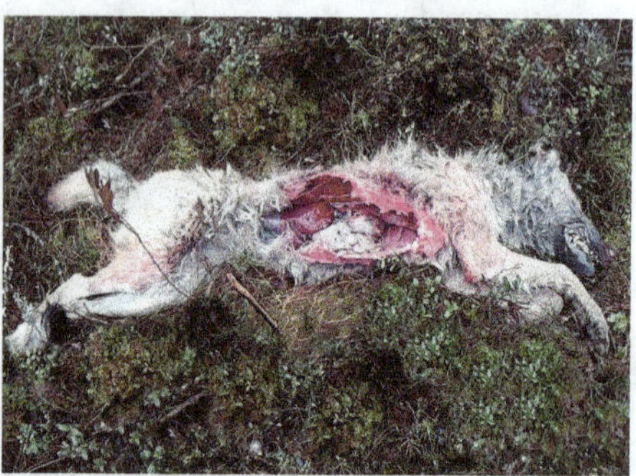

Figure 3.24. A juvenile wolf killed and eaten by its pack mates when they fought over a recently killed hunting dog.

Summary

The wolf continues hunting as it has always done. It catches what it can, and when one prey animal is killed to extinction, wolves continues with the next species. Wolves cannot see the difference in value between an elk and a sheep, nor can it see the ecological changes it causes to the fauna.

Despite all talks of applying human rights to wolves, about wolves' right to exist and to be treated as legal persons with recognized privileges, these dreams all lead to the simple statement:

A wolf can never have obligations, such as the ability to enter into contracts, to sue, or to be sued.

Figure 3.25. Family begging at a road in Finland during the famine of 1866–1868 (painting by Robert Wilhelm Ekman).

THE WOLVES' FOUR SEASONS

The wolf's life emphasizes two activities: to eat and to reproduce. When the wolf does not reproduce, it hunts, kills, and waits for the next wolf wedding.

Wolf Wedding

Wolves mature at about 2 years old and practically all females become sexually mature at the end of the second or beginning of the third year of life. Males participate in reproduction in the third and partly in the fourth year of life.

As previously mentioned, the formation of new pairs is called wolf wedding, where a group of males gather around one female in heat. During these weddings, violent clashes between young males occur as they fight for the right to mate. These confrontations sometimes end with death, and the dead wolf may even be eaten. The female bonds with the strongest wolf in these weddings, and a new pair is formed. The pair usually, but not always, lasts until the death of one of the wolves (Sabaneev 1876).

Having driven away the young, the wolves begin to mate. If there are no idle males in the area, the mating is done very peacefully. Otherwise, for the possession of a female,

Figure 3.26. A hunter ready for a wolf hunt with dogs (painting by Alfred Wierusz-Kovalski).

there is cruel squabbling among the males, and the strongest of them, driving away the others, finally remains with the female wolf. However, this rarely happens as the female prefers to mate with the wolf she has already been breeding with.

The Alpha Pair

The only female allowed to reproduce is the alpha female. It may happen, that a young mature female living with a pack enters a heat cycle, but she will be immediately expelled from the pack. Finding blood splatter of scent marks from two different females within the same territory is extremely rare and may indicate dog heritage within the pack.

The alpha male may expel the alpha female from the pack and mate with the beta female instead.

Figure 3.27. Dr. Erik S. Nyholm at a wolf's burrow (photo by U-P Kinnunen).

Several observations in Finland and Scandinavia support the fact that the wolf pack is able to replace one of the missing alpha wolves. The Norwegian researcher Lars Toverud wrote about a wolf pack living in the Julussa territory, in an article published in Nationen (Toverud 2018).

> In Julussa, there was a wolf pair having cubs in 2002–2003, but the female was shot. The following year, a new female entered the scene, and it had cubs with the old male. The female disappeared, and the next year (2004–2005) another female "married" the old male, and they had a litter. This couple was also observed in 2006 when they had another litter.

Each time a female disappears, there is another ready to mate with the male, and this male has had four litters with three different females within four years (Toverud 2018).

There was a similar observation in the Laitila territory in Finland, where the current alpha female is the granddaughter of the pack's first alpha male.

Wolves keep very stubbornly to the same wasteland, swamps, or ravines. The lost female is replaced by another, and the dead male is replaced by a former cub. This can last for dozens of years, until the entire family is completely destroyed, which is very rare, or until the swamp is dried up, a thicket is cut down, or a new village appears nearby.

The pack does not disperse due to the loss of one alpha (male or female) simply because nature does not waste resources like humans do.

Figure 3.28. Wolf pups playing outside their burrow (photo by Gisela Möller).

The Pack's Spring

Until the alpha female's rut begins, the pack hunts together, but at the beginning of rut, the wolf pack dissolves. Adults disperse first, then yearlings, and finally, juvenile wolves (Heptner & Naumov 1967). After having driven away the young wolves, the alpha male follows the female and does not leave her for a minute. In the case of the couple being persecuted, the male walks ahead and opens a trail in deep snow, periodically checking to see if the female is still following him.

At the beginning of spring, the maturing couple approach their old den where they raised the previous litter. The den is situated not more than 500 meters from a water source, and the trail from the burrow to the water source becomes noticeable when the litter starts using it. Here, they begin to live a settled life, while young couples continue to roam until the end of April in search of a place where they can establish their territory.

Even if the wolves lost the whole litter the previous year, they occupy the same den again. This attachment to the place, contrary to the usual caution of the wolf, does not speak in favor of its mental abilities, but can be justified only by the lack of convenient places for mating and by the fact that wolves do not tolerate the very close proximity of other packs (Sabaneev 1876).

During this time the pack is scattered in small groups around their territory. They don't rejoin the pack until the end of the summer, when the whole family starts its nomad life. Some yearlings may, however, join their parents when they find them—whether that is at the end of winter or in the summer. The presence of last year's young wolves is explained solely by the fact that, not knowing how to get their food yet, they try to profit from the leftover animals brought by the elderly to the den. They rarely hunt prey themselves and only later help the mother in attacks on large livestock.

This is a hard time for the pack members, and many wolves perish before summer. Some males are killed in the "wolf weddings," while others simply starve to death.

The female's pregnancy lasts from sixty-two to seventy-five days (Heptner & Naumov 1967).

The Wolves' Summer

During the first weeks after the pups are born, the female does not leave the litter, and during this time, the male feeds her, bringing prey to the den or regurgitating semi-digested meat. The female feeds the young with milk until they are 6 weeks old.

When the pups are 3 to 4 weeks old, they begin to eat food regurgitated by their parents. The reflex causing the parents to regurgitate food is activated by the pups licking their parents' mouths.

This is the main reason why it is so easy to teach young wolves to lick a human's face. A piece of meat is enough to encourage this habit because it is innate.

Research carried out by Wernher Gerhards from Germany suggests that in summer adult wolves roam in the outer part of their territory, looking for prey (*Wolfs Revir Compressed* available in German from the author).

Feeding the Litter

In June and July, wolves with cubs never touch livestock in the immediate neighborhood of the den.

Wolves avoid hunting in the neighborhood of their lairs because they are afraid to expose the den to humans, and when there is plenty of food everywhere, cattle may graze safely almost next to the wolf's lair. This led to some strange reactions against wolf hunting in the Russian Empire. The peasants in neighboring villages usually not only prevented hunters from exterminating young cubs, but they even tried to hide the locations of lairs.

Having lost their litter wolves have no need to protect the lair's location, and start to slaughter cattle nearby, sometimes without any purpose or need, simply because of their inherent instinct for surplus killing.

When cubs reach the age of 6 weeks, the parents bring various small animals to them. First the animals are dead, and then half-dead, just as a cat brings mice to kittens. Due to the distance, the adult wolves are unable to bring large prey to the lair. Thus, the wolves care primarily for themselves, eating their kill alone and bringing any excess to the lair (Sabaneev 1876).

Figure 3.29. Alpha female reguriting food (photo from www.123rf.com).

Soon, they start taking the cubs to the water hole and later, the cubs how learn to walk in a queue along the trail. At the age of three to four months the cubs are already able to kill a lamb or a young sheep, which the breeding pair will have brought to the lair (Sabaneev 1876). From August on, attacks of domestic livestock become common (Khudyakov 1937).

Howling with Wolves

Howling is used by the adults and the litter to communicate with each other. When the adult wolf approaches the den, it lets the cubs know that it is close. The cubs, hearing the adult howling, immediately raise a terrible howling and bickering audible in the dawn for a great distance.

The adult wolf's howling sounds similar to a person pulling the sound "woo" through the nose. Young wolves' howls sound like young dogs barking, with some screaming or grumbling, and every cub responds with its own specific voice. In quiet weather and with some skill it is easy to count the number of cubs in the nest simply by their response to a hunter howling. This is easily done after sunset and at dawn, when the adults are out of the nest. However, if the female is in the burrow, its curiosity forces her to approach the source of the howling (Sabaneev 1876).

Experienced whining can be taken for a wandering bachelor, and the female rushes toward the voice in order to drive the stranger out of its territory. One only need to go closer to the lair and howl. If the old wolves are still at the lair, one can be sure that they will walk ten to fifteen steps, with a favorable wind towards the suspected intruder and they can easily be shot (Sabaneev 1876).

Luring wolves by imitating their howling is possible while the cubs are young and the wolves stay in close proximity to the lair. Late in the autumn, adult wolves do not respond to a hunter's howling, which is one of the reasons why autumn hunting often fails.

Caring for Their Cubs

The alpha female is a tender mother who carefully protects her offspring from attacks by other wolves. If a person approaches the lair, the female wolf might attack him, especially if he is unarmed. In general, this happens when the cubs are small.

Many researchers have written about how wolves protect their cubs. For instance, Dmitriev-Mamonov recounted how an alpha female fought with a whole pack of dogs and rushed at hunters coming to rescue the dogs (Cherkasov 1867:159). Cherkasov tells this story:

> *An alpha female first led hunters away from the burrow, and when they began smoking out cubs, the wolf ran up to the lair, trying to grab one of the hunters. After the cubs were harvested from the burrow, the wolf appeared at a distance of 200 meters from the hunters with the alpha male. They sat side-by-side on the slope of the mountain and began a piercing, gut-wrenching howling. Both*

wolves followed all the way to the outskirts of the village, running almost on the heels of the hunters.

The earlier an alpha female is killed, the more likely it is that the cubs will not be led off by the alpha male to another place. Very young cubs perish by starving. If they are able to eat by themselves, then the male feeds them, although he never protects them. At least when he sees or hears a hunter with a dog, he always turns to flight.

As we will see, the caring changes later and the alpha couple may eat their offspring or sacrifice them for the sake of their own security.

Summary

The wolves' summer comes to an end when the pack comes back together and starts their nomad life in August.

Figure 3.30. A typical autumn attack on a herd of sheep, where twenty-six sheep were killed or injured (photo by Harri Piispanen).

Wolf's Life in Autumn

In autumn, the wolf's life gradually turns from sedentary to wandering as the wolf pack explores more remote locations further from their summer lair. The pack also does not spare domestic animals in the surrounding villages. The entire litter starts hunting when the cubs are 4 to 5 months of age and are able to join the pack in its efforts to find food. During the first weeks of nomadic life, the pack returns to the summer lair, where they spend the daytime.

The wolves' nomadic life is determined by a decrease in food. With the first strong snow, rarely earlier than the middle of October, the grazing of livestock ceases and wolves are forced to leave domestic animals (other than the village dogs) and hunt four-legged and feathered game. But since hunting these species often turns out to be beyond the power of the wolves due to their small numbers, the depth of the snow, or another reason, then packs, and especially single wolves, are forced roam up to hundreds of miles from their summer residence.

At that point, the devastation caused by wolves on sheep begins and surplus killing is triggered by the arriving winter.

The Pack's Autumn Hunting

In September, the wolves start hunting, and the autumn hunt is characterized by extensive surplus killing. Sometimes, this surplus killing is motivated by the need for young wolves to practice hunting. However, the most likely reason is that wolves, as with many other species, have an innate need to build up a stockpile for the winter.

Figure 3.30 shows the first view a sheep breeder saw one early morning after the wolves had visited his herd. Dead and injured sheep were scattered over a wide area; twenty-six sheep were lost, but only were two fully consumed. Figure 3.13, shown earlier in this chapter, is from the same attack.

In Russia, it is well documented that when wolves enter a flock of sheep, they often wantonly kill many more than they eat. During periods of inclement weather and when there is crusted, frozen snow, it is easy for the wolves to run down and kill their prey. Wolves do not need to spend much energy running, so they just keep on killing their handicapped prey until they are tired.

The Russian researchers Kutjerenko and Zubkov emphasize that wolves kill much more than they need to and during the cold autumn and winter, wolves push flocks of elk (wapiti) down riverbanks or steep cliffs into the water and simply wait for the animals to drown (Kutjerenko & Zubkov 1980).

Wolves' Pelage Changes

In autumn, there is no full replacement of the pelage, and only the underfur, which grows from the beginning of September to the end of October.

As the pelage gets thicker, the wolves also become bolder because the thick pelage prevents the wolf from sustaining minor injuries. In addition the cold weather prevents scars from being inflamed, and thus, attacks are more furious.

Young wolves pass from the cub's dark gray pelage into their first winter pelage. Its structure corresponds to adult wolves' winter pelage, but differs in the greater monotony of the grayish dirty-ocher color, with less development of black and reddish tones. The difference between an old wolf's pelage and a young wolf's (youngsters <1 year) is shown in Figure 3.31. The change in a wolf's pelage can also be seen in Figure

2.21, in Chapter 2. In Figure 3.31 the wolves shown in A, B and C exhibit the adult wolf's color setting, but D, E, and F are typical youngsters' pelts. There is an interesting story from Siberia about young wolves' pelage that was told to me during my second visit to Yakutsk.

Siberian professional wolf hunters catch their wolves using traps placed under the wolves' trail—remember that wolves tend to use the same trail in deep snow. Many wolf experts claim that when wolves are on the move, the alpha female walks first, then comes the rest of the pack, and the alpha male is the last one in the line. However, in order to avoid stepping into a trap, the alpha female forces the youngsters to walk first in the line, acting as minesweepers, cleansing the trail of traps. The hunters get paid less for the dirty grayish pelt of a youngster, something they don't like, but cannot avoid.

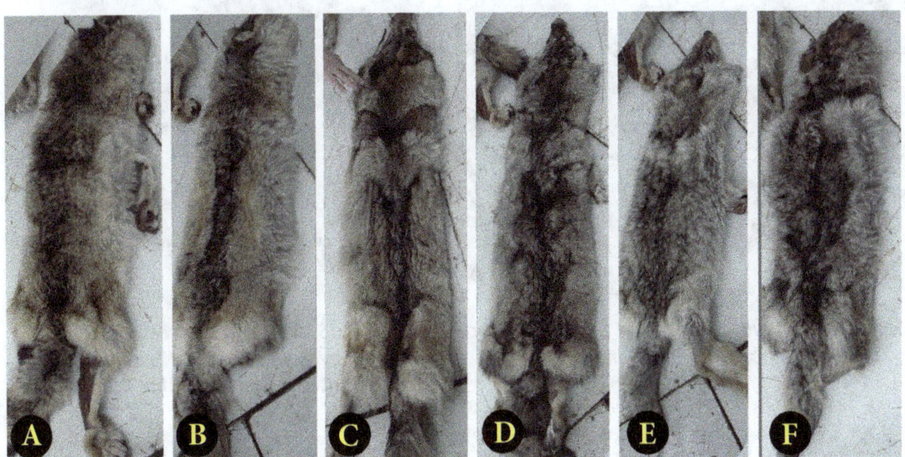

Figure 3.31. Color variation in old and young wolves' winter pelage (photos by the author).

In November, the wolf's fur becomes extremely fluffy and dense. The color of winter pelage is generally much lighter and cleaner than the summer pelage, and the black tips of the guard hairs are much larger and longer. Now the adult wolf exhibits what we might call a normal appearance.

Wolves Attacking Hunting Dogs

Finland, Sweden, and Norway have a strong hunting culture, and hunting with loose dogs is a common practice. In a study conducted in Sweden, a vast majority (86%) of wolf attacks on dogs happened in hunting situations, and in 71% of those cases, the attacked dog was killed (Backeryd 2007).

Wolf attacks on dogs are emotional issues, as dogs are not only valuable and honored hunting companions, but also close friends to the hunters and their families.

Figure 3.32. A wolf tried to get through a fence of steel net (photo by Mika Ilomäki).

Figure 3.33. A hole in a fence of steel net torn by two wolves in November 2018 (photo by Päivi Tuominen).

Attacks on dogs continue throughout the hunting season from September to February, but wolf attacks are not limited to hunting situations only. Wolves also sneak into human settlements and catch dogs in their enclosures. Indeed, they do! Figure 3.32 shows a dog's enclosure surrounded by a 2.5 mm steel net of the type that a wolf had bent apart the wires apart, even managing to cut one wire. Figure 3.33 shows another dog enclosure with a hole torn into it by two wolves. If they cannot penetrate the net, they try to dig their way under it instead. There are documented cases where wolves snatch pet dogs in broad daylight in front of the owner (Internet A7).

When a wolf approaches a dog in the yard, the dog starts barking, and the wolf pretends to retreat. If the dog follows the wolf, another wolf may be waiting to ambush the dog. Many domestic dogs are lost in this manner.

On February 25, 2017 The Guardian wrote about a typical incident in Finland where two wolves had killed a dog (Internet A7).

Määttänen's beloved previous dog, Kessu, was killed on 22 January last year. His description of the loss sounds like the abduction of a child. He saw two wolves 30 m from his window in December 2015. "They don't jog for pleasure," he says. "They were looking for food. And after that, the wolves knew I had a dog." The "wolf circle", whereby a pack of five or more wolves scour their 1,000 sq km territory for food, takes two and a half weeks in Määttänen's neighborhood. "They took one circle and the dog was not outside. But on the second circle, it was there. It was 12.30 pm, and I remember Kessu was staring into the forest. He started walking in that direction" – he points to a place where his garden blends into the forest – "and vanished from sight."

Later that afternoon, a neighbor called to warn him that two wolves had crossed the road nearby. "I went out with a gun, but it was too late." He found scuffle marks, then wolf tracks. "They had been waiting 100 m away for my dog. They had invited the dog to play, and then...", he pauses. "My dog ran into the wolf's mouth." There had been no barking. There was no blood. The wolf was so strong, it took Kessu without a sound. How does he know the wolf was big? "Because on Sunday, the hunters shot it," he says. Local hunters had quickly obtained a permit to kill this "problem" wolf.

Summary

The nomadic life of wolves starting in August, is explained by a lack of food, because they are forced to look for food in a much more extensive space and sometimes even move to very remote areas. As successful wolf hunting is possible only after the snow falls, the wolves are almost safe from hunters until the onset of winter.

Winter and Starvation

As snow falls, the number of game animals drops sharply, and hunting gets more difficult. Wolves become wicked from lack of food and lose their caution. They may even cross roads and enter human settlements. They walk along streets of villages, enter farmyards, and search for food in house yards.

A Russian hunter described in detail an attack on a young moose that took place near the village of Prisadnyj, on the Kama River (Graves 2007).

Five wolves, two mature and three young ones, came across two young moose feeding in a pine forest. The moose ran away at full speed with the wolves in close pursuit. It was winter and there was thick crusted snow. One moose ran in front, breaking the crusted snow, which was cutting its legs. The second moose ran in the tracks of the first moose, and its legs were not being cut as much as the first moose. After a half kilometer, the lead moose, with severely cut legs, turned sharply and entered thick pines. The second moose kept running straight. The wolves kept chasing after the moose which went straight.

Suddenly, this moose had its legs cut by the sharp edges of the crusted snow. Usually, the crusted snow supports the weight of the running wolves, but not all the time. When the chase reached an area where the crusted snow did not support the moose, but did support the wolves, the wolves started to gain on the handicapped moose. Until now, the wolves had been running in single line, but now they scattered, and one young wolf tried to overtake the moose, and it managed to get in front of the moose. It tried to jump on the moose. The moose struck this wolf in the skull with its hoof and the wolf crumpled and fell.

The other wolves continued the attack and some got in front of the moose. After making some huge leaps, two wolves grabbed onto the moose and stopped it. Then the other two wolves grabbed it and the moose went down. The attack area was covered with blood. The four wolves not only ate the moose, but they also ate the wolf which the moose had killed with its hoof.

This attack was unusual as the wolves (at least one) apparently attacked from the front. But this frontal attack cost one young wolf its life. Mature wolves will normally attack from the rear or side.

This article showed the advantage of wolves chasing large prey on crusted snow, and also showed that wolves will eat their own.

Figure 3.34 shows a moose and her calf, both killed by wolves in the deep snow in northeastern Finland. The adult moose was consumed by the wolves, but the calf just killed.

In wintertime, wolves never go deep into a large forest, but always lie either near the edge, or near roads and glades. In snowy winters, wolves never stay in large coniferous forests, either, but prefer to live more in deciduous or mixed small forests. When the pack is moving, they use their own trail and prefers country roads, frozen rivers, lakes, or wherever the snow is shallow.

Feeding on Carrion

In summer, when prey animals are abundant and easier to hunt, wolves do not touch carrion. However, in late autumn, when the first snow covers the landscape, wolves start using whatever they can find. After snow accumulates and feeding gets worse, the wolves turn their attention back to carrion.

In the time of greatest hunger, wolves approach populated areas, hunt dogs, attack livestock in their sheds, even by day, and willingly make use of cattle burial grounds and carrion. They travel along roads and unwillingly turn into the snow upon the appearance of a human (Heptner & Naumov 1967).

Figure 3.34. An adult moose and its calf, killed by a wolf pack. (photo by Tapani Pääkkönen).

Carrion were widely used in wolf hunts, especially in winter. Its benefits are significant. It saves a lot of time necessary for reconnaissance and tracking down the wolf. It is also convenient because it keeps wolves in place for several days so that there is time to collect beaters and hunters. Hunting with carrion minimizes the risks of accidents and makes the outcome sure.

The Pack Dissolves

The rut usually begins before the middle of the second half of winter. Old, multiparous females enter estrus first, approximately two to three weeks earlier than young, just maturing females. Before the beginning of rut, the wolf pack dissolves. Adults disperse first, then yearlings, and finally, juvenile wolves.

Later on, they may reunite, but they do not approach the adult couple, instead lying separately. After having driven away the young pack members, the adult male becomes unusually attentive to the female.

The Circle Is Closed

Rangifer tarandus fennicus: The Finnish forest reindeer is a rare and threatened subspecies of the reindeer native to Finland and northwestern Russia. They are found primarily in Russian Karelia and the provinces of North Karelia, Savonia and Kainuu in Finland, though some range into central south Finland. Unfortunately, this beautiful animal is on the top of wolves' menu. (photos by the author).

HUMAN AND WOLF

Truth has only one enemy—ideology. For centuries, new generations stumbled over old problems, and each generation presented its superior solutions, only to find out that they had to retreat as the previous generations did. Only stupidity is inherited.

Where are all those experiences collected by earlier generations and documented by them in order to give us an easier life? All gone forever because we are the superior generation, and we know the right solutions to all problems.

A HISTORY OF ATTACKS

Until the early 1970' the wolf was considered a predator and dangerous to people, as well as livestock. However, tables were slowly turning, and a new wave of research swarmed public opinion. The message was, "The wolf is not dangerous to humans," and this hypothesis came a politicized dogma from which a new religion sprang, a lethal religion based on scientific phrases taken out of context, and so the myth of the "harmless" wolf reached extraordinary proportions. Now environmentalists teach children that it is safe to pet a wild wolf.

Attacks on Facts

The Swedish biologist Dr. Elis Pålsson was one of the first to translate scientific books and articles about wolves from Russia into Swedish (Pålsson 1984). He published the book *Vargens beteende* which contains eleven research reports from professor Dmitry Bibikov's book *Povedenie volka (The wolf's behavior)*, published by the Russian Academy of Science. The reaction was astonishing!

Pro-wolf organizations started a huge campaign to discredit Pålsson and two centuries of Russian wolf science. The public was told that Little Red Riding Hood is dead, and in 1986, they printed a message on milk cartons sold in Swedish markets saying, "Information about wolves being dangerous are exaggerated and the intention of Disney's Big Bad Wolf is to scare children."

The Swedish "wolf specialist" Anders Bjärwall said in an article (Värmlands Folkblad, 15/12 84) that "there is no evidence that wolves have killed people in Russia."

In 1987, Pålsson published a book in Norway, based upon research conducted by the Russian professor Mikhail Pavlov. In August 1987, the Royal Norwegian Ministry of Climate and Environment decided to prohibit the distribution of Pålsson's book and withdrew every single copy from the market. They claimed that information from the Russian Academy of Science was unreliable and gave the Norwegian audience an inaccurate picture of wolf behavior. This book was later published in Sweden (Pålsson 2003).

So much for European "freedom of speech".

What Do We Know About Wolf Attacks On Humans

First, we have to decide whether we consider research from earlier centuries reliable or not. Let's take a look at temperatures.

The thermometer we are familiar with, was invented in 1612 by Santorio Santorii. The Fahrenheit scale was proposed in 1724 by Daniel Gabriel Fahrenheit, and in 1742, Anders Celsius proposed the temperature scale which bears his name. So we have measured the global temperatures with an accuracy less than 1 degree since the eighteenth century, and the foundation of the notion of climate change assumes that science from those days is reliable.

In Finland, for instance, the temperature was measured by the same persons who kept church records of births and deaths (as well as causes of death).

Digging into History

Aristotle, the ancient Greek philosopher and scientist, once wrote, "Lone wolves kill humans more often than a wolf pack does." Apuleius, a Latin-language prose writer, Platonist philosopher, and rhetorician who lived under the rule of the Roman Empire once wrote about wolves, saying "Huge and violent wolf packs block the roads and attack travelers."

In 1527, Álvar Núñez Cabeza de Vaca came to the New World as a member of a Spanish expedition, and his observations were published in 1542. It turns out that wolves were not entirely absent when de Vaca was in Florida. A story is recounted by de Vaca that illustrates this. Juan Oritz, a native of Sevilla, was a crew member on a ship sent to Florida from Cuba to make contact with the Narváez expedition. He was captured by Indians, but in a stroke of fortune, he survived and was picked up by the De Soto expedition twelve years later. The chief of the tribe had spared Juan Ortiz's life and had sent him to guard a temple at night against wolves, as the temple contained corpses. A wolf came and snatched the corpse of the child of an important man. Juan Oritz threw a spear, wounding the wolf, who dropped the dead child and ran away to die. For finding the dead wolf, Chief Utica spared Ortiz's life, and Ortiz became endeared to the chief.

Clearly, there were a few wolves in Florida with an appetite for human flesh (de Vaca 1542).

France

In 2013, the French professor Jean-Marc Moriceau from the University of Caen Normandy (UNICAEN) publishes his book *L'homme contre le loup, Une querre dedeux mille ans (Man Against Wolf: A 2,000-Year War)*. To date, Moriceau has found 9,031 victims, and he writes

Month	Rabid attacks Victims	Predatory attacks Victims
January	33	99
February	33	77
March	30	116
April	27	128
May	33	160
June	29	227
July	14	231
August	16	175
September	26	161
October	21	121
November	20	108
December	41	95
Total	323	1,698

Table 4.1. Predatory vs. rabid wolf attack (1578–1883).

This hostility and the fear of wolves were mainly caused by their attacks on domestic livestock, which were harmful to many sectors of the economy, even beyond agriculture, up until the 19th century. However, we should not forget that wolf attacks against people themselves were not purely a matter of legend: for a long time, they really did happen. The frequency, and the geographical and temporal distribution of these dramatic incidents varied.

If all types of wolf attack data in the sources used here are combined, the provisional total as at 15 March 2014 stands at 9031 victims. This gives us a historical database which is unrivalled worldwide. This statistical corpus includes two key types of victims, which are carefully differentiated: victims of predatory wolves (which occasionally chose human victims), and victims of rabid wolves (which attacked men during a disturbance of their behavior due to a rabies-induced seizure).

Moriceau's book *Histoire du méchant loup : 3 000 attaques sur l'homme en France (XVe-XXe siècle)* includes statistics about wolf attacks on humans found until 2007.

Age	Females.	Males	Unknown	Total
0–4	61	59	7	132
5–9	188	201	11	400
10–14	246	178	6	430
15–19	67	46	0	113
20–24	32	7	0	39
25–29	19	1	0	20
30–34	12	3	0	15
35–39	12	1	0	13
40–44	8	1	0	9
45–49	14	1	0	15
50–54	7	3	0	10
55–59	6	0	0	6
60–64	12	1	0	13
65–69	3	0	0	3
70–74	3	2	0	5
75–79	0	1	0	1
80–84	1	0	0	1

Table 4.2. Wolf predation by age from 1572 to 1824 (Moriceau 2007).

Table 4.1 shows the number of victims attacked by rabid wolves and the victims of predatory attacks.

The table covers the period from 1578 to 1883, and we can see that only 15% of all attacks came from rabid wolves.

The table also shows that the frequency of attacks from rabid wolves did not vary with the season, while predatory attacks were mainly concentrated around the breeding season.

Figure 4.1. This wolf was killed in 1854 by a poacher named Blaise Basset in La Butte-aux-Boeufs. The wolf had earlier killed a 8-year-old girl (photo by Eirik Granqvist).

Table 4.2 shows the numbers of the victims of predatory attacks during the period 1572 to 1824, grouped by age.

Again, we see that the greatest number of victims are children between the ages of 5 and 14.

Figure 4.2. Children attacked by a wolf. Painting by François Grenier de Saint-Martin in 1833 (Wikipedia Commons).

As the victims get older, the number of women clearly exceeds the number of men killed by wolves. The number of men killed between the ages of 20 and 84 is only 25% of the total number of victims in this age group.

This can only be explained by the fact that the number of wolves involved in the attack were at most two and it was probably only one. For an adult man, it should be relatively simple to defend himself against a lone wolf, while women, being smaller and weaker, had a lesser chance of surviving an attack.

Moriceau lists each victim in his book, with references to the information source (2007). This endless list of names (Marie Dupré, Philippe Arnisart, Jeanne Richard, Alphonse Martelain, Christiane Larzul, Marie Martin, Jean Turand, Denis Romyan, ...) is also an endless list of human tragedies; a husband lost his wife, or parents found what was left of their child.

Moriceau made a short note of how a wolf took two young children:

> *A big wolf, probably the beast of Orleans, killed 1697 little Franois Morand and the daughter of Remy Thierry Marguerite, both under 8 years old.*

Most exciting in Moriceau's research are the church records that have been scanned and are available on the internet describing individual wolf attacks (Internet A8). As an example, I picked a case documented by Moriceau (2014).

Marie, aged approximately 7 years, daughter of Jacques Prudent and his first wife, Tiennette Maroyer, was snatched from her doorway by a wolf and devoured in a field. Only her head, one arm and her stomach were found, and nothing besides. These pitiful remains were buried in the cemetery of this church the following day, fifth October, before my entire parish, who had gathered for Sunday Mass.

More details can be found on the internet (Internet A9).

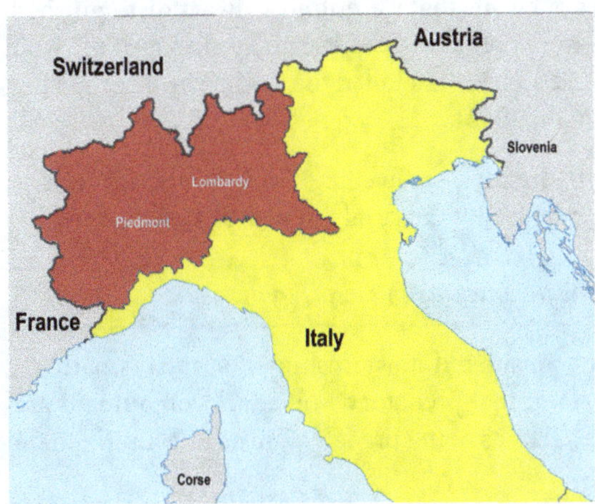

Figure 4.3. Piedmont and Lombardy in northern Italy.

From 1691 to 1695, the highest peaks were observed. This makes it easier to understand the resonance that Charles Perrault publications "Little Red Riding Hood" and "Little Thumbling" had during this period.

In France, wolves were exterminated between 1882 and 1930. The last reward for killing a wolf that had attacked a human was granted in 1896, and the last reported attack on a human took place in 1918 (Moriceau 2014).

Italy

The Italian scholars Aldo Oriani and Mario Comincini published a study that covered wolf attacks on humans in the eighteenth century. They focused on documented wolf attacks in the administrative regions of Lombardy and Piedmont, marked by red in Figure 4.3. Their study was based upon documents collected by the Italian Society of Natural Sciences (Società Italiana di Scienze Naturali). This society has archives covering wolf attacks on humans from the fifteenth century to the nineteenth century.

In the local history of the Po Valley, the wolf's presence is overwhelming. Documents describe bloody episodes of interaction, and it was the continual conflicts with wolves that inspired the scholars to take a closer look at history. They noted

> *Our initial studies made us wonder how all these numerous cases of document-ed predatory attacks could be reconciled with some naturalists' theories about the "safe" and "friendly" wolf.*

The scholars found two distinct types of events that were almost always distinguished in the documentation. The first type were predatory attacks simply aiming at the wolf feeding, and the second type were rabid attacks that killed the victims by transmitting the lethal disease (Oriani and Comincini 2002).

These two types of aggression were distinctly perceived, not only by the authorities and health care workers of the time, but also by the rural populations themselves.

Rabies had already been described as far back as ancient Egypt.

From this point of view, the scholars considered it astonishing that today's naturalists, in their biological motivations, claim that predatory wolf attacks on humans are impossible and deny any predatory attacks as being predatory, instead blaming them all on rabies.

The Victim and the Attack

The victims were almost exclusively children working as shepherds, and they took place in the summer in a field or pasture where sheep or cattle were grazing. The wolf grabbed the victim by the head or neck and immediately dragged the prey to a safe place. Predatory attacks never occurred close to human settlements (Oriani and Comincini 2002).

In general, wolves' first attacks on shepherds were accidental, but catching such easy prey soon made attacks on human more systematic. As the wolf was able to transmit this hunting method to the whole pack, predatory attacks did not remain geographically isolated incidents, but instead, spread into other counties and continued for years (Oriani and Comincini 2002).

Some Of The Predatory Attacks

The chronicles tell how sixteen people were killed and eaten in the Varese area in 1704, and despite large hunts, the wolves could not be killed. Partial confirmation of these incidents were found in the parish's archives (Oriani and Comincini 2002).

On March 31, 1705, in Viggiù, Anna Maria, 9–years–old, daughter of Giovanni Battista, was devoured by a wolf near the Aglio farmhouse, where she lived. The case did not remain isolated: on August 28, Maria Campascina (65) was killed by a wolf while she was working in the forest, and on 9 September the partially consumed body of Annunciata was recovered in Gorla Maggiore.

On July 5, 1737, a wolf came to Benna and killed the 11–years–old Caterina Messerano, while she was grazing cattle in the woods. On 4 September, in Massazza, 12–years–old Angela Maria Badone was eaten by wolves while he watched grazing cattle near the Cascina Ronco, The following day, in Vallepitola, his completely devoured body was found, and the few remains–the head and some bones–were buried on July 7. In Salussola, on October 10, the remains of Maria Azeglio of 12 years was recovered.

The winter passed without attacks, but they resumed in the summer 1738 when, in Salussola, on June 29, wolves mauled the 14–years–old Maria Lozia, and on 26 August, the wolves mauled the 12–years–old Margherita Cracco.

The above descriptions are all found in the collection studies by Oriani and Comincini (2002).

Some Rabid Attacks

For readers not familiar with rabies, a rabid wolf is unable to eat anything, and after it enters the violent phase, it lives at most one week.

There are no rabid wolves eating and continuing to kill humans for months.

During the eighteenth century at least fifty-two people were assaulted by rabid wolves in eleven different episodes. The number of deaths may not be correct because death by rabies occurs long after the biting and often in a hospital. When a wolf is running through a town, and biting everything that gets in its way, it becomes a deadly machine spreading a terrible disease. Persons injured by the rabid wolf were only treated with experimental methods that were completely useless for avoiding the lethal outcome of the disease.

The first rabies episode took place in Soncino, on April 29, 1711, when a rabid wolf emerged from the woods of the Oglio al Tinazzo and traveled along the fields of San Lino, Belvedere, and San Giovanni a Longe, biting over a hundred livestock: all died within forty days and had to be buried. At the locality Ronca, two shepherds managed to kill the wolf with spades, but they subsequently both died because of bites inflicted during the fight (Oriani and Comincini 2002).

Some fifty years later, we find another story, with more serious consequences, that took place in Orio Litta on November 21, 1765. A female wolf came out of the woods around Adda bit Paolo Angiolo Pozzone's dog. When she intervened she was bitten on the hand and arm. The animal continued on to Contrada Valisella and bit Valentino Folli on one hand. Then it went to Cascina de Strozzi and attacked Bernardo Pagano, biting him on the face, ear, and thigh. Then the wolf passed to the district of de Ratti attacked Innocente Bossi, inflicting ten bites on the head, face, and hand. Around noon, the wolf attacked a horse, but was driven away by the driver, so it went to Corte Sant'Andrea, where it wounded three men and two women (Oriani and Comincini 2002).

Then the wolf attacked a convoy of ten wagons bound for Ospedaletto, wounding two horses and two people. In Mezzana, it attacked some fishermen, biting only one man's clothes. On its way to the market of Orio, the wolf met Maria Maddalena Maroni and threw her to the ground, injuring her head. When the wolf reached Carlo Rossi's house, it threw him to the ground and bit him on the head and face. However, Carlo Rossi managed to kill the wolf with the help of his nephew Lorenzo.

Of the sixteen people bitten, at least fourteen died.

Does it really matter whether a wolf attack is rabid or predatory?

Germany

The fairy tale of "Little Red Riding Hood" was rewritten after events that happened in Germany from July 31, 1810 to July 26, 1811. During this period wolves killed eleven children, and some facts are found in the magazine *Jagd und Hund* issue 21/2004. The incidents are listed in Table 4.3.

These attacks happened within an area of 30 × 30 km except for Roetgen, which is located some 70 km away from the other villages.

The Grimms' Fairy Tales, originally known as the Children's and Household Tales (German: *Kinder- und Hausmärchen*), are a collection of fairy tales by the Grimm brothers Jakob and Wilhelm, first published on 20 December 1812. The first edition contained eighty-six stories, one of which was Little Red Riding Hood.

However, it is important to understand life in the early nineteenth century. There was no internet, no televisions, not even radios or telephones. German public schools were based upon religious education provided by the churches so that all people would be able to read the Bible.

Much of the information was transferred between generations in the form of tales told by the light of a candle. After the wolf attacks in 1810 through 1811, it is natural that children were advised not to fondle canines in the forests, and this warning was given to the children in form of a tale. After all, children spent much of their time outside in yards or the forest, and they were exposed to different threats all the time.

	Location	Date	Time	Age
1	Beesel	July 31,1810	19:00	3
2	Niederkrüchten	August 13, 1810	13:00	8
3	Helden	August 27, 1810	20:00	4
4	Brüggen	August 28, 1818	17:00	3
5	Roetgen	September 15, 1810	19:00	11
6	Bracht	September 25, 1810	18:30	8
7	Merbeck	October 31, 1810	18:00	10
8	Posterholt	November 08, 1810	20:00	9
9	Beesel	May 27, 1811	13:30	3
10	Elmpt	June 01, 1811	16:00	6
11	Kessel	July 26, 1811	18:00	4

Table 4.3. Children killed by wolves in Germany, 1810-1811.

Finland

On October 19, 2005, the historian Dr. Antti Lappalainen published his research findings on lethal wolf attacks on humans in Finland. By going through old church records and newspapers, Lappalainen found a total of 193 lethal attacks since 1710, of which 110 were children who fell victim to predatory attacks.

I have compared Dr. Lappalainen's list of victims with church records available on the internet. The church records state the name, age, parents' names, home village, and the cause of the victim's death. In my publication from 2016, I recognize three different types of attacks: children snatched by wolves (child lifting), adults most often bitten by wolves, and rabid attacks (Granlund 2016).

In the church books, I found the COD *vargbett* (bitten by a wolf), ***bort. snapp. af varg*** (snatched by wolves) and *vattuskräck* (an old Swedish word for rabies). The COD "bitten by a wolf" has a natural explanation. In those days, there was no medical care, nor were there antibiotics to treat deep inflamed wounds. Thus, a wolf bite most cer-

Date	Name	Age	Location
27.02.1710	Maria Toijainen	8	Ristiina
29.09.1714	Anna Syrjäläinen	4	Ristiina
27.02.1715	Martti Tarhoinen	4	Ristiina
27.02.1715	Maria Ukkonen	3	Ristiina
19.01.1718	Liisa Matintytär	12	Isokyrö
28.03.1718	Johanna Jaakontytär	28	Isokyrö
28.03.1718	Maria Tuomaantytär	8	Isokyrö
29.04.1718	Vaipuri Vilpuntytär	13	Isokyrö
09.02.1720	Susanna Kiikka	22	Isokyrö
20.04.1720	Maria Sippola	12	Isokyrö
02.07.1722	Markus	x	Isokyrö
05.02.1758	Liisa Heikitytär	28	Ilmajoki
12.02.1758	Matti Heikinpoika	13	Ilmajoki
17.02.1758	Anna Matintytär	5	Kurikka
18.02.1758	Maria Juhontytär	33	Ilmajoki
26.02.1758	Liisa Matintytär	36	Kurikka
28.02.1758	Liisa Markuntytär	52	Kurikka
03.03.1758	Juho Antinpoika	63	Kurikka
18.01.1756	Kalle Simonpoika	30	Sysmä
31.12.1758	Okänd flicka	9	Uukuniemi
20.12.1764	Juho Tanskanen	70	Tohmajärvi
24.12.1764	Kaapro Heikinpoika	40	Tuulos
22.01.1765	Susanna Turtinen	57	Tohmajärvi
29.12.1765	Heikki Kurvinen	5	Ilomantsi
08.01.1766	Simo Pesonen	3	Ilomantsi
21.02.1766	Markus Karhunen	12	Ilomantsi
09.02.1767	Karin Eronen	5	Kiihtelysvaara
29.11.1767	Kristiina Laakkonen	8	Ilomantsi
30.11.1767	Susanna Karvinen	8	Ilomantsi
08.01.1768	Cristian Hjerpe	3	Ilomantsi
06.06.1769	Anna Suhonen	7	Ilomantsi
17.12.1770	Kaisa Juhontytär	40	Jämsä
26.02.1773	Riitta Tuomaantytär	52	Jääski
26.02.1773	Juho Johansson	44	Jääski
03.04.1780	Antti Juhonpoika	46	Orimattila
01.06.1780	Antti Ehrsson	18	Askola
26.02.1782	Johan Charin	4	Pernaja
12.04.1784	Erkki Erkinpoika	26	Lapinjärvi
20.09.1786	Taavetti Tuomaanpoika	52	Ruokolahti
07.03.1787	Kaapro Tito	36	Kivennapa
20.06.1790	Antti Tiilikainen	16	Sortavala
13.11.1802	Antti Mikonpoika	40	Virolahti
01.11.1803	Yrjö Puukka	32	Räisälä
23.06.1807	Katariina Kelo	21	Sakkola
28.06.1807	Eeva Kurri	24	Sakkola
28.06.1807	Maria Lylander	13	Sakkola
14.01.1808	Yrjö Vesikko	33	Pyhäjärvi Vl
09.12.1812	Maria Tautila	7	Urjala
15.05.1815	Anna Matintytär	26	Virolahti
00.00.1816	Liisa Antintytär	x	Turku
24.02.1816	Martti Vero	34	Rautu
14.03.1817	Mikko Sakarinpoika	8	Koivisto
23.03.1817	Matti Yrjönpoika	38	Vehkalahti
27.03.1817	Juho Sigfridinpoika	31	Luumäki
02.05.1817	Elias Matsson	21	Koivisto
02.02.1818	Riitta Antintytär	70	Lammi
11.02.1818	Maria Vetämäjärvi	4	Alavus
27.02.1818	Juho Aktila	35	Pälkäne
25.04.1818	Katariina Samuelintytär	18	Lempäälä
30.06.1818	Ulrika Björn	23	Kangasala
10.05.1823	Simo Jaakonpoika	37	Pyhtää
13.06.1824	Juho Parikka	43	Jaakkima
18.06.1824	Anna Hjerpe	64	Hämeenlinna
19.10.1824	Pekka Leppänen	46	Ilomantsi
27.02.1824	Heikki Kuivalainen	14	Ilomantsi
24.10.1824	Matti Lemmittylä	25	Valkjärvi
30.01.1825	Berndt Hoffman	60	Kirkkonummi
17.03.1825	Matias Nyberg	26	Kirkkonummi
14.05.1825	Risto Pihlman	55	Pälkäne
09.07.1825	Simo Andersson	38	Tammela
21.07.1825	Juho Simola	55	Tammela
23.01.1826	Juho Muikku	30	Pielisjärvi
20.07.1826	Matti Antinp.Poutanen	32	Parikkala
28.07.1826	Matti Mikonp.Poutanen	28 d	Parikkala
18.08.1826	Kustaa Matinpoika	66	Kangasala
02.03.1827	Adam Hasselgren	4	Kuopio
16.02.1827	Antti Kiminki	2	Maaninka
27.04.1827	Maija Liisa Juhontytär	4 w	Jyväskylä
18.08.1826	Kustaa Matinpoika	66	Kangasala
17.04.1828	Antti Tollo	41	Jääski
24.04.1828	Antti Kuosa	18	Kurkijoki
15.05.1828	Mikko Jöransson	55	Lappee
21.11.1830	Kaisa Hannukainen	6	Kaukola
13.01.1831	Vilhelm Pillonen	7	Ruovesi
20.01.1831	Ulrika Aatuntytär	4	Sysmä
26.01.1831	Kaisa Pärnänen	4	Kaukola
17.02.1831	Heikki Everi	9	Kaukola
14.03.1831	Anna Suuronen	6	Kaukola
19.09.1831	Pekka Teräväinen	14	Kaukola
22.12.1831	Erkki Olkinuora	5	Kaukola
31.07.1832	Adam Karvanen	8	Hiitola
02.08.1832	Maria Lankinen	64	Hiitola
18.08.1832	Maria Lasonen	2	Käkisalmi
11.09.1832	Anna Ijäs	16	Hiitola
17.12.1836	Johan Lindström	6	Kemiö
29.05.1839	Juho Pukki	4	Kivennapa
15.06.1841	Elisabet Antintytär	3	Virolahti
04.04.1842	Antti Patja	20	Jääski
30.05.1843	Anna Pesonen	5	Kivennapa
12.06.1843	Pekka Mäkeläinen	26	Kivennapa
18.07.1843	Josef Vesalainen	11	Kivennapa
19.05.1844	Antti Väisänen	32	Muolaa
08.07.1844	Juho Valtonen	7	Uusikirkko
01.09.1844	Antti Walberg	6	Kivennapa
27.09.1844	Helena Breiman	11	Uusikirkko VI
22.05.1846	Juho Roponen	4	Sakkola
02.08.1846	Antti Melto	5	Kivennapa
06.05.1847	Antti Toivonen	5	Kivennapa
12.05.1847	Eeva Huhtanen	8	Kivennapa
12.05.1847	Mikko Veijalainen	5	Kivennapa
15.06.1847	Job Karvanen	7	Kivennapa
16.06.1847	Hedvig Hokkanen	3	Kivennapa
22.06.1847	Josef Erkinp.Savolainen	6	Kivennapa
29.07.1847	Josef Antinp. Savolainen	4	Kivennapa
10.12.1847	Kustaa Kustaanpoika	4	Ikaalinen
26.04.1848	Josef Nokkonen	4	Kivennapa
03.06.1848	Lovisa Susi	5	Kivennapa
28.06.1848	Maria Karhu	5	Kivennapa
15.07.1848	Katariina Paavolainen	5	Kivennapa
22.08.1848	Eeva Kääpä	7	Kivennapa
01.08.1849	Kristiina Matilainen	2	Kivennapa
15.08.1849	Juho Honkanen	5	Kivennapa
20.04.1850	Matti Veijalainen	7	Kivennapa
02.06.1850	Kristiina Mantonen	9	Kivennapa
17.07.1850	Tahvana Parikka	7	Kivennnapa
27.12.1854	Aleksanteri Pennanen	32	Pietari
14.02.1857	Maija Lindström	32	Liljendal
29.02.1857	Liisa Stoltti	44	Kirvu
21.03.1857	Matti Rouhiainen	27	Kirvu
26.03.1857	Risto Veijalainen	25	Kirvu
03.04.1857	Antti Pullinen	40	Kirvu
12.04.1857	Anna Mikont. Hynninen	20	Kirvu
19.04.1857	Anna Paavont. Hynninen	43	Kirvu
07.05.1857	Mikko Jaakonsaari	44	Kirvu
13.05.1857	Elena Häyry	41	Kirvu
22.05.1857	Eeva Reiman	65	Liljendal
13.12.1859	Vilhelrnina Rask	13	Eurajoki
24.02.1865	Taavetti Töllikkö	44	Heinjoki
17.04.1865	Anna Töllikkö	46	Heinjoki
02.03.1865	Perttu Räikkönen	60	Heinjoki
28.03.1865	Tuomas Myyrä	36	Heinjoki
09.04.1865	Antti Myyrä	19	Heinjoki
22.04.1865	Tuomas Räikkönen	9	Valkjärvi
30.05.1877	Oskari Aakku	3	Hämeenkyrö
04.06.1877	Kaarle Turunen	3	Hämeenkyrö
30.07.1877	Johan Johansson	7	Ylöjärvi
17.10.1877	Kalle Elinanpoika	3	Pirkkala
25.10.1877	Kaarle Avola	5	Hämeenkyrö
10.11.1877	Eeva Huhtamaa	2	Hämeenkyrö
25.12.1877	Kustaa Juhonpoika	33	Punkalaidun
28.12.1878	Edla Hanhikoski	8	Ylistaro
18.01.1880	Kaarle Hömberg	8	Kaianti
23.04.1880	Johanna Wiik	2	Laitila
25.04.1880	Maria Tapomäki	6	Nousiainen
26.04.1880	Maria Helin	2	Mynämäki
15.05.1880	Amanda Latvala	3	Aura
03.08.1880	Anna Lindberg	10	Mynämäki
06.10.1880	Ida Eufrosynentytär	4	Paimio
07.10.1880	Serafina Granfors	5	Laitila
15.10.1880	Paul Grönroos	5	Vehmaa
14.05.1881	Juho Vähätalo	5	Nousiainen
15.05.1881	Matilda Heikkilä	4	Karjala
10.06.1881	Mauri Leppäoja	9	Nousiainen
29.06.1881	Kustaa Niittumaa	4	Mynämäki
15.07.1881	Juhani Matinpoika	7	Nousiainen
22.07.1881	Gustaf Hartman	9	Karjala
31.07.1881	Konrad Åkerman	2	Masku
03.08.1881	Mathilda Savon	8	Laitila
15.08.1881	Gustaf Nummelin	5	Karjala
10.09.1881	Kaarle Forsström	7	Mynämäki
04.09.1881	Varpu Paakki	32	Uusikirkko
15.09.1881	Mikko Määttänen	31	Uusikirkko
01.10.1881	Kalle Santala	8	Mynämäki
31.10.1881	Alina Juhontytär	6	Vehmaa
07.11.1881	Kalle Grönroos	5	Vahto

Table 4.4. Humans killed by wolves in Finland 1710-1881.

tainly resulted in septicemia (blood poisoning), which if untreated with antibiotics, is most often lethal.

Table 4.4 lists all known incidents where wolves have killed humans in Finland. A map with each victim can be found on the internet (Internet A20). The Finnish "green pro wolf expert" Dr. Erkki Pulliainen dismisses these cases because, according to him, there is no evidence that these killings ever happened.

Most of the incidents in Finland are documented and can be verified by church books. Several cases are reported by journalists and found in newspapers. Below are two reports from those days (Karjalatar 32, August 10, 1877):

In July, a wolf appeared at the beach where three children were swimming in a lake in Ylöjärvi. The oldest child took the youngest with him and ran home for help. The wolf took the remaining nine year old boy. The father came running to help and the wolf then released its prey in a field of oats. The boy was still alive but died in the arms of his father.

A 12–year–old boy was taken by the wolf when herding cows. People heard him shout but thought he was shouting at the cows. As he didn't return home people went looking for him and found only one leg with the boot on.

I cannot even imagine the parents' pain when they found the remains of their child.

Russia in the Nineteenth Century

Professor Mikhail Pavlov stated, "Facts about attacks of wolves on people are not myths but reality." He continues, "Wolves primarily attack children since children sometimes mistake a wolf for a dog and try to pet the wolf. Such actions can end in tragedy. There are countless documented cases of wolves attacking people in Russia. Usually, rabid wolves do these attacks; however, there is plenty of documentation about attacks by non-rabid as well. Nevertheless, there are still some people who claim that a non-rabid wolf will not attack a human. That simply is not true. Non-rabid wolves also attack humans."

However, we have to go back to the 1840s to understand the magnitude of wolf attacks on humans. In 1873, the Russian hunter and author M. P. Vavilov wrote:

Think about living in a Russian village in a hut when one could only barely see over the snowdrifts. You are sitting in candlelight when you suddenly hear a wolf howl, and then there is a commotion in the village. The cattle become restless, the horses snort, the dogs begin to howl, and humans become uneasy— no matter how brave you are, an unsettledness springs up in you as a result of these sounds. The wolf is the greatest and most dreadful scourge of humans in our countries ... and there are many peasants who have been utterly ruined by wolves. Our peasants, barely becoming free from slavery, hardly being able to pay the heavy duties of the landowners, carrying their burdens, but not carrying people but carrying predatory animals—wolves (cited in Graves 2007).

Wolves deprived the peasants of their main accomplishments, their welfare, the main achievements of their simple and poor lives—which were their cattle and horses.

From 1849 to 1851 according to the Ministry of Interior, wolves killed at least 376 people or more each year. In the 1870s, wolves roamed on the streets of large cities in Kazan, Voronezh, and Tver, grabbing dogs on the streets and attacked people. Wolves were also in Moscow and St. Petersburg. According the Russian Central Statistical Committee, from 1870 to 1887, in the forty-nine provinces of European Russia and in the Privislyandskij region, 1,445 people were eaten by wolves. By the end of the nineteenth century, 50 to 100 people were killed by wolves in European Russia each year.

People should not shed tears over wolves which some people somehow manage to call, "the sanitarians of nature"; rather, they should shed tears over the large numbers of domestic and wild animals, domestic fowl, and pet dogs which wolves destroy–and for the people the wolves attack (Sabaneev 1876).

Zemstvo was an institution of local government set up in 1861 by Emperor Alexander II of Russia. This local government succeeded in solving many problems of general education, public medical service, construction and maintenance of roads, and sponsoring local economic development.

They also investigated and documented most of the wolf attacks in Russia. This documentation has served as a source for many scientific studies.

Research by Sergei Korytin

Sergei Korytin is a doctor of biology, professor, and director of the Prof. Zhitkov department of ecology and ethology at VNIOZ, the All-Union Scientific Research Institute for Hunting Economy and Fur-bearer Raising. In 1990, Korytin published an article in a leading hunting magazine *Ohota i ohotnitshje hozjaistvo* Volume 6, "Wolves as Man-Eaters". We shall spend some time with his article.

Sources

Korytin collected the material from the annual publications of the Russian Ministry of the Interior (Zhumal Ministerstva Vnutrennih Del). These publications contained reports of all (reported and investigated) wolf attacks against humans during the period 1840 to 1861. The original material was collected by local governors. Korytin selected attacks carried out by healthy wolves only, and he found 273 attacks, of which 221 were on children and 52 on adults.

Each case included a detailed description of the place, time, victim's name, victim's father's name, age, social status, behavior of witnesses and wolves, and victim's injuries. Also, if the victim was eaten by the wolves, the remains were described.

Korytin writes about the material

> *This shocking, but at the same time unique material gave us an opportunity to perform a quantitative analysis of wolves' attacks on humans.*

The Outcome

Korytin made the following observations:

- Children either survived or died. If they died, they were either killed or killed and eaten. If the wolf carried the child away it was considered dead unless later found alive.

- An adult either survived or was killed, and if killed either eaten or not. Contrary to children, a wolf was unable to carry away an adult.

- 73.4% of the 221 children were killed, while 26.6% survived. Of the adults, 13.5% were killed, and 86.5% survived.

- In most of the cases, the wolves carried away the child, and the high number of survivors is due to the simple fact that adults persecuted the wolf, and it had to abandon the child to be able to escape. However, most often, the wolf had enough time to finish its "dinner," and the victim was not found until the day after the attack.

- Of the thirty-eight children found, 50% were fully eaten, 23.7% partly eaten, and the remaining 26.3% simply killed. Statistically, the difference between killed and fully eaten children is significant. Thus, Korytin assumed that attacks against children were not always triggered by hunger (surplus killing).

- Most often, wolves attacked children between 2 and 13 years of age but rarely older. In most of the cases, the child was between 4 and 10 years of age, and the reason is simple. The wolf has to be able to carry the victim, and older children were just too heavy. Some 100 years ago, the average weight of a 1–year–old child was 8 kilograms, while a 5–years–old child weighed 15 kilograms, and a 10–years–old child 27 kilograms. Girls made up 59.4% of the killed children.

- The majority of attacks were on lone children (61%). The wolves rarely snatched a child from a group of other children (only 26%). In 9.5% of cases the child was intercepted when it was with one of its parents.

- In 100 cases out of 172 (58.7%) the wolf came looking for food (children) in human settlements. The rest of the attacks, 41.3%, happened outside the villages. In three of 100 cases, the wolf had snuck into the house in broad daylight and intercepted a sleeping child in its bed. In thrity-nine cases, the wolf intercepted the child in the yard and in the remaining fifty-eight cases, from places next to the yard or village.

- The distance from the victim's house were in direct relation to the victim's age. Farther from the house or the village, the average age of the victim was 8.8 years; children intercepted from the yard were, on average 6.6 years old, and children intercepted in their home were an average 5.3 years old.

- Most of the attacks took place in broad daylight. In seven cases, the wolf attacked late in the evening.

- In 68% the attack was carried out by one lone wolf. Three times, there were two wolves involved in the attack; in six cases, the number of wolves was not known, and in the remaining sixty-five cases, the report mentions wolves (plural) without specifying the exact number participating in the attack.

- In 60% of the cases, the wounds caused by the wolf attack are found on the victim's head, and 25% of the children were killed by a bite to the neck or throat.

- When a wolf intercepts a child, it usually takes it into the forest, approximately 1.5 to 3 km from the place where the child was intercepted.

Below, I list some of the documented cases by the document reference.

Zhurnal Ministerstva Vnutrennih Del, 1846, part 16, page 563

In the government of Livonia, Yuri Tuba's children Jaan and Katrine were collecting berries some fifty paces from their home when a wolf appeared. Jaan grabbed his sister in order to save her from the wolf, but the wolf attacked him, tore the girl away, and escaped with the victim into the forest. Despite the parents' pursuit, the wolf killed the girl, and they only found a shredded shirt and some bones.

Zhurnal Ministerstva Vnutrennih Del, 1848, part 24, pages 161-162

From the government of Moscow, we can read how a 3–year–old peasant boy was with his sister in a pasture when a wolf approached, grabbed the boy by his head, and ran toward the forest. The girl pulled the boy from the wolf when the wolf tried to grab the boy at the hip. The wolf went into a fury and attacked the girl, but she was rescued by people rushing to help her. The wolf ran to the nearest village, killed one calf, and escaped. When the tsar was informed of this event, he awarded the girl with 150 silver rubles.

Summary

Wolves seem to intensify their attacks on children in the spring and summer, while attacks on adults occur all year. The first to notice wolves' summer attacks on children was P. A. Mantifel, when he studied wolves' behavior during WW II. Mikhail Pavlov claims that this is a part of young wolves' training. However, there is a logical explanation that supports Mantifel's reasoning. During the cold period, children spend most of their time inside while summer is a time when they play in yards and forests close to the villages. This is also supported by the fact that most of the attacks are carried out by lone wolves, meaning they are either young wolves forced to feed themselves while their parents take care of the new litter, or an alpha looking for (fast) food far away from the den.

It also seems as if it takes some time for a wolf to get used to human flesh. In Mogilev (Belarus), attacks against children continued from 1844 to 1847, then they started again in 1850 and continued for some time. During these periods, nine children were lost to wolves. The first victim lost her ear, and her left flank was opened. The second victim lost his legs. With the third victim, a 4–year–old girl, the wolf left only her head, her hands, her chest, and some bones. The fourth victim was a 2-1/2–year–old girl who was intercepted by a wolf. The girl's father found the partly eaten victim before she was totally consumed by the wolf. The fifth victim was a 6–year–old boy, and the remains (one foot) was found 1 kilometer from his home.

I hope the evidence collected and reported by Sergei Korytin is enough to prove that wolves treat humans as prey.

Russia in the Twentieth Century

After the Russian revolution in 1917 until the Second World War, it seemed as if the Lenin–Stalin regime wanted to suppress any problems with wolves because everything was perfect in a communist state, and the regime would not tolerate any misfortune being published. It wanted to look perfect.

Instead of helping the rural people in their fight against wolves, scholars began to de-demonize the wolf. In 1933, Kaverznev dismissed all talk about wolves attacking humans. He used statistics from the time before the revolution to support his opinions. The same statistics were used by the Russian hunting experts Generozov and Solovjov when they proved the opposite.

The Russian communists needed to disarm the civilian population, thus, any publication of wolf attacks on humans were banned.

This more or less useless debate continued until the period after World War II when the number of wolves markedly increased, particularly in the regions that suffered from the German invasion.

The first attacks on children were reported in Kirov (Kirovskaya Oblast) at the end of September 1944. A wolf grabbed a 1–1/2–year–old boy near the village of Burakovskij and carried him off into the forest. Fortunately, collective farm workers were able to rescue the boy and drive off the wolf. The boy survived. A few days later two wolves attacked a 12–year–old girl who was tending horses in a pasture. The wolves badly tore her clothes, but caused only a few light wounds.

These two incidents show how wolves had entered stage seven of Professor Valerius Geist's famous list of seven stages leading to an attack on people. Professor Geist wrote

> *Wolves attack people. These initial attacks are clumsy, as the wolves have not yet learned how to efficiently take down the new prey. Persons attacked can often escape because of the clumsiness of the attacks.*

After these two attacks, wolves started to systematically hunt children. On November 6, 1944, on the road to the collective farm The New Derevnya near Aleksandrovsk, wolves tore an 8–year–old girl named Perfilov to pieces. Only scraps of clothing remained of the girl. On November 12, 1944, nine wolves bit to death 14–year–old Musinovu Tamaru. In a forested area named B. Ramenskij on November 19, 1944, two wolves killed 16–year–old Maria Polyakova as she was returning home from work.

Beginning in the spring of 1945, wolf attacks on people increased, and the attacks became more bold and spread to other regions of the Kirovskaya Oblast. On April 29, in the village of Golodaevshchina, a wolf attacked 17–year–old Maria Berdnikovu, who was working with her sister 50 meters from a cattle yard. Maria did not see the wolf because of weeds. The wolf grabbed her by the throat. People ran up shouting, but the wolf paid no attention and tossed the girl several times. B. M. Pashkin ran up, and the wolf snarled at him. When other people ran up, the wolf took the victim in its teeth and dragged her toward the forest. On the way the wolf jumped over a fence with the victim, and the fence was more than a meter high!

From 1946 through 1950, man-eating wolves were especially active in the Darovskij, Lebyazhskij, Sovetskij, Nolinskij, Khalturinskij, and Orichevskij regions of the oblast. In July and August of 1948, in the Darovskij region wolves carried away nine children aged from 7 to 12 years. Then in July and August of 1950, one boy and three girls from 3 to 6 years of age became the victims of wolves in the Lebyazhskij region (Graves 2007).

After restoration of the destruction caused by World War II, the number of wolves was reduced to a fraction of the pre-war population, and in some districts, the wolves were entirely eradicated.

The World in the Twenty First Century

On February 13, 2006, a wolf attacked a Russian lumberjack named Sergey Tambovsky while he was cutting wood with a chainsaw in the Ural Mountains. The wolf attacked him from behind, bit his leg, and a tried to bite him a second time. Sergey killed the wolf with the chainsaw. A second lumberjack named Pavel Tonkushin was a witness to the attack.

The local veterinarian, Mikhail Pidzhakov, said it was very cold and that the wolf was probably hungry. He added that when wolves are hungry, they "forget their fear." (Graves 2007).

In January 2012, a "super pack" probably consisting of many different large packs, surrounded the remote town of Verkhoyansk, forcing locals to mount patrols on snowmobiles until the government could send in extra help.

The Telegraph wrote in January 2013 how Yegor Borisov, head of the Sakha Republic, called for an urgent cull of wolves after the predators swamped populated areas in search of food. The local government announced a three-month "battle against wolves" to be launched on January 15.

In China, a pack of starving wolves attacked villagers, seriously injuring two persons. One victim had an ear torn clean off, while others suffered scratches to the face. This happened when up to five of the animals surrounded the small farming community before viciously mauling the six people living there, leaving two seriously injured, in a previously unheard of attack (Gillman 2014).

In the Russian republic of Bashkortostan, students have to walk through a snow-covered forest because no bus was provided to get them from their home village of Verkhny Nugush to their classes in Galiakberovo. On their way to school, they are armed with axes for their dangerous walk (Stewart 2016).

Wolf hunters on their way. Painting by Alfred Wierusz-Kowalski.

Victim(s)	Date	Type	Country	Victim(s)	Date	Type	Country
Valery Vinokurov	April 14, 2018	UP	Russia	Lima Ankudinova (†)	April 6, 2015	PR	Russia
2 People	February 20, 2018	UP	Iran	6 People	April 6, 2015	PR	Iraq
Lydia Vladimirovna	January 19, 2018	RA	Ukraine	5 People	March 24, 2015	PR	Armenia
Anna Lushchik, Vladimir Kiryanov, &&	January 4, 2018	UP	Ukraine	Giorgi Gogiberidze	March 7, 2015	UP	Georgia
2 Men	January 2, 2018	UP	Belarus	Two families on a snowmobile ride	January 25, 2015	RA	Canada
4 Residents	December 11, 2017	UP	Russia	Tagir Atajev, Anatoly Sonich, Vera Sonich	January 21, 2015	RA	Belarus
Mirbek Kelgenbaev	November 7, 2017	UP	Kyrgyzstan	Amankhan Amirov, Ozat Kyrykbaev	January 16, 2015	PR	Kazakhstan
Madi Utegenov	October 14, 2017	UP	Kazakhstan	2 Residents (†)	January 14, 2015	RA	Kazakhstan
Celia Hollingworth (†)	September 9, 2017	UP	Greece	Man	December 23, 2014	PR	Kyrgyzstan
Khasrat Gurbanov, Fikret Aliyev	August 7, 2017	PR	Azerbaijan	Resident	December 20, 2014	PR	Russia
Elderly Woman	August 1, 2017	UP	Greece	3 People	December 10, 2014	PR	Russia
Alyeva Aida Abbas	July 25, 2017	PR	Azerbaijan	Bolot Zhunushaliev	November 23, 2014	UP	Kyrgyzstan
Matin Bashiri (†)	July 24, 2017	PR	Iran	Şükran Aliyev	October 29, 2014	UP	Azerbaijan
Rajab Gadirov	July 20, 2017	PR	Azerbaijan	Nurçiçək Yusif, Əfsanə Yusif, Vüsal Yusif, &&	October 27, 2014	RA	Azerbaijan
Mohammad Mammadov, Bakhshish Asgarov	July 19, 2017	PR	Azerbaijan	Dijanu Kurtović	September 26, 2014	UP	Croatia
Beekeeper	July 7, 2017	RA	Russia	Vinod, Yograj, Sewaram, Perkasha, Bablu, &&	September 26, 2014	RA	India
3 People	July 4, 2017	UP	Georgia	Khem Chand, Kamlesh, Rita, Baljore, Maksood	September 25, 2014	RA	India
3 Children, 4 adults	June 13, 2017	UP	Iran	Abdurrahman Kara, Ahmet Topçu, Zehra Topçu	August 26, 2014	PR	Turkey
Tahira Habulla, Nazli Mammadaga	June 10, 2017	UP	Azerbaijan	Zhao Duoba and 5 other people	August 13, 2014	PR	China
Fatima Karami	May 6, 2017	PR	Iran	Nuriye Alacahan, Gaziye Can	July 8, 2014	RA	Turkey
Mohammad ?	April 18, 2017	PR	Iran	Cuma Dalbudak, Selahattin Öcal	June 3, 2014	PR	Turkey
Sultan Hasanoğlu, Mürteza Hasanoğlu, &&	April 2, 2017	RA	Turkey	Öner Kırdar, Erdek Karsiyaka	April 21, 2014	UP	Turkey
Farmer	March 15, 2017	PR	Kyrgyzstan	Nikolai Mikhailov	December 1, 2014	RA	Russia
Vusal Abbasov	February 21, 2017	PR	Azerbaijan	Ruslan Nuritdinov	January 6, 2014	RA	Russia
Marcelo Vanzuita	February 2, 2017	PR	Canada	Meryem Öztürk, Elif Sevinç, Baki Gündoğdu, &&	January 3, 2014	PR	Turkey
3 People	February 5, 2017	RA	Ukraine	8 People	10, 20, 2013	RA	Iran
Kadyrzhan Sharshenbek uulu	February 5, 2017	PR	Kyrgyzstan	Yura Arushanyan	October 17, 2013	PR	Armenia
Skiers	December 7, 2016	UP	Canada	Michelle Prosser	October 15, 2013	RA	Canada
Child	December 30, 2016	PR	India	8 People	October 10, 2013	UP	Iran
2 People	December 4, 2016	PR	Iran	Zeki Cane	October 7, 2013	UP	Turkey
Oil worker	December 2, 2016	UP	Kazakhstan	Daulet Tuyeshiyev	September 5, 2013	PR	Kazakhstan
Sivam Kewat (†)	November 24, 2016	UP	India	Noah Graham	August 24, 2013	UP	USA
A child	November 8, 2016	PR	Kyrgyzstan	Adil Ahmad (†)	July 13, 2013	PR	India
11 children	November 7, 2016	RA	Azerbaijan	Aadil Hameed Sheikh (†)	July 13, 2013	PR	Kashmir
2 Adults, 1 child	November 4, 2016	UP	Pakistan	William "Mac" Hollan	July 6, 2013	UP	Canada
Brent Woodland	November 1, 2016	UP	Canada	Mevlüt Özcanlı (†), Fikriye Pişkin, &&	June 12, 2013	UP	Turkey
Resident	October 31, 2016	RA	Azerbaijan	Feyzullah Aydin, Pınar Aydın, Gülgez Aydın &&	April 26, 2013	PR	Turkey
Andrew Morgan	October 8, 2016	PR	Canada	Vitaly Vanadze	April 23, 2013	PR	Georgia
Worker	August 29, 2016	UP	Canada	Dawn Hepp	March 8, 2013	PR	Canada
Alexander Chausov,Ivan Golub, Vadim Golub, &&	July 7, 2016	RA	Belarus	Ziya Kerdige, Sercan Ceco, Kamber Altun	March 5, 2013	PR	Turkey
2 Children	June 8, 2016	PR	Iran	Elderly Woman (†)	February 5, 2013	PR	Tajikistan
Bülent Taşçı	June 8, 2016	UP	Turkey	Lance Grangaard	December 10, 2012	RA	Alaska
Sahib Mamedov	May 31, 2016	PR	Azerbaijan	Muratbek Bakhtygali, Aigul Espentayeva, &&	December 6, 2012	PR	Kazakhstan
Zlyva Hussein, Gôld Hussein, Sarab Ghazanfar	April 22, 2016	UP	Iran	Aishat Maksudova	November 2, 2012	UP	Russia
Aslan Shauhalovu	April 13, 2016	PR	Russia	Meryem Kara (†), İsmail Atmaca	October 15, 2012	RA	Turkey
5 People	April 2, 2016	RA	Iran	Abbas Mohammed (†)	September 24, 2012	PR	Iraq
A couple with a boy	March 25, 2016	RA	Mongolia	Rukmanna (†)	August 1, 2012	PR	India
Rosa Harutyunyan	March .21, 2016	UP	Armenia	Jeffrey Kartsivadze (†)	July 10, 2012	PR	Georgia
Valiko Tagiashvili (†)	March , 20, 2016	PR	Georgia	Stanislav Biennale (†)	July 1, 2012	PR	Ukraine
2 People	February 24, 2016	RA	Russia	Zhagor Imangaliyev	April 25, 2012	UP	Kazakhstan
Seyed Hassan Mousavi.	February 22, 2016	UP	Iran	Varlam Butskhrikidze (†)	February , 2012	PR	Georgia
A shepherd	January 30, 2016	PR	Macedonia	1 Adult	June 17, 2012	PR	Sweden
Bejshebaj Turgunbayev, Kanykei Aktanbaeva	December 21, 2015	RA	Kyrgyzstan	Seven people (††)	March , 2012	PR	China
Musa uulu Taalaybek.	December 2, 2015	UP	Kyrgyzstan	Surik Isayan	March 15, 2012	PR	Armenia
Elchin Mamishov	November 30, 2015	PR	Azerbaijan	Grigory Gerasimovich, Valentin Shevchuk	February 1, 2012	RA	Belarus
6 People	November 29, 2015	UP	Iran	4 People	January 5, 2012	UP	Kazakhstan
Ilham Mammadov, Padar Behramov	October 26, 2015	PR	Azerbaijan	Rene Anderson	September 25, 2011	PR	USA
A Resident	October 16, 2015	RA	Turkey	5 People	June 24, 2011	RA	Belarus
2 People	October 4, 2015	RA	Russia	Kezban Kartalmış, Şerife Erkip (†)	April 14, 2011	RA	Turkey
Matthew Nellessen	September 23, 2015	PR	USA	Asylhanov Mukhtarov and 3 men	January 31, 2011	PR	Kazakhstan
Mahaneh Shams	July 31, 2015	PR	Syria	Karen Calisterio	November 27, 2010	UP	USA
Dhakira Ghasemi, Abolfazl Rahimi	July 6, 2015	PR	Iran	3 mAdults, 1 child	October 25, 2010	PR	Iran
Mehmet Karasu, Ali Yasar	June 20, 2015	PR	Turkey	Zhyidyz Bakasova, 1 child	October 29, 2010	PR	Kyrgyzstan
Yamanurappa Basappa Mushigeri, Sakrappa	June 9, 2015	PR	India	10 People (†)	September 27, 2010	RA	Russia
Amir Menkes and 4 more people	May 9, 2015	RA	Israel	Ali Şahin, Kıymet Şahin, İsmet Bozkurt	September 9, 2010	RA	Turkey
2 People	April 26, 2015	UP	Belarus	Candice Berner (†)	March 8, 2010	PR	Alaska

Table 4.5. Attacks on humans after 2010 (Wikipedia)

ABOUT ATTACKS ON HUMANS

The politically correct view about wolves is that they are "harmless" and of no danger to humans. This view arose from the early research of eminent North American biologists who, confronted by historical material contradictory to their experiences, greatly mistrusted that material (Valerius Geist).

However, I have presented indisputable facts from the nineteenth and twentieth centuries that wolves may, under certain conditions, attack humans.

Mature Age and General Aggression

Until wolves become mature, they behave like dogs, giving the false impression that wolves are playful and kind to humans. However, scientific publications and practical evidence show that at the age of 2 to 3 years, most wolves become aggressive toward humans. This is verified by both Mikhail Pavlov and Dmitry Bibikov in their books about the wolf.

We know from captive wolves living in zoos that at an age of approximately 3 years, wolves become aggressive toward the personnel. In Stockholm Zoo (Skansen), the wolf Silva was euthanized in 1991 after reaching maturity and exhibiting aggressive behavior. In Kolmården Wildlife Park, a pack of wolves attacked and killed a zookeeper at the park in June 2012. Although the management of the Wildlife Park said it was unclear why the pack of wolves attacked a human, nobody realized that the whole pack had just reached the critical age of 3 years. The woman they killed had raised the wolf pack since they were cubs, but despite this, the wolves treated her as an alien (Berg 2018).

Maturity is one of the main reasons why people abandon wolf–dog crosses that were purchased as pets (Dethlefsen 2016). An example of how the wolf's heritage lives on in mature wolf–dog hybrids comes from Salem Township, Pennsylvania, where, on July 17, 2006, a captive pack of nine wolf hybrids kept as pets killed their owner, Sandra L. Piovesan, although she treated her wolves like children. In fact, she used to say that her dogs give me unqualified love (Fuoco & Harlan 2006).

According to Dimitry Bibikov, 30% of all mature wolves exhibit aggressive behavior and do not hesitate to attack humans.

L. Krushinski studied the role of aggression in wolves and forms of aggressive displays toward other animals. He noted, "Cubs under one year generally were not aggressive toward strangers. Later, aggression increased, especially during the mating season. Adult wolves show more and more aggression. For example, a tender and happy wolf that was raised in a cage became dangerous for humans after three years. Krushinski concluded,

> *European wolves raised among humans from pups display a wide variety of levels of aggression toward humans. All possibilities occurred, from very aggressive males to very nice females that readily took to any stranger.*

Generally, the wolf is an aggressive animal, and only its fear of humans prevents it from attacking humans more often in nature.

When Krushinski wrote this conclusion, he did not yet have access to most of the information on man-eating wolves. There were few data available on the problem when his seminar on the behavior of wolves took place in 1979. Nevertheless, at that seminar, Krushinski reported that a third of all middle Russian forest wolves are potentially dangerous for humans because of their defensive reactions. These wolves feel fear toward men, less toward women, and are not threatened by children.

So there seems to be particular animals among wolf populations that become successful and experienced at attacking large prey like moose and wild boar, and, accidentally, humans. Wolves can then be expected to progress in specialization, sometimes solo, sometimes as a team. Each man-eater has appeared under particular circumstances. One of the favorable conditions seems to be a sharp increase in wolf numbers so that the number of daring, aggressive wolves also increases proportionally (Krushinski 1980).

Therefore, it is apparent that aggressive animals are much more common in some wolf populations than in others. Elevated aggression toward humans might be a consequence of poor fauna, poor foraging opportunities, or having available food connected mostly with human activity. Where wolves occur in such places, they are potentially dangerous for humans. If, for some reason, wolf numbers increase under such circumstances, wolves can be particularly troublesome.

On March 19, 1821, Lars Backmark recorded that a tamed wolf started to kill and eat humans. Backmark was visited by Mr. Ferner from Öresund, Sweden, who told him that many people were wounded and killed by wolves in localities of Öresund, and other parishes in the county of Dalarna. People believed that the wolf was taken as a cub from a den in 1817 and was kept as a pet at the Gusinge estate. After about three years the animal reached maturity and escaped.

The Ring Game

Wolves live in a cage of innate instincts. Love, friendship, or partnership mean nothing. They don't care about capitalism, feminism, or global warming. The only things they care for are food, sex, and survival, in that order. If they smell prey, they kill and eat; if they smell a possibility to have sex, they fight to get sex; if they have to escape to survive, they flee.

To trigger a wolf attack, you just pull the wire anchored to one of these three instincts.

I mentioned the cubs' ring game, where a pack of cubs encircle one of the cubs and try to make it stumble. When it does so, the whole gang jumps on the cub in the middle. Several events show how this mechanism works with adult wolves.

Wolves do not know if the person or animal lying on the ground is there accidentally, and why should they care. They simply see prey (dinner), ready to be consumed, and greediness triggers the attack.

Patricia (Trisha) Wyman was a Canadian wildlife biologist working as a caretaker in the Wolf Centre of the Haliburton Forest & Wildlife Reserve in Ontario. On April 18, 1996, she was found dead in the wolf enclosure. Investigations carried out by Erich Klinghammer came to the conclusion that Wyman was probably encircled by the wolves and accidentally tripped on one of the many broken branches in the enclosure, and the wolves then attacked her. The official version talks about the taste of blood, but I am more or less convinced that it was the innate instinct to attack a tripping prey animal that triggered the attack (Wikipedia).

Back to Kolmården Wildlife Park in Sweden, where similar events have been reported.

In May 2011, one of the wolf keepers went into the enclosure to socialize with the wolves. She sat on a stone, and the wolves approached her. Suddenly, one of the wolves bit her on the head and pulled her hair until she fell on the ground. In a testimony to the court in Norrköping, Sweden, she said that this triggered an immediate attack from the wolves. When she miraculously succeeded to get back on her feet, the wolves had encircled her and started to make fast attacks, as they do in the ring game. There was no kindness or friendship, just ice-cold yellow eyes staring at her. She tried to make contact with the lead wolf, all in vain. The leader stared at her with large yellow eyes, its tail held straight slightly bent upward and the head lowered. It was prepared for an attack on her. After several attacks by the wolves, she managed to get out of the enclosure when a tractor caught the wolves' attention for one second (Berge 2018).

On April 22, 2012, a group of young girls visited the wolf enclosure, where it was possible to socialize with the wolves. The girls were sitting on some stones when one of the girls was pulled to the ground by one wolf from the pack. Immediately, the pack attacked her, but she was rescued and taken to hospital by her parents, where she stayed for four days. The management dismissed this by saying that the wolves just wanted to play with the girl (Berge 2018).

In June 2012, another wolf keeper (Karolina) was killed and probably eaten by the wolf pack in Kolmården Wildlife Park. It is uncertain how the wolves attacked her, but I assume that she was too confident around the wolves because she believed in the "politically correct truth" that wolves are not dangerous.

Figure 4.4. A socialized and well-fed wolf–dog in Ähtäri Zoo, Finland (photo by the author).

Don't Show Debility

When confronting wolves, avoid any signs of weakness, fear, unsteadiness, or illness, and instead act bold, calm, and resolute.

Don't ever turn your back on wolves!

The wolf is a coward, and it avoids direct fighting where the risk of being injured by an unknown animal is overwhelming. However, it does not hesitate to attack an animal that turns its back and offers an opportunity to taste it.

Again, we have an excellent example from the Kolmården Wildlife Park, where a deaf girl was let into the wolf enclosure in 2008 and was immediately attacked by the wolf pack. More about this attack can be found in Swedish (Internet A10).

In his book Man and Wolf, Harry Frank highlights the fact that socialized wolves may be obstreperous, even with familiar, experienced handlers. Such behavior is likely to uncover any debility in its object. He also writes that wolves are likely to respond to signs of debility with testing and possibly attacking, even if they have a long history of friendly interactions with their victim. Thus, he strongly recommends that anyone who is debilitated in some way should avoid contact with wolves (Frank 1987).

Don't Show Fear

Animals sense fear, and this is especially true of large mammalian carnivores like wolves, bears, lions, and tigers. The trick is to never show fear, because if you do, you are dead.

It Was a Rabid Wolf

When all else fails and the politically correct experts run out of explanations, they use the "rabid excuse". They claim that it was a rabid wolf, and that a healthy wolf is safe to pet.

Who knows if an approaching wolf is rabid or not?

Contrary to documented facts, these experts claim that the majority of "attacks" by wolves on humans stem from rabid wolves which, because of the disease, have lost their caution and fear. One may ask if it matters whether someone is attacked by a rabid or healthy wolf. If the victim dies, the outcome is the same.

Wolves frequently suffer from rabies, and they act as a source of this infection for people. Although more than 70% of the total cases of rabies among humans stem from bites from dogs, and bites from wolves are less than 3% (Rudnev 1950), wolves are the principal host (reservoir) of the rabies virus in nature.

The Lore of The Harmless Wolf

Unfortunately, the consensus that wolves are harmless led to the tragedies described above. Kolmården is an excellent example of how wrong this lore is. The first reactions throughout Sweden were "This is impossible! Wolves do not behave like this," although many earlier incidents, as described above, gave indications of what was coming. Still, at the time of this writing, Swedish "wolf experts" cannot understand why these attacks happened in Kolmården. Domesticated wolves are allowed to roam in human settlements all around Sweden with the simple explanation: "Wolves are not dangerous".

When do we fully understand the risks a wolf population brings to human?

In Finland, the lore of the harmless wolf came to an abrupt end in February 2017, when two wolves attacked a 7–year–old boy at Ähtäri Zoo. The boy probably tried to pet the wolf through the fence, and the wolf managed to grab his hand and mauled it severely, with another wolf joining the attack. The boy suffered serious injuries and was taken to the hospital for treatment.

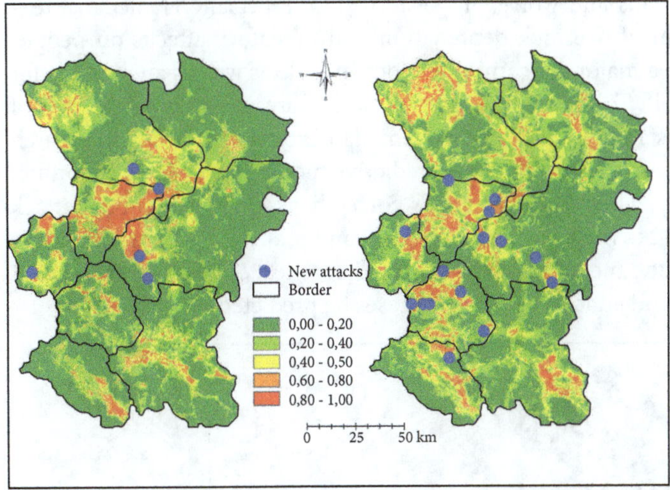

Figure 4.5. Probabilities of a wolf attack in Iran.

The boy had somehow gotten past a first wooden fence, making it to the edge of the animal enclosure, before he was attacked.

The boy visited the zoo with his parents, and there were crowds of spectators watching the wolves, but no one reacted when the boy got past the first fence. There is only one reasonable explanation.

The politically correct media, schoolteachers, the great audience, and parents, believed that it is safe to pet a wolf.

Wolves Continue Attacking Humans

Ironically, we need scientific evidence produced by politically correct scholars, whose research is funded by, for instance, Greenpeace, WWF, Animals Rights, or Rewilding Europe, to be used as references if we want to publish "facts" about wolves.

I have several times been criticized for my use of Russian wolf research because it is "obsolete" and gives the wrong picture of the wolf. However, the wolf does not know it and, thus, continues as it did in Russia.

Wolves in Iran

In Iran, wolf attacks have been reported for millennia. Many cases of wolves snatching small children have been reported and adults have been attacked on occasion.

Conflicts between humans and wolves in western Iran, especially Hamedan Province, occur in the form of livestock depredation and predatory attacks on people. Conflicts have become a major concern of the local people as well as an obstacle for conservation of the wolf. To identify the distribution of areas with potential risk of wolf attacks on humans and livestock in the Hamedan Province, an Iranian research team employed maximum entropy to build predictive models with reported conflict data from 2001 to 2010. The resulting models correctly assigned subsequent attack sites from 2011 and 2012 to high-risk areas (Behdarvand et al. 2014). Figure 4.5 shows the outcome of this study, and although this was a theoretical estimate, it proves that wolves attack humans and attacks can in some cases be predicted.

Figure 4.6. Child lifting, a French lithography from 1839.

In Iran, a total of fifty-three wolf attacks on humans were recorded in the Hamedan Province, between April 2001 and April 2012. Most attacks were classified as predatory (68%) and pet-related (19%). The majority of victims were children (12 years old or younger). Most incidents (70%) took place during the wolves' pup-rearing season. The most frequent human activities at time of attack were recreation based (57%), and the locations of attacks were frequently in the farmlands (43%) and outskirts of villages (41%) (Behdarvand & Kobani 2015).

In the Iranian wolf attacks, we notice the same behavior as Russian scholars did in the nineteenth century.

Attacks on children happen during the rearing season.

Child Lifting and Wolves in India

Indian wolves have a history of preying on children, a phenomenon called child-lifting. In 1878, 624 people were killed by wolves in Uttar Pradesh, and fourteen others were killed in Bengal during the same period. In 1900, 285 people were killed in the Central Provinces. Between 1910 and 1915, 115 children were killed by wolves in Hazaribagh, and 122 were killed in the same area in 1980 through 1986 (Rajpurohit 1999).

Rajpurohit analyzed the problem of child lifting in the Hazaribagh West, Koderma, and Latehar forest divisions of Bihar State, India. The evaluation was based upon records of the Forest Department, interviews, and a survey. Five wolf packs had created problems in sixty-three villages. From April 1993 to April 1995, eighty children were attacked of whom only twenty were rescued.

All the children were taken from settlements primarily between March and August between 5:00 and 7:00 pm. There were more female victims (58%) than males, and 89% were between 3 and 11 years old.

Researcher / country	Time	Victims	Age	Rescued	Season	Female
Moriceau (France)	1572–1824	933	0–14	N/A	Mar-Nov	53.0%
Sergey Korytin (Russia)	1840–1861	221	2–13	29.4%	Summer	59.4%
Rajpurohit (India)	1993–1995	80	3–11	25.0%	Summer	58.0%
Behdarvandi (Iran)	2001–2012	53	0–12	N/A	Summer	N/A

Table 4.6. A summary from three centuries.

What We Learned from History

Table 4.6 summarizes some common features in wolves' attacks on children during the ages. This information supports the assumption that wolf behavior has not changed during the last three centuries. Nor is there any significant difference in behavior between wolves from different parts of Europe and Asia. It seems as if boys have a better chance of surviving an attack than girls do. Most of the children were less than 13 years old, and the majority of attacks happened during wolves' pup-rearing season.

Although prey is available during the pup-rearing season, attacks on humans (children) are more frequent then than in winter, when food resources are scarce. This observation does not support the common belief that only when wolves run out of food and search for alternate prey do they become dangerous to humans.

I add another theory to the debate. In summertime, packs are dispersed within their territory. The breeding pair look for food far from the lair in order to not reveal the location of the lair. This, along with the fact that they hunt alone and need fast and easy food, takes them closer to human settlements, where a child is easy prey.

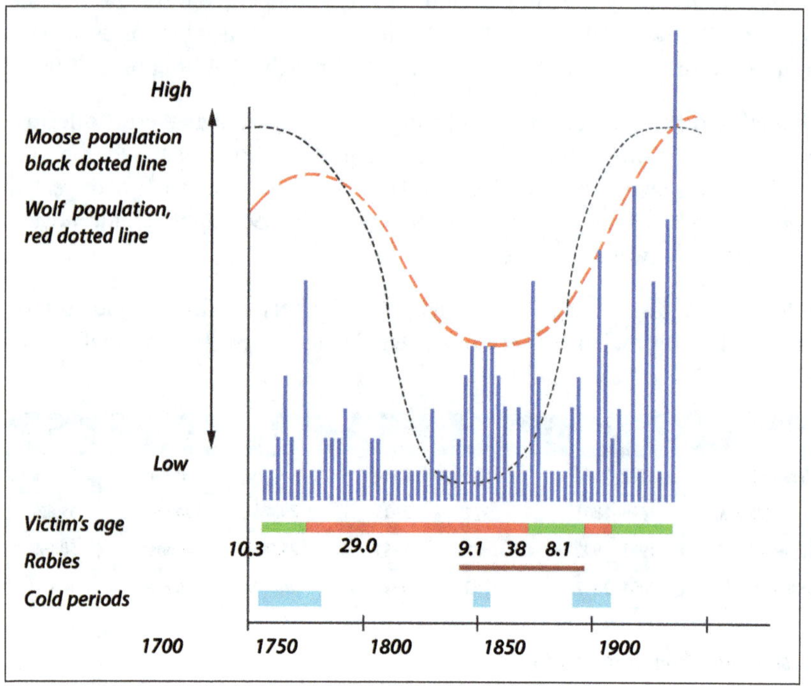

Figure 4.7. Variations in moose and wolf populations from two centuries compared to wolf attacks on humans, climate, and rabies epidemic.

Figure 4.7 was originally created by professor Pjotr Danilov from Petrozavodsk State University and the Finnish large carnivore specialist Dr. Erik S. Nyholm. In this chart they compare variations in the Finnish–Russian wolf population to variations in the moose population. This drawing shows the relative changes on the y-axis rather than absolute values. I added the wolves' victims from Table 4.4 in order to show correlation between the wolf population, moose population, and wolves' attacks on humans. No direct correlation between moose abundance and wolves' attacks on humans can be found. During low moose population, there are certainly cases of rabies among adult victims, increasing the total number of victims. However, the number of children killed by wolves seems to correlate with a high moose population, except in the early 1800s when an epidemic of rabies was spreading among Finnish wolves.

Habituated Wolves

Wolves habituating to humans is not a new phenomena although wolves' strict protection encourages them to approach human settlements. The result has been an intensifying frequency of wolf attacks on humans although the consequences are less lethal than two centuries ago.

Marc Leblond, 5 years old, was killed by a wolf in 1963 north of Baie-Comeau, Quebec, Canada. Death by wolf attack was confirmed by the district coroner and police chief and reported by T.R. Mader in "Wolf Attacks on Humans," Abundant Wildlife Society of North America, undated.

In 2015, wolves attacked two families on snowmobiles in Labrador City. In 2013, a pack of wolves attacked Michelle Prosser in Merritt, BC, and William Hollan was attacked by wolves while cycling in the Yukon.

On December 7, 2016, a wolf aggressively stalked a man at Mount Norquay, Alberta, after killing his dog. On October 8, 2016, 26-year-old Andrew Morgan was attacked by a wolf near Canmore, Alberta. On August 29, a young worker was attacked at the Cigar Lake Mine in Saskatchewan. In June 2016, officers shot a wolf at Banff National Park because it was harassing park visitors.

In the spring of 2018, three roaming wolves terrorized Drezdenko and neighboring municipalities of the southwestern Polish Lubuskie province, attacking humans.

One of the victims told a Polish national broadcaster that the wolf approached her from behind and bit her calf. Despite the painful injury, the victim started shouting, and the wolf backed away and fled.

"This wolf is lurking out there for us around our households," complained another citizen, saying that the wolf was bent on attacking not only children but also adults.

Habituation is a growing concern as wolves sooner or later start treating humans as potential prey. In Europe, the situation seems to escalate when wolves roam in human settlements without showing any fear.

Figure 4.8 shows a wolf in the middle of a suburb in Sweden. The photo was taken in 2011. Now, seven years later, things are even worse all over Europe.

In January 1999, a man was jogging with his two dogs near Ucluelet, BC, when two wolves attacked the smaller of his dogs. The man grabbed the dog away from one of the wolves, and the wolf lunged toward the man but did not make contact. The wolves then followed the man as he returned to his vehicle (McNay 2002)

A similar incident occurred in March when a woman walking her dog encountered a wolf on a trail. The woman immediately picked up her dog and retreated to a nearby parking lot with three wolves following her (McNay 2002).

Figure 4.8. Wolf roaming in a human settlements (photo by Angelika K).

The Kenton Carnegie Case

I would not typically write about the Kenton Carnegie case because our history is full of identical incidents. However, this case is an excellent example of how deadly the myth of the harmless wolf is.

I let Professor Emeritus Valerius Geist have the word for the next couple of pages as I paraphrase his 2008 article on the subject.

On November 8, 2005 a 22–year–old student in Geological Engineering, Kenton Joel Carnegie, from the University of Waterloo, Ontario, Canada, was killed in northern Saskatchewan by a pack of wolves. While he was almost certainly not the only victim of wolf predation in North America in the past century, judging from conversations with native people, and a closer review of case histories, this was the best-investigated case to date.

Mr. Carnegie was in a university co-op program that allowed students to gain hands-on experience from visits to mining operations. He was flown into Points North Landing, a mining camp close to Wollaston Lake in northern Saskatchewan. Bad weather delayed his return. On November 4, 2005, Todd Svarchopf, an experienced bush pilot, and Chris Van Galder, two of Kenton's camp companions, had an encounter with two aggressive wolves on the airfield close to camp. The two young men beat back the attack, photographed the wolves, and told everybody in the camp.

Two days before Kenton was killed, the young men were warned at a dinner at a local lodge by an experienced northerner, Bill Topping. He admired the pictures and told his guests that they were lucky to be alive!

On November 8. 2005, at about 15:30, Kenton Carnegie notified Van Gelder that he was going for a walk along the lake and expected to return by 17:00. Kenton had gone to the west shore of Wollaston Lake before when going fishing. This area is isolated and not open to unauthorized traffic. At about 18:15, because Kenton had failed to appear for dinner, Chris Van Galder and Todd Svarchopf went in search of him, but could not find him in camp. Todd saw Kenton's tracks in the fresh snow leaving camp, but not returning.

About 18:30, Chris and Todd, along with Mark Eikel, co-owner of the camp, drove out in a truck to search for Kenton. Fresh snow had fallen, and the party followed the clear footprints, which headed south from camp.

Kenton's tracks headed towards the shore of the lake. When Eikel and companions encountered wolf tracks, they reversed and headed back to camp so Eikel could get his rifle, a more powerful flashlight, and a radio. The party then drove to a nearby cabin, thinking Kenton might be there, but found none of his footprints. They returned by truck to where they had been earlier and they soon saw that Kenton's footprints left the road and headed down a trail toward the lake.

There were wolf tracks on the trail.

Then they saw Kenton's footprints doubling back, and found a concentration of wolf tracks. Mark Eikel shone the flashlight, and saw what he thought was Kenton's body. He ordered everybody back to the truck, not wanting the others to see the sight. On the way back to camp, Eikel radioed Robert Dennis (Bob) Burseth, an employee of the camp, long-term resident of the north, and an experienced hunter.

Burseth realized something tragic had happened and contacted his wife, Rosalie Tsannie-Burseth, who was the local coroner at Wollaston Lake, to ask her to contact the Royal Canadian Mounted Police (RCMP). Next, Chris Van Galder called the RCMP from camp, and the company office was notified. About 19:30 Eikel and Burseth returned by truck to check on Kenton. Eikel believed that Kenton was dead, but he wanted to make sure that his mind was not playing tricks on him and he also wanted to get a second opinion. They parked the truck and walked down the ridge on the edge of the lake, noting the many wolf tracks. Mark Eikel shined the flashlight around until both could see Kenton's body.

They saw exposed flesh and ribs from the belt up. The pants appeared to be on. Eikel and Burseth approached to within 30 feet, but they stayed only a couple of minutes before returning to camp to await the police and coroner, who arrived about 21:35 pm

Figure 4.9.

Right: Wolves' paw prints from the place where Kenton Carnegie was killed (photo RCMP).

Left: A bear's paw prints.

When they returned, they found that Kenton's body had been moved from the location where Mark Eikel and Bob Burseth had seen it some two hours earlier. The distance moved was about 20 yards. Officer Noey indicated the move on his hand-drawn map and confirmed the distance by pacing it out the next day. Much more of the body had been consumed.

There had been four wolves running together near camp earlier. The four had been seen on the runway the day before, November 8. Burseth also saw three wolves running across the lake toward the kill site at about 7:45 am the morning following Kenton's death, that is, November 9. Eikel confirmed that four wolves had been seen near the camp and garbage dump site.

About 21:50, Constable Noey and coroner Rosalie Tsannie-Burseth begin securing and inspecting the site. They examined and photographed the body and surroundings for 40 to 45 minutes. Then Constable Marion authorized the removal of Kenton's body, and the party returned to Points North Landing.

The following day, November 9, 2005, between 13:00 and 14:14 Constable Noey, coroner Tsannie-Burseth, and Bob Burseth returned to take pictures, and analyze the scene. The following are their joint results, as summarized in Constable Noey's report.

1. Kenton's footprints, heading south, were followed by a wolf who stepped into Kenton's footprints. Constable Noey surmised that the wolf had been stalking Kenton.

2. Constable Noey followed Kenton's footprints, which continued past the kill site for a distance of about 60 to 80 meters to the shoreline.

3. At this point, more wolf tracks converged on where Kenton stood. The wolf tracks were coming from the south along the shore of the lake. It looked like a hunting strategy had been executed by the wolves, and it was surmised that Kenton was thus killed by at least three wolves and possibly by all four!

4. At that point Kenton's footprints turned back toward the road.

5. From that point it was an additional 10 to 20 meters along the trail before the snow was disturbed, indicating an altercation.

6. Footprints now headed across the trail and a little way into the muskeg. The footprints indicated that Kenton was running half on the trail and half on the muskeg. There was a lot of disturbance of the snow.

7. From there it was a short distance north to the kill site, where the body and pieces of clothing had first been discovered before it had been dragged the extra 20 yards.

8. In between were two sites where the tracks indicated that Kenton stood, shedding a lot of blood. A third place where he had apparently stood, dripping blood, was where the search party found the body.

The coroner's inquest in Saskatchewan, unfortunately, did not touch on policy matters. It only answered the narrow question of who killed Kenton Carnegie, to which the answer was wolves. Change the question slightly, to *what* killed Kenton Carnegie, and the answer becomes

The myth that wolves do not attack people.

Two Conservation Officers from the Saskatchewan game department (SERM), Kelly Crayne and Mario Gaudet, arrived on the 10th in order to do their investigation. They stated in their report that "officers investigated the site and found numerous wolf tracks in the area. No other large animal tracks could be found."

The Myth Must Survive

The tracks and signs at the scene were thus examined by two senior native persons highly experienced in tracking, two experienced northern hunters, two conservation officers, a seasoned bush pilot, and a highly trained physical scientist. Svarchopf, Van Galder, and Eikel, who were first on the scene, identified only wolf tracks. They were vindicated by Bob Burseth, as he insisted that he, too, saw only wolf tracks. In turn, Buirseth was vindicated by RCMP Constable Noey and coroner Tsannie-Burseth, who not only saw only wolf tracks at the site but also saw and heard wolves so close to Kenton's body that Constable Noey fired his shotgun twice and also asked Eikel to discharge his rifle to spook the wolves away. Conservation Officers Crayne and Gaudet also saw only wolf tracks. In addition, Constable Noey and coroner Tsannie-Burseth were able to decipher the track pattern left by the wolves, showing a classic hunt pattern for wolves.

Wolves Don't Kill Humans

The Saskatchewan coroner asked for the case to be re-examined by the scientists, Dr. Paul Paquet, a wolf researcher, and Professor Ernest G. Walker of the University of Saskatchewan. Before their confidential report was submitted, Paquet informed the popular news media that he recognized immediately that a black bear had killed Carnegie. "The problem was bias right from the start," Paquet asserted, then he added, "When I looked at the photos, I immediately saw bear tracks," The National Geographic Society sent a team to film a re-enactment of Kenton's death, and Dr. Paquet acted as consultant.

Victims of wildlife tragedies in North America tend to be blamed for the event, and it was not different in Kenton's case.

Paquet claimed that a number of forensic signs identified the responsible predator as a bear. His claims included the following:

- Wolves do not drag their prey from the kill site but consume prey in situ. Yet Kenton's body, he claimed, had been dragged some 50 paces. However, European accounts of how wolves deal with prey, livestock, and humans as well are that they carry or drag prey into cover, away from where they attacked closer to human habitations. The resolution of what appears to be opposites is quite simple: if undisturbed, wolves consume their kill at the kill site. But if the wolves are disturbed or in danger, they move their kill. And that's what happened in the Kenton Carnegie case. The wolves fed at the kill site until they were disturbed by the first search party. By the time the second party arrived, the wolves had dragged Kenton's body about 20 meters—not 50 meters.

- Paul Paquet is quoted in the *National Wildlife* article on page 30, saying, "The clothes and skin had been stripped away, indicating the so-called banana-peel eating technique common to bears." How could Paquet know that? How many clothed human bodies handled by wolves have been available for examination in North America?

- The wolves had not consumed the victim's liver and heart, which is also very uncharacteristic of wolves.

However, ALL forensic signs of a bear presume that the bear was standing or moving in about 1.5 inches of fresh snow. For instance, if a bear peeled away the clothing, then the bear must have had his paws on the ground in the snow. Also, the bear would have moved in on the kill site, leaving tracks; dragged the body, leaving tracks; ran way when the first search party arrived, leaving tracks; returned to the carcass, leaving tracks; and left again when the second party arrived–again leaving tracks. There would have been massive bear track signs of multiple entries and exits and a tremendous amount of trampling around the body.

There were no bear tracks!

My Finnish colleagues spontaneously identified a lone fox track beside the abundant wolf tracks. If they found the track of a fox, could they have missed the tracks of a bear?

The Verdict

The coroner ruled that only one expert witness would be allowed to testify on behalf of the Carnegies', and they chose Mark McNay. After listening to eyewitnesses at the scene, to Paul Paquet, and to the presentation by Mark McNay, the six-person jury rejected Paquet's presentation unanimously, despite his being assisted by counsel.

The jury ruled that the cause of Kenton Carnegie's death was wolves.

The United States Against Europe and Asia

It is all about arms. Professor Charles Kay explains this in an email to me, saying:

So why the difference in wolf behavior and man-eating in Europe, Russia, and India compared to North America? Simple, did the Czars want the peasants armed? Did the Communists want the peasants armed? Does the present Russian oligarchy want the peasants armed? Do the rulers in India want the peasants armed? Did the French kings want the peasants armed? Not on your life!

Conversely, here in North America early Europeans and Americans were armed to the teeth! Not because America's forefathers feared grizzlies, wolves, or mountain lions, but because early settlers were stealing the continent from its original owners, Native Americans.

The same of course is true in Africa. In general, African lions only kill and eat people where the populace is unarmed. European invaders even confiscated bows, arrows, and spears leaving many people totally unprotected. The Maasai, though, never gave up their spears and Maasai still kill lions with spears! Elephants too! Man-eating is non-existent among the Maasai. Other people, however, are not so fortunate.

If Kenton Carnegie had had a Smith & Wesson or a Glock, chances are that he would still be alive today, but the general public is prohibited from carrying or even owning handguns in Canada.

COUNTERING AN ATTACK

Because the opposition is an animal, it is impossible to predict anything, but there are some common rules, that may be useful.

Remember the wolves' weaknesses and be prepared to make use of them. They may be utilized as long as the wolf pack have not decided to attack. While the wolves persecute someone or something, they are simply "accelerating". The "point of no return" (V1 in the airline industry) comes when the pack encircles the prey or the prey is injured and the wolves feel bold and confident. From this point onwards, the pack turns into a killing machine. The wolves start attacking the victim to inflict wounds, then they retreat while the prey is weakened by blood loss.

Single wolves sneak up on the prey and try to take it by surprise. This is not less lethal, but a single wolf is much easier to confront.

Fast as a Lightning

Although the wolf has a strong, almost straight and relatively inflexible spine, it is an extremely fast animal. In 2015, I was immobilizing a wolf and a wolf–dog hybrid with a tranquilizer gun, using darts with hypodermic needle tips, filled with a dose of sedative tranquilizer solution. I had to hit them in the thigh muscle with the dart, but two times, the wolf snatched the dart from the muscle within fractions of a second. The wolf's quickness was astonishing. However, the anesthetics from the two previous darts had an impact on the wolf, and the third dart remained where it was supposed to.

Don't count on being quicker than a wolf, because you will not be.

Trying to hit a wolf with, for instance, a stick can make matters worse. The wide movements of swinging a stick appears to increase the wolf's arousal and, even worse, a wide horizontal movement leaves the victim's torso open to attack. Unless the wolf is rendered unconscious by the blow, hitting is seldom effective when the wolf is highly aroused (Frank 1987).

The 92–lb. Concrete Bag

Imagine someone dropping a 92–lb. bag of concrete from a pick-up truck onto your lap as you try to catch it on the fly and you'll get an understanding of how heavy a wolf is and what the impact of a wolf's leap could be. When we mentioned that Trisha

Wyman might have tripped on one of the many broken branches in the enclosure, it was not necessarily purely an accident. It could have been the result of a wolf's hard leap at her that brought her to the ground.

Figure 4.10. A wheelbarrow to fight wolves (photo by the author).

Neophobia

Neophobia is the fear of anything new, especially a persistent and abnormal fear. In the context of wolves, it is the main reason why wolves don't prey on unknown animals.

Russian researchers reported on a case where wolves used to prey on confined livestock. Once, a herd of livestock panicked and ran though the fence into the nearby forest. While in the forest, they were safe from the wolves simply because their environment had changed, and the wolves did not realize they were prey animals.

Although a wolf can smell carrion at a distance of 10 km, it never approaches the carrion immediately after it has been placed. A pack may send a scout to investigate the carrion, and the rest of the pack appears at the carrion weeks after the scout has visited it. The carrion then keeps wolves in place for several days. Hanging a glove or a scarf on a branch close to the carrion makes the wolves abandon it for weeks.

The unwillingness to try new things or break from routine is typical wolf behavior.

Harry Frank tells about an incident:

> *On one occasion we rescued the victim of a mobbing wolf pack by charging it, roaring, and pushing a wheelbarrow in front of us. This panicked the pack very effectively.*

In Russia, a young boy caused panic among attacking wolves by playing hard rock on his mobile phone. I tested this with my hunting dog using low-quality and noisy music for the test. As soon as I played the music for my dog, it "pissed its pants."

One can always rely on wolves' neophobia. It is just a question of finding the right tools or methods for this purpose.

The Wolf Is a Coward

The wolf is bold as long as it feels safe and confident. It increases its confidence by analyzing the other animal for a short while before deciding whether to attack or flee. If someone threatened by wolves makes a counterattack against the pack, the attack will probably be suspended. Depending on the situation, the wolf or pack either backs away a couple of paces, giving the victim some extra seconds, or they simply remain in place. However, if the wolves back, they usually do not flee, but, stop and evaluate the situation before they consider a new approach.

Usually, younger wolves retreat farther while older wolves are bolder.

If the intended victim is a child, the rescuer(s) should move in between the wolf and the victim. The wolf will have decided earlier that the victim is what it wants, and it will not turn on the rescuer, but will instead try to get around or between them to the victim. However, if the victim has already been bitten by the wolf, it may try to protect its prey, the way dogs guard their food.

The degree of habituation is of importance. The habituated "city wolf" might not show any fear of humans at all.

The best way to save a person is to have as many people as possible shouting all the while and throwing objects such as stones if it can be done without injury to the wolf's victim.

What If?

If the victim cannot escape and starts expressing fear, an attack may be some seconds away. To counteract an attack, Harry Frank (1987) proposes some strategies.

If the victim is grabbed by a wolf, he should not pull his hands away, but instead he should go with the direction of the pull. Struggling at this point would only exacerbate wounds already received and increase the intensity of the wolf's attack by increasing its head-shaking to get a better grip.

The victim could straddle the wolf from behind and hold its windpipe shut–see Figure 4.11. In about 20 seconds, the wolf should become weak and groggy, relaxing its grip. If alone, the victim should hold the wolf until it is unconscious or dead.

Don't hesitate to kill a wolf. It has just shown that it is prepared to kill you!

An effective choke can also be achieved by grabbing all the loose skin over the wolf's scruff and twisting. This compresses the carotid arteries, reducing the supply of blood to the brain and causing considerable loss of motor control, if not consciousness. However, both methods of choking should be carried out bare–handed. Gloves afford a significantly poorer grip.

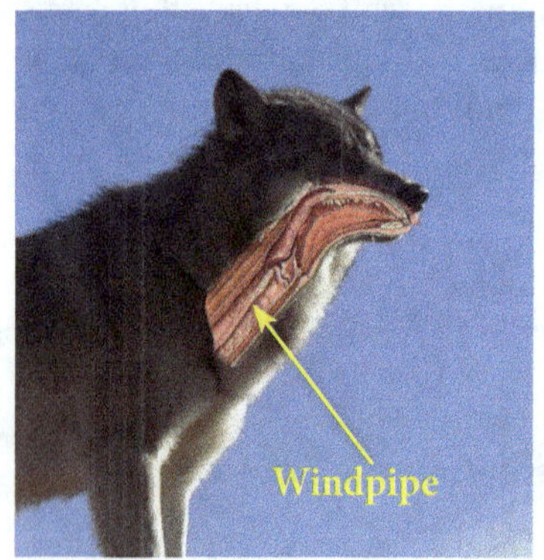

Figure 4.11. The location of a wolf's windpipe.

The natural response to an attacking wolf is to block it with the forearm, which is then first bitten. It helps to parry such an attack with a "bite stick". The bite stick must not be used for hitting. Typically, the wolf will snap at or grab the stick and then let go. A defensive wolf is unlikely to press the attack after one or two grabs (Frank 1987).

Screaming when bitten hard is a common impulse. It has two effects. First it excites the wolf, and second it brings any humans in earshot running with their 'fight or flight' responses already aroused. Thus, screaming should be employed only when there are humans in the vicinity.

Harry Frank writes

A person who has been knocked down and converged upon by several wolves should go limp, curling into a fetal position, head tucked in, neck protected by the hands and chest and belly protected by the drawn-up legs. He should try to remain as still as possible even if snapped at or grabbed. Lying still increases the chances that the wolves will wander off after investigating their victim and trying to elicit a response.

I am doubtful, because when the victim is down, it turns from prey to dinner.

On the Horseback

I have received several inquiries about wolves following young girls on horseback. Although the wolf is probably most interested in the horse, there is a potential risk that the situation could escalate as the horse panics. Experienced riders are presumably able to handle the horse, but for young riders, injuries caused by falling off a panicking horse are possible.

The problem is that a horse is less intelligent than a wolf and, under some circumstances, it may be even more intelligent than the rider. If possible, avoid riding in areas where wolves move and, if necessary, harness the horse with blinders. Blinders do not necessarily prevent the horse from panicking, but they do reduce.

Summary

Although attacks on humans are extremely rare, there is no reason why a wolf could not accept humans as prey. There is enough of evidence showing it has done so and probably will continue to do so whenever the situation triggers it in the wolf's mind.

Let's keep our community safe.

PROTECTING LIVESTOCK

Every wolf pack will switch to livestock from their traditional prey if cattle or sheep are available within the wolves' territory. However, this fact has never been reported by the media or pro-wolf advocates in either the United States or in Europe. Based on data collected by the Idaho Wild Life Service, wolves were twenty times more likely to kill cattle than individual mountain lions and 170 times more likely to kill cattle than black bears or coyotes (Kay 2015).

To get compensation for killed livestock, the wolf-killed livestock has to be found. Then it has to be verified that it was killed by wolves. Unfortunately, most of the victims are never found, and it is estimated that less than 10% of livestock killed by wolves are ever verified as such. Reindeer herding people have experienced the same problem with wolves in Scandinavia, Northern Finland, and Russia. Not only do wolves kill reindeer but they scatter the herds around the wide tundra, causing thousands of animals to disappear never to be found.

An interesting study was carried out in Oregon, where cattle and wolves were equipped with GPS radio collars. A rancher was told to tend the cattle every day, but wolves simply went nocturnal and started killing calves at night. When the GPS data were analyzed the researchers could watch how wolves harassed the cattle all night making the cattle avoid the best feeding areas, just as deer and elk did. In places where cattle were harassed by wolves, the calving rates declined from an average of 95% to 70%. For a medium–sized ranch, this decline in calving rates would cause annual economic losses of roughly $50,000.

Livestock Protection

Wolves are dangerous animals and tend to lose their fear of humans if not hunted regularly. Requirements, that large carnivores must be conserved in multi-use landscapes surrounding houses, farms, villages, and cities, can be satisfied only by complete isolation between wolf habitats and human settlements.

Traditional Fences

Fences are proposed each time wolves attack free–ranging cattle and dogs. I once asked the owner of Kuusamo Wildlife Park in Finland, Mr. Sulo Karjalainen, why he had 4–meters high (12 foot) fences and a net of rebar above the wolves' enclosure. He said that without a net above, they would climb over the 12–foot fence.

Mikhal Pavlov (1982) wrote about a case where a full-grown wolf—after killing a sheep about 6 months old—threw the young sheep over its shoulder and jumped a fence about 2 meters high. The wolf's body cleared the fence, but it hit its hind legs and thus dropped the sheep. Also remember what happened with the fences in Figure 3.32 and Figure 3.33 of Chapter 3.

Figure 4.12. Typical type of steel net that was shredded by a wolf pack in Skåne Zoo 2010 (photo by the author).

Concrete Walls and Nets of Steel

In 1976 a wolf named Lajka jumped over the 3-meter high (9 feet) concrete wall surrounding the wolf enclosure at the Skansen Zoo, in Stockholm. The wolf escaped into the city of Stockholm, where it was shot outside the Spanish Embassy (Berge 2018).

In 2007, two young male wolves (10 months old) escaped from Kolmården Wildlife Park by simply digging a tunnel under the fence. To prevent this type of escape, the fence had a concrete basement that reached 1 meter below ground, but the wolves dug the tunnel under this basement. Two days later, one of the males was euthanized outside the zoo and the other wolf was euthanized by a peasant some 100 kilometers (60 miles) north of the zoo, where it had killed some livestock (Berge 2018).

While these two youngsters were on the run, a wild wolf got into Kolmårdens Wildlife Park from outside. Nobody knows how!

Skåne Zoo used to host wolves, and in December 2010, their entire wolf pack decided to escape from the wolf enclosure. With their strong jaws, they shredded the steel fence into pieces and escaped from the enclosure into the zoo area, where they killed a number of animals before the whole pack was euthanized. The escape was so furious that they left blood stains on the fence (Berge 2018).

Pavlov wrote that in the Kirovskij Region, there were at least seven incidents where wolves had chewed through the metal chains attached to a trap. He also found three wolf jaws that showed evidence of how the wolves had tried to chew through the chains.

Digging its way under a fence and the fence's basement is an easy task for an adult wolf.

Figure 4.13. A typical electric fence for carnivores.

Electric Fences

Some European countries promote the use of electric fences. This type of fence creates an electrical circuit when touched by a person or an animal. One terminal of the power releases a short electrical pulse along a connected wire about once per second. The other terminal is connected to the ground. The voltage varies, but fences used with livestock usually release a pulse of 5,000 to 12,000 volts. In order to not be lethal, the current is limited to 100-150 milliampere (mA).

The effect of the electrical shock depends upon the voltage; the energy of the pulse; the degree of contact between the recipient, the fence, and the ground; and the route of the current through the body.

However, there is one problem with the electric fence. To work properly, it has to be kept clear of the ground. A single straw touching a wire makes the whole fence useless because the straw closes the electrical circuit, creating a flow from the wire to the ground. The reduction in current flow results in the fence having only a fraction of the original effect.

For the fence to work, the wolf has to touch both the wire carrying the voltage and the ground. Jumping through the fence between two wires does not close the electrical circuit.

We know from the above examples that it should not be difficult for a wolf to jump over an electrical fence carrying a sheep.

A study conducted in Denmark at the University of Aalborg suggests that the minimum fence height should be 115 to 145 centimeters (3.7–4.7 ft) and the voltage level should be at least 5 000 volts (Jensen, Pagh, & Vik Stronen 2017).

The popularity of electric fences is rapidly growing, although there are no studies evaluating any long-term advantages of this solution.

Wolves are extremely adaptive, and they may learn how to avoid electrical shocks from the wires.

Confining Livestock Every Night

Confining animals every night is one proposal made by the EU Commission to improve the protection of animals against wolf attacks (EU Commission 2014).

Confining a large herd of sheep that are scattered around the alps is a time-consuming task for a single shepherd and a couple of herding dogs. It might even be impossible as confining it requires a safe place large enough for the sheep to spend the night.

Confining dairy cattle is easier, as these cows are housed indoors throughout their lactation and may only be put to pasture during their 60-day dry period before, ideally, calving again. The EU requires farmers to keep cattle on pasture for most of the summer. In these cases, the herd is usually grazing in an area surrounded by a fence and in the proximity of the farm.

Beef cattle are expected to live in a low–stress environment. They must have access to shelter from extreme weather, safe handling and equipment, veterinary care, and humane slaughter, none of which are satisfied if wolves roam in close proximity.

As we can see, while confinement is a solution for a limited number of cases, it is practically impossible to confine free-ranging livestock kept in large pastures, such as cattle or sheep in the Alps.

Livestock Guard Dogs

An alternate solution to confining animals is using livestock guard dogs (LDG). Landry et al. (2014) studied internal and external factors that may influence livestock guard dogs' efficiency against wolf predation in the French Alps (Alpes Maritimes Department). Wolves were observed passing a flock of sheep, feeding on freshly killed sheep, or attempting to attack sheep, despite the presence of LGDs.

Wolves were apparently not afraid of the LGDs, and although the wolves were chased by or had agonistic encounters with the LGDs, these experiences did not prevent them from returning on the same subsequent nights. Several occurrences were recorded in which a single LGD faced a wolf and exaggerated its behaviors instead of attacking (Landry et al. 2014).

Figure 4.14. Free–ranging sheep in the Pyrenees (photo by the author).

Therefore, Landry considered it likely that wolves would become habituated to LGD's, suggesting that no long-term avoidance learning occurs in this case (Landry et al. 2014).

In addition, there are several cases where LGDs have been killed by wolves. On September 24, 2018, wolves from the Rogue pack in southwest Oregon killed one of the guard dogs brought in to protect livestock (Internet A11).

Fladry–A Proposed Solution

Fladry is a rope mounted on poles or trees and that has strips of colored flags attached. These flags will flap in a breeze, which is intended to deter wolves from crossing the fence line. Fladry have been used all over Europe and Russia in traditional wolf hunting for several centuries. More about this in Chapter 7.

There are studies proposing fladry as a tool to ward wolves away from domestic livestock. However, it has some limitations.

In an article published in Sweden (Internet A12), experiences with jingle bells and fladrys were examined. The bells were meant to keep wolves away from dogs, so they were tested with hunting dogs. Peter Nilsson, a wolf tracker from Sundsvall, Sweden, claims that this method has been tested for ten years, and the bells have worked as expected keeping wolves away from the dogs.

On the other hand, the well-known Russian scholar Ivan Pavlov, whose contributions to animal behavior were about learning, demonstrated how dogs learn the meaning of a bell calling them for supper. I don't expect wolves to react differently.

According to Alexander Gomonov from the Russian Hunters Association, bells have no effect in protecting dogs from wolves. Wolves kill dogs regardless of what kind of bells dogs wear and, he says, wolves are too smart to experience bells as a treat.

The same article claims that fladry is effective up to four weeks, after which wolves ignore it. Again, Alexander Gomonov has a different opinion. He says that fladry works for a couple of hours when hunting young and inexperienced wolves, but adults don't care.

My experiences from wolf hunting suggest that a fladry works for 24 hours at most, after which the wolves escape through it. Usually, adult wolves escape first, while juveniles may remain behind the fladry for some time.

Ann Eklund analyzed 562 scientific articles from 1990 to 2016 that covered losses caused by large predators. Only 4% of those publications analyzed the effects of different methods of protecting livestock. Her conclusion was that there is no scientific support for different methods to protect livestock from predators (Eklund 2017).

The Ultimate Solution – Culling Wolves

Despite all efforts to protect livestock, wolves seem to learn how to avoid both fences and LDGs. On July 20, 2017, the French government approved a cull of forty wolves to save sheep. Of these forty wolves, thirty-two were shot during organized hunts, while the remaining eight were shot in efforts to protect sheep from an imminent attack.

Farmers demanded the cull to protect their sheep against wolves because "electric fences and fearsome dogs are powerless in the face of the predators" (Phys.Org 2017).

Norway allowed a large cull that started on January 1, 2018, in order to reduce damages to sheep and goats. At the same time, a large wolf hunt was arranged in Sweden in order to control the growing population.

Other European countries allow the killing of habituated wolves that repeatedly visit settlements. In this case, a separate permit is issued for each wolf.

The Habitats Directive and Wolf–Livestock Conflict

Council Directive 92/43/EEC of May 21, 1992 (the Habitats Directive), allows for viable solutions to wolf–livestock conflict. Article 16 of the Directive states

> *Provided that there is no satisfactory alternative and the derogation is not detrimental to the maintenance of the populations of the species concerned at a favorable conservation status in their natural range, Member States may derogate from the provisions of Articles 12, 13, 14 and 15 (a) and (b):*
>
> *a) to prevent serious damage, in particular to crops, livestock, forests, fisheries and water and other types of property;*
>
> *b) in the interests of public health and public safety, or for other imperative reasons of overriding public interest, including those of a social or economic nature and beneficial consequences of primary importance for the environment.*

NOTE the wording: "To prevent serious damage to livestock"; "in the interests of public health and safety"; and "including those of a social or economic nature."

These provisions should be enough to prevent wolves from habituating to humans and preying on domestic animals, thus eliminating the main sources of wolf–human conflict.

On November 14, 2017, I wrote a proposal to the Finnish prime minister's party suggesting that the government should allow the euthanizing of wolves approaching settlements and livestock without prior permission. My objective was to revert the ongoing habituation process and force wolves back into the wilderness, where they belong. My proposal would also give rural inhabitants the chance to effectively protect their properties and increase their personal security.

"If humans can be linked to something that predators fear innately and that they cannot habituate to, then predators will avoid humans and their habitations" (Geist 2016).

But who cares

Soon, these cows will be replaced by wolves and beavers!

Typical landscape in the Pyrenees, where free-ranging cattle are grassing on the slopes of the Alps (upper photo). In the lower photo, it is possible to distinguish small white spots, which are sheep scattered around the slope (photos by the author).

CONSERVATION AND WOLF MAN-AGEMENT

Science has evolved, from being the force pulling mankind forward to being the number one tool in political rhetoric. This becomes obvious when studying the European Union and the United States in their struggle to promote the coexistence of people and large carnivores.

The EU Commission provides funding to projects and initiatives that promote its policy priorities throughout the European Union.

The Directorate-General for Environment makes funding available through the LIFE program and, occasionally, some pilot projects and/or preparatory actions related to environmental policy. This funding is included in the annual EU budget.

The LIFE program is the European Union's financial instrument supporting environmental and nature conservation projects throughout the Union. Since 1992, LIFE has funded some 4,000 projects, many of which have been about coexistence with wolves. So far, however, all the all publications have only strengthened the rhetoric.

LIFE also finances some grants for non-governmental organizations active in the field of the environment because such organizations are key players in the development and implementation of environmental policy. They are important channels of information about the concerns citizens have regarding the environment, and they contribute to raising citizens' awareness of specific environmental issues and policies. But is this all doomed to fail?

Valerius Geist wrote (2007)

Yet where in their search have they found one example of wolf packs existing for a long time in harmony with humans close to "houses, farms, villages and cities"? Had there been a way to coexist with wolves, would not the Europeans and Asians have discovered it long ago? Had there been a way to coexist with wild wolves would Western Europeans have gone to the high economic and social costs that were entailed by the massive, yet inefficient methods of destroying wolves?

Wolves and Conservation

Wolf conservation involves stakeholders such as livestock producers, sheep and reindeer herders, hunters, rural people, and the greater urban public. These groups are influenced by wolves in different ways, and in many cases, the differences are the foundation of conflict between the groups. Experience has shown that the people with the most positive attitudes toward wolves are those with the least experience.

The research team of Williams et al. (2002) analyzed attitudes toward wolves and found that 51% of respondents thought positively of them, and 60% supported wolf restoration. Furthermore, they noticed that attitudes about wolves had a negative correlation with age, rural residence, and ranching and farming occupations and a positive correlation with education and income. They expect that progress in education and urbanization will lead to increasingly positive attitudes over time (Williams, Ericsson, & Heberlein 2002).

In the United States, as in Europe, it seems as if the objective is to create a sandpit where scholars can play with toys they call wolves. We know from the histories of Russia, Siberia, and Asia what a wolf should look like and how it is supposed to behave. Despite the overwhelming volume of documents from past centuries, everyone wants to invent a new wolf, like releasing new editions of the Adobe Flash® player.

From the EU's point of view, wolf conservation is simply a question of creating an animal and calling it the pure wolf.

The Sandpit

Research has taken over conservation, and animal welfare is forgotten. Instead, scholars are sitting at their computers watching the movements of collared animals and writing scientific reports for their colleagues. Hunters, farmers, and people working in the fields and forests are spectators of this huge computer game. The photos shown in Figures 4.15, 4.16, 4.17, and 4.18 give a clear view of what this is all about.

It is obvious that many wild animals suffer from wearing GPS collars, and these collars cannot provide such new information about wolves that it would justify this suffering, especially when a majority of these collars remain on the animal's neck even after they have ceased working.

It would be easy to continue tracking these animals after the GPS battery runs out because each collar is or can be furnished with a VHF beacon that would works for another two to three years. The GPS collar can also have a drop-off mechanism that would allow the operator to release the collar from the animal's neck.

But science is more important than animal welfare.

Collared	Type	Sex	Age	Name	Notes
29.3.2018	GSM	female	adult	Nala	Last observation June 24, 2018
24.3.2018	GSM	female	adult	Vana	Last observation March 11, 2018
15.3.2018	Iridium	female	adult	Pinna	Last observation June 18, 2018.
16.2.2018	Iridium	male	juvenile	Saka	Last observation May 26, 2018
14.3.2017	GSM	female	juvenile	Sani	The collar ceased in July 2017.
14.3.2017	Iridium	male	adult	Saro	Last observation April 21, 2018
11.3.2017	GSM	male	juvenile	Penne	Last observation March 3, 2017
3.3.2017	GSM	male	adult	Peltsi	Last observation April 27, 2018
14.2.2017	GSM	male	adult	Varo	Last observation April 12 2018.
16.3.2016	GSM	male	juvenile	Elo	Last observation June 3, 2016
16.3.2016	GSM	male	juvenile	Emppu	Collar failed to work
9.3.2016	GSM	female	juvenile	Mella	The collar ceased in 2016.
3.3.2016	GSM	female	adult	Pinna	The collar ceased in July 2017.
3.3.2016	GSM	male	adult	Pele	The collar ceased in March 2017.
23.2.2015	GSM	male	adult	Tami	The collar ceased in November 2016.
4.2.2015	GSM	male	juvenile	Sorro	Last observation in February 2015
3.4.2013	GSM	female	adult	Julla	Last observation in May 2014
26.3.2013	GSM	male	adult	Iko	Last observation in March 2014
23.3.2013	GSM	female	adult	Inla	Last observation in January 2014
20.3.2013	GSM	male	adult	Loppi	Last observation in September 2014
14.3.2013	GSM	male	adult	Julle	Last observation in February 2014
11.3.2013	GSM	male	juvenile	Seri	Last observation in August 2013
7.3.2013	GSM	female	juvenile	Rita	Last observation in August 2013
5.3.2013	GSM	female	adult	Kara	Last observation in November 2014
28.2.2013	GSM	male	juvenile	Kojo	Last observation in May 2015

Table 4.7. Twenty-five of seventy-two collared wolves lost in the forests of Finland (Internet A13)

Between 2013 and 2018, seventy-two wolves were collared in Finland, and of those wolves, destinies of twenty-five are unknown. They may or may not carry a malfunctioning collar for the rest of their lives (Table 4.7).

Information About Wolves is Classified

The United States and most European countries have implemented Freedom of Information laws that give the general public access to data held by national governments. The emergence of this legislation was a response to increasing dissatisfaction with the secrecy surrounding government policy development and decision–making.

For instance, the Finnish Act on the Openness of Government Activities from 1999 extends the principle of openness to computer documents and to corporations that perform legally mandated public duties, such as pension funds and public utilities.

Under this law, any person may access any record in the possession of a governmental authority. There are, however, a few reasons for withholding a document, some of them which relate to conservation issues.

1. Documents containing information on endangered species or valuable natural resource areas if the release would endanger their preservation

2. Documents, records, and data used as a basis for or concerning an academic thesis, scientific or scholarly research, or product development unless it is obviously clear that the research, development, or study; their proper evaluation and the student, researcher, or the sponsor of the work are not harmed.

In practice, all information about wolves in Europe is classified. Thus, there is no possibility for the general public to obtain any type of information about large carnivores, and especially wolves.

And the Final Confession

John Linnell from the Norwegian Institute for Nature Research (NINA) makes an admission in an email to Magnus Hagelstam, Finland, dated February 2, 2007.

At the end of the twentieth century we were forced to play with peoples' emotions, try to catch their attention and push the governments. And we succeeded!

Now at the twenty-first century the focus has changed. Now we have to make people accept the wolf as a part of our nature. We do not deny the facts that wolves are dangerous as we don't deny the Holocaust or Srebrenica. Wolves do kill people, there is no doubt about it. Through history lots of people have been killed in both rabid and predatory attacks.

No further questions.

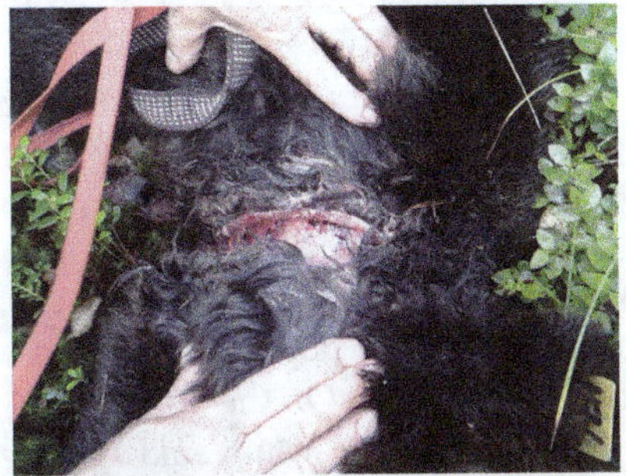

Figure 4.15. The neck of a collared bear shot in 2013. The GPS collar had sunk deep into the flesh as the bear grew toward autumn. I have seen similar injures on four other bears.

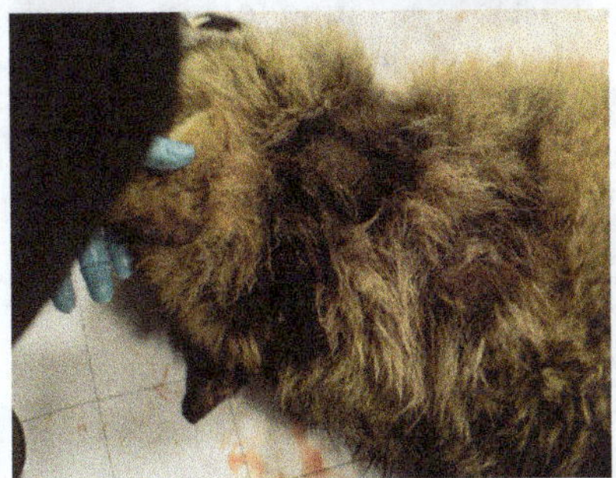

Figure 4.16. The neck of a collared wolf shot in Norway in January 2018 (photo by the author).

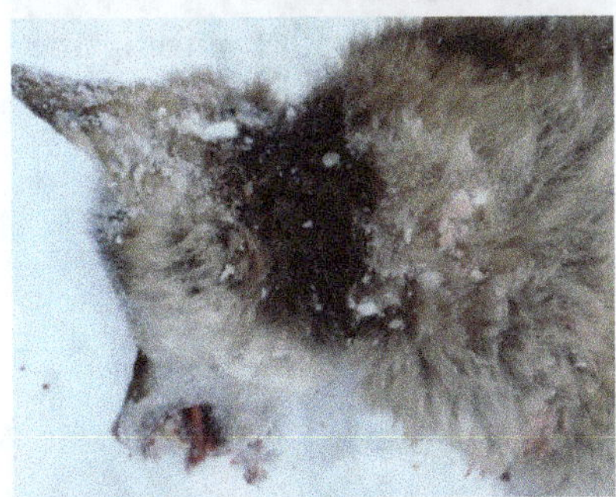

Figure 4.17. The neck of another collared wolf shot in Norway in January 2018. The fur was wet and squeezed by the GPS collars. For the fur to keep the neck warm, it must be fluffy. The temperature at the time these were shot was −20°C (photo by the author).

Figure 4.18. This Finnish Forest reindeer was killed by wolves, and it wore a dead GPS collar when I found it. This is evidence proving that some of the collared animals wear the collars until they die (photo by the author).

REWILDING THE WESTERN WORLD

City dwellers worldwide enjoy many advantages over the rural population, including better job prospects and better access to food and healthcare. On the other hand, however, mental health problems such as schizophrenia, depression, and anxiety disorders are more common in urbanites. Urban living has been found to raise the risk of anxiety disorders and mood disorders by 21% and 39%, respectively (Internet A14).

The German psychiatrist Andreas Meyer-Lindenberg studied two brain regions: the amygdala and the perigenual anterior cingulate cortex (pACC). The amygdala is known to be involved in assessing threats and generating fear, while the pACC, in turn, helps to regulate the amygdala. In stressed city dwellers, the amygdala appeared more active; in people who lived in small towns, less so; and people who lived in the countryside had the least activity of all, according to an article on *The Guardian's* website (Internet A14).

In the urban population, there did not seem to be the same smooth connection between the behavior of these two brain regions that was observed in the others. An erratic link between the pACC and the amygdala is often seen in those with schizophrenia (Internet A14).

Is this study proof that life in cities makes us go mad?

Why is it that the larger the settlement you live in, the more likely you are to become mentally ill? German researcher and clinician, Dr. Mazda Adli says

Obviously our brains are not perfectly shaped for living in urban environments.

The state of equilibrium maintained by living organisms is called homeostasis. This optimal functioning includes variables such as keeping body temperature and fluid balances within certain limits. Other variables include the concentrations of sodium, potassium, and calcium ions, as well as blood sugar levels, and these need to be regulated despite changes in the environment, diet, or level of activity (Wikipedia).

To what extent does the human mind try to equalize the disequilibrium in city dwellers' brains by creating an imaginary relationship with the nature, thus trying to smooth the erratic link between the pACC and the amygdala? Does the brain manipulate a city dweller's mind to make this imaginary connection to nature indispensable?

We know from prisons, where young men are held isolated from women for years, that they often collect photos and paintings of nude girls on their walls. Do they have something in common with some urban city dwellers?

The Urban Solution

A Dutch foundation calling itself Rewilding Europe announces on their website

> *We want to make Europe a wilder place, with more space for wild nature, wildlife and natural processes. In bringing back the variety of life, we will explore new ways for people to enjoy and earn a fair living from the wild.*

> *There is a growing realization that connecting with wild nature makes us feel good and keeps us mentally and physically well.*

> *Rewilding boosts local economies where alternatives are scarce. We work towards situations where nature tourism flourishes and local people earn a fair living from nature-based enterprises. This will help revitalize both rural and urban communities.*

Does this mean that more people can be stuffed into large cities, and their mental health is guaranteed by providing widespread wildlife tourism?

The New Nature Is on the Way

In the Serengeti, millions of animals live in a park that covers over 60,000 square kilometers. There, you can watch lions with a fresh kill or have close encounters with cheetahs, watching how they hunt large game. This is where the majority of wildlife videos presented on TV are produced.

Serengeti

Sinclair et al. wrote in their book *Serengeti III 2008*, "The Serengeti is one of the premier natural ecosystems in the world," and "The Serengeti is a large, mostly pristine ecosystem [and] as such is one of the most positive examples of conservation in the world, and is a treasure for the entire planet." Charles E. Kay writes in his review of the book

That is to say, the book's fundamental premise is that the Serengeti is a wilderness without a human history of any importance. However, according to the authors, this idyllic state of nature is threatened by the indigenous people surrounding the park, who as the authors admit are some of the poorest people on Earth and who receive few benefits from western preservation. "The main conclusion is that unless human population increase in areas surrounding protected areas is stopped, or even reversed, the future of conservation in both the community areas and the protected areas will be seriously compromised."

Far from being a 'natural' ecosystem, Serengeti is entirely an artifact of colonial processes. It began when the British government in Kenya forced the Maasai from their ancestral lands. ...This ethnic conflict created a no-man's land or buffer zone in the Serengeti and led to an abnormal increase in wildlife. ... At the same time European-introduced livestock diseases decimated local cattle herds, which led to the starvation of untold numbers of indigenous people, along with renewed violence between ethnic groups.

More importantly, "these new landscapes of 'planned wilderness' created by Britain's hunting elite in fact became the image [of Africa] itself in European paintings and literature," an image that dominates western ecological thinking to this day. ... Based on the archaeological and genetic data, there can be no denying that hominids evolved in Africa, as did our species, Homo sapiens, approximately 100,000 years before the present time (Kay 2009).

Thus, what is more unnatural than an African ecosystem without hominid hunters and fire-starters?

An Open–Air Zoo

In northern Europe, wildlife tourism flourishes. At the eastern border of Finland, it is possible to watch "real wolves" from a hide. **The Telegraph** writes

There are a few bear watching bases in Finland: they're like pit stops for the animals, who come to snack on occasional meaty scraps before continuing on their way. They're wild, but the set-up gives researchers the chance to track them – and lets binocular-toting tourists have a good look too

"They are wild ..." Without understanding animal behavior and the huge business beyond these spectacles, it is easy to believe that what you see is real nature. Even worse, photographs taken from these hides are presented to the public as showing wild animals in the Finnish wilderness.

A photo taken from one of these "feeding places" shows another view. In Figure 4.20 we see a typical overfed carrion bear completely unable to live in nature simply because it is overweight. These bears typically spend their time 1 to 2 kilometers from the hide and obtain their daily food from the same carrion in front of the hide. The carrion is placed behind a log or slope to hide it from the spectators and photographers.

Figure 4.19. A hide and carrion in front, not visible from the hide (photo by Tapani Pääk-könen).

Figure 4.20. An overfed bear living in the proximity of a wildlife hide, feeding on carrion (photo by Tapani Pääkkönen).

In order to prevent wolverines from dragging away the carrion, they are tied to the ground using reinforced steel bars. Unfortunately, bears and wolves wrench the carrion without caring for the steel bars, thus breaking their teeth. The local veterinarian in the city of Kuhmo once told me she had collected over 100 broken teeth from commercial carrion.

What kind of wolves do we find dwelling at a carrion? As usual, these wolves belong to the same pack, and the pack has been around for years. It is likely that the current wolves are second- or third-generation carrion wolves, completely unable to feed themselves in the wild.

Figure 4.21 shows a pack of "carrion wolves" at a commercial hide in Finland. The photo shows how these wolves exhibit a variety of different colors within a single pack.

It is up to each of us to decide whether these wolves are just mongrels or real wolves.

Figure 4.21. A pack of "wild" wolves dwelling at a commercial carrion in Finland (photo by Esa Hirvonen).

When Extreme Religion Turns into Terror

Long ago, the protection of nature was a part of everyday politics, and the legislation guided our actions. Today, nature protection has turned into a bloody battle with harassments and death threats. The environmentalists' targets are not states, governments, or companies, but ordinary people depending on livelihoods close to nature, and a typical case is described in the "New American" (Internet A15).

In many European countries, trained hunters are tracking animals injured in traffic accidents. In most cases, the animals have to be euthanized because of severe injures. In Sweden, such a hunter had his car burned and he was assaulted by environmentalists after he had been ordered to kill a wolf injured in a traffic accident (Internet A25).

These "terrorists" rarely identify themselves as such, preferring to use other terms, which are sometimes specific to their situation, such as separatist, freedom fighter, or nature protectors.

A typical terrorist organization is Animal Liberation Front (ALF) and their "hang around gangs." Their activities are financed by private donators and public funding, although they don't support democratic and peaceful methods to achieve their goals.

The Finnish ALF hang around group calling itself EVR (from the Finnish translation of Animal Liberation Front) terrorizes society by burning properties and movables, killing animals–yes they do, and harassing people.

Clashes are promoted by organizations like Defenders of Wildlife saying that people who oppose wolf reintroduction are "aggressively anti-science" (Kay 1993). Experience also suggests that opposition to wolf control is seldom ultimately based on scientific evidence, but rather on ethical and moral concerns.

We Communicate with Wolves

During the process of domestication, the dog developed a limited ability to read and express feelings in such a way that its owner at least believes the dog is able to express its will using facial communication. However, this trait owes more to domestication than any shared biological capability of canids. Humans may be able to interpret some of an animal's facial expressions, but no wild animal ever understands the difference between a smile and a frown. In spite of this, wolves communicate with each other using body language such as eye contact, facial expressions, posture, and tail positions, all of which can have specific meanings to wolves but definitely not to humans.

Figure 4.22. Four faces, four facial expressions (Photos Kolmården, Wikipedia Commons).

We can take a look at the expressions in Figure 4.22 and try to interpret the wolves' messages from left to right.

Wolf A: "You are going to take a photo of me? Sorry, but I'm a little bit shy."

Wolf B: "Back off, I'm busy!"

Wolf C with its head tilted: "Please hug me!"

Wolf D (the same as C): "Are you a wolf or a prey animal?"

We (me and you) tend to analyze the facial expressions of wolves just as we do with dogs and humans. We raise wild animals to our level, believing that nature adapts to our society and works within our rules. What is even worse, we believe that wolves are able to read our faces and understand our intentions. Earlier in this chapter, we learned about the girl attacked at Kolmården Zoo. When she was attacked by the wolf pack, she tried to make contact with the leading wolf. What an attitude from a professional wolf keeper!

Believe or not, wolves can only sense fear and weakness. Love or empathy do not exist in the wolf's world, not even within a pack.

New Scientist from April 15, 2015 presented a discovery made by Japanese researcher Miho Nagasawa at Azabu University in Japan. Human eye contact with dogs leads to release of the "love hormone" oxytocin, which elicits caring behavior, and this in turn causes the release of more oxytocin. This loop has been shown to be important for human bonding, for example, between mothers and their children. It turns out that dogs may have hijacked a uniquely human bonding mechanism to ensure that we love and care for them. The researchers also found out that oxytocin levels rose not just in the humans–but in the dogs too.

In contrast, when Nagasawa's team tested hand-reared wolves, they found no such effect, and wolves spent little time gazing into their owners' eyes. This means that the tendency to gaze into eyes must have evolved during the domestication of dogs, according to Nagasawa.

Wolves Habituate to Humans

Habituation is a form of learning in which an organism learns to stop responding to something that is no longer biologically relevant. For instance, wild animals habituate to repeated noises from cars and forest harvesters when they learn these have no consequences. Habituation can be described as a process of non-associative learning, where a new experience does not involve associating it with either a reward or a punishment (Wikipedia).

As far as wolves are concerned, habituation is simply a reduction of innate behaviors like, for instance, cowardice and cautiousness.

Habituation should not be confused with taming. Taming is the deliberate, human-directed process of training a wolf against its initially wild or natural instincts to avoid humans so that it instead learns to become tolerant of humans (Wikipedia).

The Finnish Wildlife Agency collects information about animal observations in the wild. One part of their database contains information about observed wolves or wolf tracks. Figure 4.23 shows the total number of wolves observed between 2011 and 2018. Adults are printed in blue and young wolves in red. The monthly variations can be explained by the following

- The lack of snow reduces the number of observations as 60% are based on paw prints.

- The observations follow the wolf pack's annual cycle. The pack disperses in March at the latest. During the summer months, the alpha pair are nursing the pups and avoiding human contact, while the rest of the pack members are scattered around the territory living in small groups. As the pack members come together in August, the hunting season begins, and wolves become bolder. More about this cycle in Chapter 3.

Figure 4.24 compares the number of wolves observed close to human settlements (within <500 m) to the total number of wolves observed. To fully understand these changes in the wolves' behaviors, these observations should be compared against the total wolf population (in black).

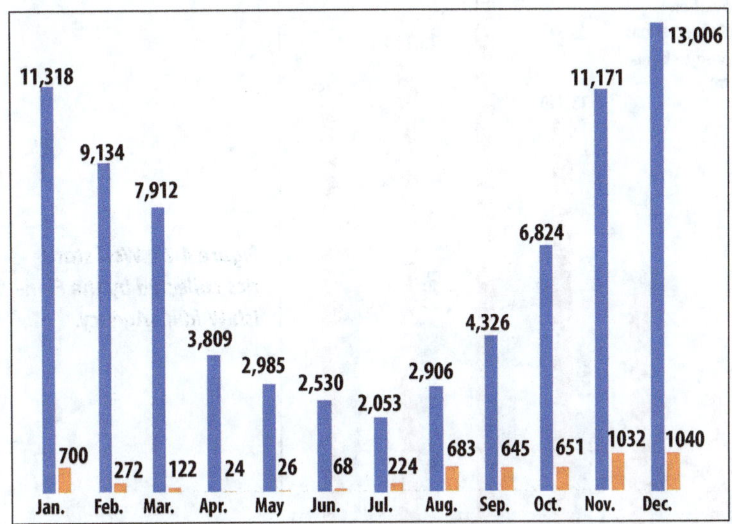

Figure 4.23. Monthly wolf observations from 2011 to 2018.

There is only one interpretation: The wolves have habituated to a level where they completely ignore human settlement and treat these as a natural **part of their habitats**. However, the European Union recognizes something called "favorable conservation status" which is defined as (EU Commission 2016):

*Population dynamics data on the species concerned indicate that it is maintaining itself on a long-term basis as a **viable component of its natural habitats,** and the natural range of the species is neither being reduced nor is likely to be reduced for the foreseeable future, and there is, and will probably continue to be, a sufficiently large habitat to maintain its populations on a long-term basis.*

The above statistics predict changes in wolf behavior and habituation within near future. In the end, we repeat the mistakes the Russians did when wolf packs roamed the streets of Moscow and St. Petersburg.

Summary

The current debate about wolves challenges the cultural legacy underlying our previous perceptions of these animals.

For some administrators, particularly those within national parks in regions directly affected by the return of wolves, "political" considerations dictate a degree of reserve.

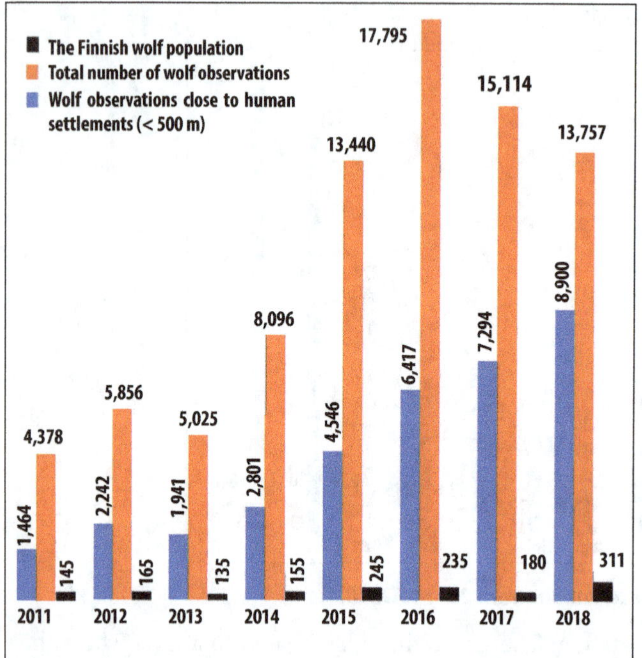

Figure 4.24. Wolf statistics collected by the Finnish Wildlife Agency.

This is perplexing for the observer, and raises the question of whether the wolf recovery campaign necessarily entails withholding certain available information about the animal's relationship with humans (Moriceau 2014).

The connection between the "man-eating" wolf stereotype and real events, long considered self-evident, has consequently become a sensitive and sometimes even taboo question.

The noted philosopher George Santayana penned one of the great truths about human history:

Those who cannot remember the past are condemned to repeat it.

YELLOWSTONE EXPOSED

One evening, I received an email from Professor Charles E. Kay. It is a description written by a person having seen Yellowstone before and after the wolves.

When I lived in Montana, I often made a trip to northern range in Yellowstone National Park (YNP) during late November to photograph rutting mule deer and bighorn sheep, as well as post-rut bull elk. Although I have read all the scientific reports, I was still shocked to see how things have changed. Gone are the bighorns, mule deer, and bull elk. So are all the professional wildlife photographers I once met on the winter range. Once I photographed thousands of elk in the Lamar and on Hellroaring, while today there are NONE. I did see a few elk around Mammoth, but I actually saw more elk in the town of Gardiner than in YNP.

Gone too were all the wolf packs as there are few animals for the wolves to eat left in the park aside from each other. The wolves, though, have still not figured out how to effectively kill bison, and bison have clearly increased and on my recent visit were distributed from Soda Butte Creek and the Lamar all the way down to just above Mammoth.

Things have changed outside the park too. There are now 100's of elk on private ground all the way down the Yellowstone Valley and into the Paradise Valley, where there were none before the wolf came. The state wildlife agency having cut two weeks off the general elk hunt and closed the late cow hunt many years ago when wolf predation first impacted the northern herd. Contrary to what one might expect, I saw very few mule deer outside the park despite the fact that two week had been cut from that general season, as well as for bighorns, I saw sheep where I had never seen them before as, for instance, on the road by the airport and by the Devil's Slide. Apparently the sheep are using the roads as an anti-predator device to avoid wolves.

Luckily, I had other business to attend to, but the wildlife of yesteryear is long gone. Blame it on Climate Change, as a recent writer in the New York times did.

Introduction

When the Europeans arrived, they started to eliminate Native Americans. These Native Americans were the keystone predators and they determined the distribution and abundance of elk, deer, and other ungulates, not carnivores. As the Native Americans were eliminated, it led to an abnormal increase in elk and other ungulates, while the ungulates, in turn, destroyed aspen and willows, causing the ecosystems to collapse and change states (Kay 2013).

The plan to reintroduce wolves in Yellowstone was motivated by the wrong belief that large numbers of wolves inhabited the ecosystem before they were eliminated by predator control efforts. However, evidence suggests that there were only a few wolves in Yellowstone between 1835 and 1876 because there were few ungulate prey. Early explorers reported seeing bison only three times, none of which were in the park, and they reported seeing elk on only forty-two occasions, or an average of one elk observation per party in eighteen days. When only one of the early explorers reported having seen a wolf, the most that can be said is that wolves were rare in the Greater Yellowstone Ecosystem during the period from 1835 to 1876 (Kay 1995).

During the 1920s, the US National Park Service exterminated wolves from Yellowstone National Park, while other federal and state agencies eliminated wolves from the remainder of the Greater Yellowstone Ecosystem.

In 1933, National Park Service policy stated, "No native predator shall be destroyed on account of its normal utilization of any other park animal" (Kay 1995).

In 1963, the National Park Service biologists said they were having a terrible problem with too many elk and deer. They talked about how they really needed to get wolves in there to reach a balance of nature. They had a sort of fantasy notion that if we had a few wolves, we could effectively control them. And in turn, the wolves would control these elk and deer, and they would have the willows back.

Under provisions of the Endangered Species Act of 1973, the US Fish and Wildlife Service (1987) formulated a recovery plan for wolves in the northern Rocky Mountains including Yellowstone. The plan called for reintroducing wolves into the Yellowstone Ecosystem and was supported by the Fish and Wildlife Service, the Park Service, and various environmental organizations (Kay 1995).

In 1987, the Recovery Plan for these creatures was completed and a draft *Environmental Impact Statement* was published, recommending experimental wolf populations be reintroduced to the three areas. The statement caused activists and stockmen to gnash their teeth and slobber at the mouth. The former didn't like the plan's provisions to permit shooting troublesome wolves, and the latter didn't like wolves, period. But unheard above this cacophony were scientists who harbored serious doubts about the proposition (Kay 1993).

Prof. Charles E. Kay (1993) gives voice to those concerns. In the August issue of "Peterson's Hunting Journal" he raised the question:

> *If wolves are brought back, how many are enough? The Recovery Plan announced that when 10 breeding pair of wolves remain three successive years in each area, wolves would be considered recovered and be removed from the Endangered Species list.*

In 1988, the Senate-House Interior Appropriations Committee appropriated $200,000 for the National Park Service and the US Fish and Wildlife Service to address issues related to restoring wolves to Yellowstone.

A simulation model of gray wolf recovery for Yellowstone National Park was developed based on observations of wolf predation in other areas. Based upon the behavior of this computer model, they reached the following conclusion documented in ***"Wolves for Yellowstone? Vol. II, Research and Analysis, United States Forest Service, forwarded to Congress, 1990."***

A Basket of Wishes and Clashes

There is no combination of choices where wolf predation has devastating consequences to elk (*Cervus elaphus*) populations in the park. The reason is that social behavior limits wolf densities so that the wolf population cannot attain total numbers high enough to depopulate the elk herd (Mark S. Boyce, from the University of Wyoming, Department of Zoology and Physiology, Laramie, WY 82071. (p. 3-5))

> *Research by Will Graves on Russian wolves showed that when the wolf population went up, prey population went down.*

The US Fish and Wildlife Service concluded that potential conflicts with hunting would be of no concern: ***"It does not appear necessary that wolf predation requires that hunting opportunities be reduced (pp. 3-42)."***

> *Hunting in an area fifteen miles wide and sixty miles long north of Yellowstone has been ruined, because wolves have decimated elk in the area.*

The Executive Summary on *"Potential Impact of a Reintroduced Wolf Population on the Northern Yellowstone Elk Herd"* states that the elk population would decrease somewhat, but that the decrease would not exceed 10% under the conditions modeled. The report concluded that if other factors remained within normal bounds, the relationship between predator and prey would be relatively stable and could therefore continue indefinitely (pp. 3–61)

"Effects of Restoring Wolves on Yellowstone Area Big Game & Grizzly Bears—Executive Summary, Opinions of Fifteen North American Experts." If wolves are reintroduced, extinction of any prey species, elk, mule deer, moose, bison, pronghorn, bighorn sheep, and mountain goats, was thought to be extremely unlikely (pp. 4–54)

The report stated that there should be moderate to little change in elk behavior and distribution if wolves reintroduced. (p. 4-56)

Elk now cluster around park buildings. Elk have moved from mountains to lower levels into hay fields of private ranches.

General Impact on Ungulates, Prediction: "Since wolves prey upon weak and inferior animals, overall prey population condition would benefit from wolf introduction." *(pp. 4–68)*

In the Mologo–Sheslshinskil Mezhdurech area the bodies of 63 moose killed in a five year period were examined. Of the 63, only nine had any defects. Five had defects in teeth, three defects in antlers, and one defects in its fore and hind hooves. The technical work done in a controlled area showed that the sanitizing role of the wolf in nature is overemphasized. (Graves 2007).

In 1994, there were 19,760 elk in Yellowstone; in 2010, only 4,600. Wolves have decimated many species of wildlife in Yellowstone. Now there are only about twenty to thirty moose in the park.

The Reintroduction

In 1991, Congress directed the US Fish and Wildlife Service to develop an Environmental Impact Statement for the purpose of reintroducing wolves into Yellowstone National Park (**Yellowstone Science volume 13, number 1, winter 2005**). In January 1995, fourteen wolves were captured from east of Jasper National Park, Alberta, Canada, and the wolves arrived in Yellowstone the same month. Seventeen additional wolves captured in Canada were released into the park in April 1996.

Again, all experts had forgotten the most important rule of evolution. It optimizes all species to adapt to their natural environment, and moving Canadian wolves to the United States is just another example of humankind's ability to mess with nature.

"Hell is full of good intentions, but heaven is full of good works."

Robert T Fanning Jr. wrote (2007)

There are hundreds of cases of man monkeying around with the balance of nature and screwing things up. One of the best examples is the introduction of the mongoose into the Hawaiian Islands as a means for dealing with a huge and troublesome rat population. Those conscientious biologists, however, neglected to realize that the rat is a nocturnal animal, while the mongoose preys during the day. Their paths simply never cross, so today, Hawaii not only still has its rats, but it also has 100s of thousands of mongooses creating mayhem with rare ground nesting birds and other native species. This is just one example of the law of unintended consequences in dealing with wildlife. The unintended consequence to the Rocky Mountain States of the non native gray wolf is much more serious and not simply the consequence of a couple thousand extra wolves roving the countryside, but rather a much greater problem caused by the level of depredation of native species–elk and deer–than originally claimed.

Not only has the wolf program been the equivalent of a dangerous invasive species but elk counts are just in from the Lolo Districts 10 and 12 in Idaho. In District 10, the official elk count in 1995 was 9,729. The count just released is 1,473, — a population decrease of 85% from the pre-wolf program era. The adjacent District 12 yields a similar loss of 82% from its pre-wolf program days (Fanning 2007).

With the Wolves Comes the Diseases

Gray wolves are carriers of worms and parasites and pose significant danger to animals and humans. The problem in the western United States is the large wolf population, which is heavily infected with tapeworm, up to 63% carry *Echinococcus granulosus,* and regionally, it is up to 100%.

The deer and elk become infected with hydatid cysts in the lungs and liver before these big game animals come into the valley bottoms where they spend the winter. It is fairly common in the west that elk and deer dwell around ranch buildings, farm buildings, and close to rural towns. Under those circumstances, there will be animals dying throughout the winter and the offal of these animals left outside. Rural dogs from nearby towns and ranches will surreptitiously go out and feed on the infected offal. When that happens, within a few weeks, the tapeworm develops in the gut of the dog, and the dog begins spreading millions and millions of eggs into yards, around homes, and on verandas, and of course, because we allow dogs into the house, also in our homes.

Wolf Reintroduction Changes Ecosystem

There is a flood of stories and videos convincing the greater audience how healthy Yellowstone is after the wolf reintroduction in 1994 and 1995. Yes indeed, wolves do change the ecosystem, and as one example, beavers spread and built new dams and ponds. These dams had multiple effects on stream hydrology. They even out the seasonal pulses of runoff, store water for recharging the water table, and provide cold, shaded water for fish, while the now robust willow stands provide habitat for songbirds.

We also know that a vast web of life is linked to carcasses abandoned by wolves. Among others, wolverines benefit from wolves' leftovers even though they are capable of killing prey animals by itself. The raven is a typical visitor preying on wolves' leftovers.

This all is called a trophic cascade, where a keystone predator causes a major reduction in the herbivore population, which then causes a major rebound in the associated plant community. What happened in Yellowstone was that wolf predation significantly reduced the numbers of mule deer, elk, and moose.

Charles Kay wrote (2013)

> *This, though, creates a problem because wolf advocates have repeatedly stated that wolves have no major impact on ungulate numbers or hunting opportunities! How can they have it both ways? Because wolf supporters have been talking out both sides of their mouths at the same time. To date, this fraud has been successful because the media, the public, and even federal district court judges are ecologically incompetent. In other words, a lot of people have been using the term keystone predator in regard to wolves, without knowing what that term actually means.*

> *Now, however, you know the truth. A keystone predator is one that significantly reduces the numbers of its prey, elk and deer, in the case of wolves.*

Tables are slowly turning from the time with abundant reserves of prey animals toward an opposite condition. As prey become scarce, wolves have to switch from their traditional prey animals, such as moose and elk, to smaller animals. Beavers are probably among the first to go, and as prey disappear, the wolves starve, intensify their attacks on livestock, attack visitors, and finally kill each other or leave the park.

However, it may take some decades before Yellowstone's ecosystem reaches its negative minimum, but it will happen as it has in other places around the world.

David L. Mech wrote (2012)

Either the elk reduction or the behavioral changes are hypothesized to have fostered growth in browse, primarily willows (Salix spp.) and aspen (Populus spp.), and that growth has resulted in increased beavers (Castor Canadensis), songbirds, and hydrologic changes. The wolf's image thus has gained an iconic cachet. However, later research challenges several earlier studies' findings such that earlier conclusions are now controversial, especially those related to causes of browse regrowth.

Toby Bridges wrote in an article on "lobowatch.wordpress.com":

It is no secret among the residents of the Greater Yellowstone Area that the National Park Service and the US Fish and Wildlife Service have been less than honest about the impact wolves have had on the park and the area in general, or how those involved with the Northern Rockies Wolf Recovery Project have manipulated science to achieve a fast track to a successful wolf recovery.

Summary

The federal and state agencies responsible for this program promised that there would be a finite, manageable number of wolves. The entire program, built on the Mark S. Boyce computer model using predictive science as the cornerstone, promised seventy-eight to one hundred wolves over a 10 to 20 year period, maximum!

The computer model obviously failed in estimating what happens to the states around the Park. From Yellowstone, the wolves have spilled over into Wyoming, Idaho, Utah, and Montana and have become a huge problem. According to US Fish & Wildlife Service, the number in these states is slightly more than 1,500, but they did not lie.

There are less than 150 wolves in Yellowstone!

At that time, a simulation model of gray wolf recovery for Yellowstone National Park was developed based on observations of wolf predation in other areas. The outcome was:

> *There is no combination of choices where wolf predation has devastating consequences to elk (Cervus elaphus) populations in the park. The reason is that the social behavior limits wolf densities so that the wolf population cannot attain total numbers high enough to depopulate the elk herd (Mark S. Boyce, University of Wyoming, Dept. of Zoology and Physiology, Laramie, WY 82071 (pp. 3–5)*

Russian data reveals that, on average, a gray wolf kills one deer a week, or ninety saiga (Eurasian antelope), fifty to eighty boar, or eight to ten moose per year, yet the same animal in Yellowstone would supposedly rein in its appetite and only kill one deer every twenty-three days.

Why such a significant difference? I don't feel there was any kind of responsible evaluation at all, and the consequence is significantly lower elk counts in high density wolf areas throughout the mountain West.

The conflict remains.

5
CHAPTER

WOLVES AND MONGRELS

The species Canis lupus was first recorded by Carl von Linné in 1758. The Latin classification translated into English was "dog wolf." Now the nominate subspecies is the Eurasian wolf (Canis lupus lupus), also known as the Canis lupus linnaeus. Since 1758, the Eurasian wolf's physical appearance, as well as its behavior, has been described in detail. We know what a wolf should look like and how it behaves.

We also know from the Darwinian theory of natural selection that if, and only if, a canine looks like a wolf and behaves like a wolf, then it is a wolf.

IS THE WOLF AN EXTINCT SPECIES

The gray wolf is the product of nature sculpted by evolution for millions of years. By contrast, the dog is not a species but an artifact of human creation using the genetics of the wild wolf and other canids. Dogs have been created by humans to fit with human needs, our habitations and professional activities. The way wolf protection is practiced in the United States and the European Union leads to a slow hybridization with dogs, golden jackals, and coyotes, and thus there is a loss of the real wolf (Geist 2018).

To understand what is going on, we have to remember what was said about Darwinian evolutionary theory in Chapter 4. Being the basic mechanism of evolution, natural selection NEVER produces the variety of different physical traits that we see in wolves in Yellowstone or in the different parts of Europe. Evolution optimizes all species, and if there is variation within one species, it depends solely on variations in the environment. Thus, the Mexican wolf is different from the Canadian gray wolf, and wolves in Spain differ from wolves in Russia.

Wolf–Dog Crossbreeds

Hybrids are bred by mating two *Canis lupus* subspecies, and the offspring display traits and characteristics of both parents. While it is possible to predict the genetic composition of a backcross on average, it is not possible to accurately predict the composition of a particular backcrossed individual due to the random segregation of genetic traits. In a species, a twice backcrossed individual would be predicted to contain 25% of one species' genome and 75% of the other's. However, it may in fact still contain 50% of both, but never less. Tables 5.1, 5.2 and 5.3 illustrate the problem.

Each dog and wolf has inherited two genes, one from its father, and the other from its mother. When a purebred dog interbreeds with a pure wolf (Table 5.1), their offspring exhibit four possible combinations, each with a slightly different makeup (Table 5.2).

In Table 5.2, one of the pups from Table 5.1 interbreeds with a pure wolf. The outcome is a hybrid generation (F_2).

Again, an F_2 hybrid interbreeds with a wolf, and the outcome is an F_3 hybrid. However, if we had interbred the yellow F_2 cub with a wolf, the result would have been a pure wolf as far as this gene is concerned. Because the selections are random, the makeup of the F_2 hybrid would on average be, as mentioned above, 25% of the dog's genome and 75% of the wolf's. The percentage for the F_3 hybrids in Table 5.3 would be, respectively, 12.5% and 87.5%.

However, it is interesting to note that the makeup of each wolf–dog crossbreed that has been backcrossed toward wolf could be anything between 50% and 100% wolf.

Dog breeders use statistical estimates, meaning that they take an average of each backcrossing, which may be correct or not.

Another fact to be taken into consideration is that two hybrids can interbreed as well, but without knowing their parents' history, there is no way to estimate the final genetic makeup.

Dog + Wolf		$Wolf_{Father}$	$Wolf_{Mother}$
A purebred dog	Dog_{Father}	Dog_{Father} $Wolf_{Father}$	Dog_{Father} $Wolf_{Mother}$
	Dog_{Mother}	Dog_{Mother} $Wolf_{Father}$	Dog_{Mother} $Wolf_{Mother}$

Table 5.1. The first generation.

Hybrid F_1 + Wolf		$Wolf_{father}$	$Wolf_{Mother}$
F_1 Hybrid wolf + dog	Dog_{Father}	Dog_{Father} $Wolf_{Father}$	Dog_{Father} $Wolf_{Mother}$
	$Wolf_{Father}$	$Wolf_{Father}$ $Wolf_{Father}$	$Wolf_{Father}$ $Wolf_{Mother}$

Table 5.2. The second generation.

Hybrid F_2 + Wolf		$Wolf_{Father}$	$Wolf_{Mother}$
F_2 Hybrid wolf + dog	Dog_{Father}	Dog_{Father} $Wolf_{Father}$	Dog_{Father} $Wolf_{Mother}$
	$Wolf_{Mother}$	$Wolf_{Mother}$ $Wolf_{Mother}$	$Wolf_{Mother}$ $Wolf_{Mother}$

Table 5.3. The third generation.

Evolution Through Hybridization

Hybridization influences evolution in a variety of different ways, and there is every reason to believe that new species may arise by hybridization. The geographical area of divergent populations may be limited, and thus, pre-zygotic barriers may be reinforced. In some cases, hybridization makes a positive contribution if there are hybrid genotypes better suited to an environment than their parents. From that point on, evolution decides which of the crossbreeds survive, because further speciation involves natural selection among hybrids as well. As natural selection requires genetic variation, genetic variation might be enhanced by hybridization.

Introgression

Introgression means gene flow from one species into the gene pool of another by repeated backcrossing of a hybrid with other hybrids or their parent species. Introgression differs from simple hybridization and results in a complex mixture of parental genes. It takes place over a long period of several generations.

The wolves' world has a long history of hybridization. Primarily, the first hybridizations took place at the time when wolves were reintroduced into the United States and Europe. For instance, the wolf population in Yellowstone is most probably suffering from large-scale introgression. The variety in appearance can be explained not by evolution but only by introgression.

A similar phenomena is observed in Italy, where Ettore Randi's research team discovered that 87.5% of the Italian wolf population exhibited genetic signs of introgression from dog genes (Randi et al. 2014).

A paper published by Robert Wayne's research team reveals the presence of small blocks of dog ancestry in the genomes of 62% wolves sampled from all Eurasian populations analyzed. This suggests that hybridization has occurred in different parts of Eurasia throughout multiple generations (Wayne et al. 2018).

Dr. Malgorzata Pilot, one of the co-writers on Wayne's team, said

> *We found that while hybridization has not compromised the genetic distinctiveness of wolf populations, a large number of wild wolves in Eurasia carry a small proportion of gene variants derived from dogs, leading to the ambiguity of how we define genetically "pure" wolves.*

> *Our research highlighted that some individual wolves which had been identified as "pure" wolves according to their physical characteristics, were actually shown to be of mixed ancestry. On the other hand, two Italian wolves with an unusual black coat color did not show any genetic signatures of hybridization except for carrying a dog-derived variant of a gene linked to dark coloration.*

This statement shows how difficult it is to separate purebred wolves from hybrids, especially when Dr. Pilot says they "did not show any genetic signatures of hybridization, except for a dog-derived variant of a gene linked to dark coloration."

So the only method of removing hybrids is to use morphological traits. Hidden "dog ancestry" pops up sooner or later as an atypical trait in the wolf's appearance or behavior.

How They Interbreed

The reproductively isolating mechanism between wolves and dogs that prevents fertilization is "behavioral isolation." At first, we recognize the fact that a dog approaching a wolf or a wolf pack will probably be eaten. The simple reason is that the dog does not understand wolf behavior, and when it finally does understand, it is too late to escape. A wolf preparing for an attack lifts its tail a little bit above the back and starts wagging it as it approaches the dog with its head lowered. This is not a welcoming ceremony but an indication that the wolf is feeling excited and looking for a weak point or an opportunity to grab the dog by its neck. The dog wants to say hello, as it does to humans, but being weaker and slower, it does not have a chance to counteract the attack.

So, how do they interbreed?

Male Wolf and Female Dog

There have been observations of a lone male wolf mates with a female dog. Usually this happens when the dog's owner is walking the dog unleashed in the forest. Mating happens within a couple of minutes without the owner being aware of the incident. The hybrid pups are most often undesired and euthanized soon after their birth (personal interview with Dr. Erik S. Nyholm). Most likely no wild hybrids are produced this way.

Female Wolf and Male Dog

Old female wolves (former alpha females) are sometimes dismissed from the pack by a younger female–typically their daughter. This happens in February–March when the females come into heat. Being dismissed from the pack, the old female takes whatever is left, and it might be a male dog reacting to the smell of the female's pheromones.

However, it is unlikely that this crossbreeding creates viable offspring because the dog is presumably unable to feed the nursing female during the first weeks, when the alpha female does not leave the den. If the litter survives the first three weeks, most of the cubs may live on, as wolf cubs do.

There is no scientific evidence suggesting that first generation hybridization (F_1) is common in nature, but it happens.

Humans in the Middle

The main reason why wolves and dogs interbreed is that the first generation of wolf–dog hybrids are created by man to be used as pets. Eugene M. McCarthy says there are currently approximately 300,000 captive hybrids in North America alone (Internet

A17). As the wolf–dog reaches maturity, it will most likely start exhibiting aggression toward its owner and become difficult to handle. For the wolf–dog owner, instead of just eliminating his/her former pet with an injection, many prefer to release their pet into nature. A high-content wolf–dog does not have the same limitations as purebred dogs have when encountering another wolf in the wild. Thus, mating between the two is possible (Dethlefsen 2016). This is probably the reason why wild F_1 hybrids are rare.

In a large-scale study involving about one hundred animals, Iljin (1941) reported that all F_1 hybrids, as well as the F_2 and F_3 generations, were capable of producing offspring. Wolves enter heat once a year, in winter, while dogs do so twice, or in some breeds, three times annually. Iljin reported that all F_1, and most F_2 hybrids enter heat once a year, in late fall. The gestation period in hybrids was about the same as that of a wolf or dog.

Figure 5.1. A purebred mongrel. Compare the head of this wolf with the dog in the upper left corner (photo Asko Kettunen).

Figure 5.1 shows a typical mongrel from northeast Finland. It should be obvious that this mongrel has more in common with the Karelian Bear Dog in the upper left corner than with a pure wolf. We recognize similarities such as, for instance, the shape of the wolf's head, pointed ears without fur inside, and an orbital angle greater than 50 degrees with eyes pointing forward.

I sometimes used to call this type of head a "bowling pin."

There are also documented incidents where wolf–dogs have escaped from their enclosures at wolf–dog breeder's kennels. A typical case is shown in Figure 5.2, where a Russian military wolf–dog was captured by a game camera and later shot by Finnish border guards.

Figure 5.2. A Russian military wolf-dog on the loose.

My Wolf Genetics Explained

In order to reveal the possibilities of genetic analysis, we shall take a look at some values collected in Table 5.4. This table contains some (not all) genetic traits collected from Finnish, Scandinavian, and Russian wolves between 1981 and 2018.

Species ID

This is the wolf's identification which usually contains the year 19XX or 20XX and the sequence number within the year. Thus, K1405 is the fifth wolf tested by me in 2014.

Color Locus E

The dominant form of the gene, the E allele allows the dog to produce eumelanin, which is a black pigment. This locus has three possible forms: black (E), melanistic mask (E^m), and yellow (ee). If it contains two values of E, the wolf is likely to express the coat color defined by the K and A loci. With E^m the canine is likely to have a dark facial mask. Figure 5.3A shows wolf K1424 in Table 5.4. We can see from the photo that the wolf indeed exhibits a dark facial mask, exactly as predicted by its genetic makeup. This trait is atypical to wolves.

Color Locus K

Color locus K is dependent on the E locus. If the E locus genotype is e/e (recessive), the K locus is not expressed. However, if the E locus is coded as E/E or E/e, the K locus is expressed. This locus can contain the dominant K^B allele that codes for solid black, as with, for instance, black wolves.

The k^y allele allows the agouti gene to be expressed without brindling. If a wolf is k^y/k^y at the K locus, the A locus then determines the wolf's coat color. The k^y allele is recessive to K^B.

Color Locus A

Agouti signaling protein (ASIP) controls the localized expression of red and black pigment in the domestic dog. Dayna Dreger and Sheila Schmutz suggest that there are four ASIP alleles and they demonstrate a dominance hierarchy of: $a^y > a^w > a^t > a$ (Dreger & Schmutz 2011). The a^y allele (fawn) is considered dominant to black-and-tan (a^t) and the wild type allele (a^w). Tan points (a^t) is the almost bottom gene in the agouti series gene, which means that in order for it to be expressed, the dog must be homozygous, containing two a^t alleles. The gene under the tan points gene is the recessive black, which is very rare. Solid black color is associated with the color locus K allele K^B.

A Shetland Sheepdog such as the one in Figure 5.3C has at least one a^y allele, thus expressing fawn. A pure Malamute as like the one in Figure 5.3D expresses a^w (wolf sable). A wolf should always be homozygous a^w/a^w. Note, if it has a^w/a^t, as, for instance, some of the P17XX hybrids, then it still expresses wolf gray.

Notice the fawn color setting in Figure 5.3B, and this wolf, K1423 in Table 5.4, has color locus A = a^y/a^w.

Figure 5.3E shows two siblings (K1618 and K1622), of which one expresses a^w/a^w and the other a^y/a^w. Finally, the wolf in Figure 5.3F is K1506 in Table 5.4 and again we find the color locus A = a^y/a^w.

Color Locus S

When cells are unable to produce any pigment, the result is a white color. The black color in a wolf's coat is produced by the black pigment called eumelanin and the red pigment called phaeomelanin. Both pigments can vary in intensity and color shade.

The column Color Locus S shows two alleles, the S allele (no white, solid) and the s^P (piebald or extreme white).

Curly

This locus tells us if the wolf has curly coat or not. The allele T = the genetic variant typically associated with a curly coat, and it dominates the variant C typically associated with a non-curly coat.

Species ID	Locus E	Locus K	Locus A	Locus S	Curly	Ears
K1417	E/E	k^y/k^y	a^w/a^w		C/C	T/C
K1418	E/E	k^y/k^y	a^w/a^w		C/C	C/C
K1419	E/E	k^y/k^y	a^y/a^w		C/C	C/C
K1420	E/E	k^y/k^y	a^w/a^w		C/C	C/C
K1423	E/E	k^y/k^y	a^y/a^w		C/C	C/C
K1424	Em/E	k^y/k^y	a^w/a^t		C/C	T/C
K1425	E/E	k^y/k^y	a^w/a^w		C/C	C/C
K1426	E/E	k^y/k^y	a^w/a^w		C/C	C/C
K1501	E/E	k^y/k^y	a^w/a^w		C/C	C/C
K1502	E/E	k^y/k^y	a^w/a^w		C/C	C/C
K1503	E/E	k^y/k^y	a^y/a^w		C/C	C/C
K1504	E/E	k^y/k^y	a^w/a^w		C/C	C/C
K1505	E/E	k^y/k^y	a^w/a^w			C/C
K1506	E/E	k^y/k^y	a^y/a^w		C/C	C/C
K1508	E/E	k^y/k^y	a^w/a^w		C/C	C/C
K1511	E/E	k^y/k^y	a^w/a^w	sp/sp	C/T	C/C
K1515	E/E	k^y/k^y	a^w/a^t	S/S	C/C	C/C
K1605	E/E	k^y/k^y	a^y/a^w	sp/sp	C/C	C/C
K1611	Em/E	k^y/k^y	a^w/a^w	S/S	C/C	T/T
K1612	E/E	k^y/k^y	a^w/a^w	S/sp	C/C	C/C
K1613	E/E	k^y/k^y	a^y/a^w	S/sp	C/C	C/C
K1614	E/E	k^y/k^y	a^w/a^w	S/sp	C/C	C/C
K1616	E/E	k^y/k^y	a^y/a^w	S/sp	C/C	C/C
K1617	E/E	k^y/k^y	a^w/a^w	S/sp	C/C	C/C
K1618	E/E	k^y/k^y	a^w/a^w	S/S	C/C	C/C
K1619	E/E	k^y/k^y	a^w/a^w	sp/sp	C/C	C/C
K1621	E/E	k^y/k^y	a^w/a^w	S/S	C/C	C/C
K1622	E/E	k^y/k^y	a^y/a^w	S/S	C/C	C/C
K1625	E/E	k^y/k^y	a^w/a^w	S/sp	C/C	C/C
K1626	E/E	k^y/k^y	a^w/a^w	sp/sp	C/C	C/C
K1808	E/E	k^y/k^y	a^w/a^w	S/S	C/C	C/C
N1801	E/E	k^y/k^y	a^w/a^w	S/S	C/C	C/C
N1802	E/E	k^y/k^y	a^w/a^w	S/S	C/C	C/C
LA-2-81	E/E	k^y/k^y	a^y/a^w	S/S	C/C	C/C
PK 1208-97	E/E	k^y/k^y	a^y/a^w	S/S	C/C	C/C
PK-1203-97	E/E	k^y/k^y	a^y/a^w	S/S	C/C	C/C
PK-1250-97	E/E	k^y/k^y	a^y/a^w	S/S	C/C	C/C
P1701	E/E	k^y/k^y	a^w/a^t	S/sp	C/C	C/C
P1702	Em/Em	k^y/k^y	a^w/a	S/S	C/C	T/T
P1703	Em/E	k^y/k^y	a^t/a	S/S	C/C	T/T
P1704	Em/E	k^y/k^y	a^t/a	S/S	C/C	C/T
P1705	Em/Em	k^y/k^y	a/a	S/S	C/C	T/T
P1706	Em/Em	k^y/k^y	a^w/a^t	S/S	C/C	T/T
P1707	Em/E	k^y/k^y	a^t/a	S/S	C/C	T/T
P1708	E/E	k^y/k^y	a^w/a^t	S/S	C/C	T/T
P1709	E/E	k^y/k^y	a^t/a	S/S	C/C	T/T
P1710	Em/Em	k^y/k^y	a/a	S/S	C/C	T/T

Table 5.4. Some genetic traits of Finnish, Scandinavian, and Russian wolves and hybrids.

Ears

In Table 5.4 we notice two alleles, T = typically associated with pricked ears, and C = typically associated with floppy ears. Usually, wolves are homozygous C/C (floppy ears) even though they don't have floppy ears!

Figure 5.3. Genetic traits expressed (photos A & B by an anonymous hunter, C & D from Wikipedia Commons, E by an anonymous hunter, F by the author).

Summary

The wolves P17XX are hybrids, and we can see a clear difference in their genetic makeup compared to the wolves. We also know that the wolves K1423, K1424, and K1425 are hybrids by their appearance, and these wolves were shot because they were suspected to be hybrids. Further, the K1611 is putatively a feral Tamaskan dog shot as a wolf.

Dog heritage can last for generations within a wolf population. The best evidence of this are the black wolves in Yellowstone. Genetic research from the Stanford University School of Medicine and the University of California, Los Angeles revealed that wolves with black pelts owe their distinctive coloration to a mutation that occurred in domestic dogs and was carried to wolves through wolf–dog hybridization (Anderson et al. 2009).

How Do We Know These are Wolves?

By grouping canines into distinct groups using fragments of their genetic makeup, it is possible to separate pure wolves from dogs and hybrids. It is even possible to separate different dog breeds from each other. Formally, the populations chart in Figure 5.4 is based upon 7,000 markers covering each of the thirty-nine chromosome pairs in the dog genome. The test contains on average 160 SNP markers per chromosome, with a median intermarker distance of 269 kilobases. Additional markers are selected on chromosome 12. A complete description of the components and methods can be found on the website www.mydogdna.com.

The data is presented as a two-dimensional diagram using a method called multi-dimensional scaling (MDS).

From this chart, we notice wolf K1611's population, and it is obvious that it is outside the wolves, all represented by blue circles. We find the Russian and Finnish wolves at some distance from each other. Further, we notice that some "wolves" appear between German Shepherds and Russian wolves. They are all hybrids, and most of them belong to the P17XX population.

Challenges in Wolf Identification with DNA

The system of biological classification (taxonomy) was set up by Carl von Linné in 1735. Taxonomy groups organisms together into taxa, and these groups are given a taxonomic rank, thus creating a taxonomic hierarchy. Today, the Linnaean system has progressed to a system of modern biological classification, based on the evolutionary relationships between organisms, both living and extinct.

Still, all species are defined by their expressed traits!

Unfortunately, specification with the use of genetic markers seems to deviate from reality as wolves exhibiting doggish traits pass the genetic evaluation as pure wolves. We can take a look at some examples.

In 2015 and 2016, some seventy wolves were culled in Finland, of which the hunters provided me with documents for thirty-eight wolves. Of these wolves, six had white or yellow claws, a trait that is unusual in many wild animals for the reasons explained earlier in this book. These wolves are marked with yellow in Table 5.4 and all have the a^y allele in color locus A, indicating fawn color setting, which might have been inherited from dogs sometimes in the past (Schmutz et al. 2007).

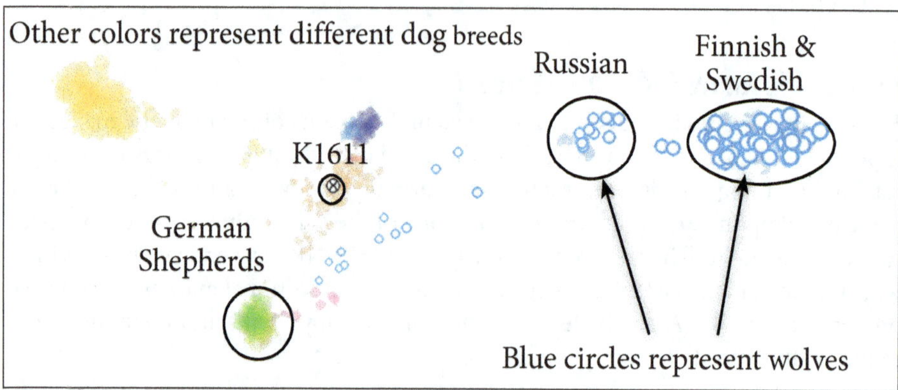

Figure 5.4. A two-dimensional population chart.

Earlier in this chapter, we read a statement from Dr. Malgorzata Pilot where she said:

On the other hand, two Italian wolves with an unusual, black coat color did not show any genetic signatures of hybridization, except for carrying a dog-derived variant of a gene linked to dark coloration.

Her statement "did not show any genetic signatures of hybridization, except for carrying a dog-derived variant." caught my attention.

The logical interpretation of this statement is that a wolf's genetic makeup can exhibit dog ancestry but still be considered a pure wolf.

Similar reasoning has been used by the Finnish Supreme Court, who decided that a F_3 hybrid should be considered a pure wolf because it does not endanger the wolf population. The simple reason for this verdict was that the genetic methods used to separate wolves from dogs were unable to distinguish F_3 hybrids from pure wolves.

If we look at the blue circles in Figure 5.4, all wolves having a^y in color locus A are found within the Finnish–Swedish wolf population.

Humans Altering Evolution

The perfect Western society has long ago abandoned evolution and started to twist nature to its own wishes. Extinct species are recreated human and animal DNA is "repaired" and modified as if evolution had done something wrong.

Figure 5.5. A red wolf (photo by Jett Fereby).

The Red Wolf

In 1967, the red wolf was listed as an endangered species (under a law that preceded the Endangered Species Act of 1973), meaning it is considered in danger of extinction throughout all or a significant portion of its range. In 1973, the US Fish and Wildlife Service (USFWS) established a breeding program for the red wolf. Biologists began to remove all red wolves from the wild. Over a period of six years, more than 400 wolf-like canids were captured in Louisiana and Texas, but only forty-three were considered pure red wolves and placed in captivity. Crossing these forty-three and analyzing the litters to find hidden traits, the biologists revealed that only seventeen were supposed to be true red wolves, of which only fourteen successfully bred in captivity (Wikipedia).

In 1987, four pairs of red wolves were reintroduced to the wild in northeastern North Carolina. Each wolf was equipped with a radio transmitter so that biologists could monitor their movements. Additional releases were made, and the first wild reproduction occurred in 1988. Of sixty-three red wolves released between 1987 and 1994, the population rose to as many as 100 to 120 individuals in 2012 but has declined to forty individuals in 2018 (Wikipedia).

Now it is time to ask, is this species just a mongrel? We must not forget that the red wolf is an artifact of intense captive breeding programs by the USFWS. They are not a species that is a product of evolution or natural processes. They are an artifact of human making. Calling them species confounds different categories. They were recreated in good faith, no doubt, but they are consequently an artifact of human ingenuity and not a natural or Darwinian species.

William Bartram, a naturalist, botanist, scientist, and author undertook expeditions lasting years around the time of the American Revolution (1776), spending time in the Carolina, Florida, and Georgia west to the Mississippi. The only wolves he saw were "perfectly black," but he was reliably informed that there were also white wolves, pied ones, and other mixtures. He saw no red wolf! (See :*Tales of the Wolf,* compiled by Denise Casey and Tim W. Clark, Moose Wy, Homestead Publishing, pp. 56-59, *The Travels of William Bertrand.* Naturalist's Edition, edited by Francis Harper, Yale University Press 1958).

The Eastern Wolf

Canis lupus lyacon, or the eastern wolf's taxonomic classification, has been under review, with various suggestions having been presented as to its derivation, including it being a subspecies of gray wolf. At the moment, the eastern wolf is recognized as a gray wolf subspecies by *Mammal Species of the World.*

The eastern wolf is currently listed as a threatened species, and it is particularly susceptible to hybridization due to its close relationship to the coyote and its ability to bridge gene flow between coyotes and gray wolves.

Furthermore, human persecution over a period of 400 years caused a population decline that reduced the number of suitable mates, thus facilitating coyote gene swapping into the eastern wolf population (Wikipedia).

However, a 2016 study concluded that even the "eastern wolves" have about 32% coyote ancestry.

The question remains, how can a species with 32% coyote be considered a pure wolf?

Does Protection Work Against Nature?

Genetic studies provide some theories about wolves in North America. One theory proposes that there exists only two species: the gray wolf (*Canis lupus lupus*) and the coyote (*Canis latrans*). These two species have produced hybrids, including the Great Lakes wolf, the eastern coyote, the eastern wolf, and the red wolf (Wayne et al. 2016).

Another theory proposes that there are three species, with the addition of the eastern wolf as the species *Canis lupus lycaon*, and the red wolf being considered the same species. Hybrids include the Great Lakes wolf that are the product of gray wolf × eastern wolf hybridization, and eastern coyotes that are the result of eastern wolf × coyote hybridization (Rutledge et al. 2015).

Figure 5.6. An eastern wolf (Wikipedia Commons).

Surprisingly, some scientists claim, based on morphology, that the red wolf should be considered a separate species *Canis rufus*.

Some questions still remain:

1. Who is qualified to define these animals as endangered species?

2. Are the managers of these endangered species free to choose among the various taxonomic systems and pick one of the many species definitions available?

3. Do we believe that destroyed natural environments and extinct species can be restored by human intervention—and should they be restored?

There is common agreement on accepting the fourteen ancestors' DNA as the base material for all future DNA analysis, thus allowing scientists to decide what the red wolf should look like.

Siberian Wolves

In 2016, our research team analyzed nineteen Siberian wolves in order to find reference material for further genetic research on the European wolf populations. At that time, we assumed that the only pure wolves were found in Russia. Surprisingly, we found the ASIP a^t allele (color locus A) in 60% of the tested wolves, something we have not observed in any of the European wolves we have tested.

Despite the atypical color loci in some Siberian wolves, their appearance was typical to gray wolves simply because their genetic makeup was either a^w/a^w, or a^w/a^t, and the a^w is dominant to a^t.

Summary

Domestic dogs have been shown to have multiple alleles of the ASIP, while wolves are (and should be) homozygous to the a^w allele. However, the a^y allele seems to spread within the Finnish and Scandinavian wolf populations suggesting introgression of dog genes.

In my research, the first observation of the a^y allele in wolves was in Lapland (Finland) as early as 1981, where one tested wolf carried this allele. This wolf is found in Table 5.4, as LA-2-81 (Lapland, #2, 1981). Later, in 1997, this allele was found in three wolves (PK-1208-97, PK-1203-97, and PK-1250-97). The letters PK stand for North Karelia, and the year was 1997. The samples I have collected from wild wolves between 2014 and 2016 carrying the a^y allele all came from North Karelia as well. I have not yet observed this allele in wolves from western and southwestern Finland.

An interesting photo was sent to me in the winter of 2018. This photo shows an almost red wolf, again in north Karelia. Although this wolf had black-tipped guard hairs on its back, the overall color tone was red (Figure 5.9).

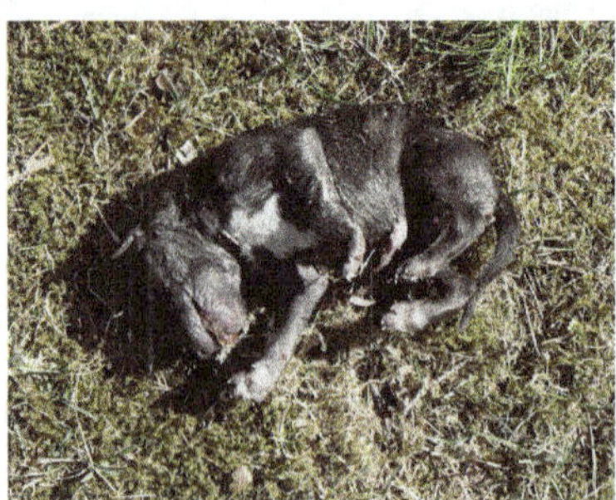

Figure 5.7. This cub was found dead and sent to the Finnish Food Safety Authority for investigation. They wanted to return it to the hunters because they claimed it was a dog. It looked like a dog, and it had large white spots atypical of wolf pups. However, genetic tests at the University of Oulu revealed that it was a pure wolf (photo Ari Kirjanen).

VARIATIONS IN PHENOTYPE

Originally, the wolf was specified by its expressed traits, and this was the basis for current taxonomy. At the moment, the wolf is classified as an endangered species in most Western countries. In Europe, Council Directive 92/43/EEC (the Habitats Directive) defines the framework for member states' legislation, and in Article 12 of the Directive reads as follows

Member States shall take the requisite measures to establish a system of strict protection for the animal species listed in Annex IV (a) in their natural range, prohibiting: (a) all forms of deliberate capture or killing of specimens of these species in the wild; (b) deliberate disturbance of these species, particularly during the period of breeding, rearing, hibernation and migration;

Figure 5.8. A hybrid with solid black hair on the back (photo by Asko Kettunen).

Figure 5.9. A "true" red wolf in Finland.

Killing a wolf (listed in Annex IV) is a serious criminal offense, which under Finnish or Swedish law is punishable by imprisonment for a maximum term of four years. Further, the hunter's hunting license is suspended for up to five years.

The wording "deliberate disturbance" in particular causes confusion because postmortem DNA analyses decide whether the killed animal was a wolf, a hybrid, or a dog. This, in turn, has led to situations where loose dogs have harassed and killed sheep, but the farmer (and the police) were unable to intervene due to the question of whether it was a wolf or a dog.

For this reason, I advise not using descriptions in this chapter without being aware of the consequences of the contradiction between phenotype and genotype in EU member states' legislation.

Genotype vs. Phenotype

The relationship between phenotype and genotype can be described as

Genotype + environment → phenotype

A phenotype is any property of an organism that is easily observed and is the result of an interaction between the genotype and environment. This relationship develops and changes over a long period (adaptation), during which the species in question undergoes specialization influenced by changes in the environment. For instance, the development of modern **Homo sapiens** diverged from chimpanzees at least 12 million years ago.

Despite big differences in phenotype, the genetic difference between Homo sapiens and the chimpanzee is less than 2%.

Evolution automatically strives toward species with coloration, physical size, behavior, and other traits optimal for their environment. In the same way as a carnivore's phenotype adapts to the environment, the prey animals do whatever is needed to survive. For a prey animal it is important to have optimal camouflage to be able to hide for the carnivores.

How to Recognize Introgression

Depending on the environment, there are variations within all species. The willow grouse's adaptation to different seasons is typical to some species. Within wolves we find different nuances in the color setting, but as Russian scholars point out

Despite variation in nuances, the color setting is the same (Bibikov 1982; Heptner & Naumov 1967).

The Tail

The original purpose of the wolf's tail was for balance. It prevents the wolf from toppling over as it makes sharp turns while hunting, fighting, or escaping. The tail also plays an important role in wolves' social behavior. Heptner and Naumow wrote (1967),

The tail is fairly large, fluffy, and hanging down to the tarsal joint. It looks as if broken at the base and in the standing and calmly moving wolf, it hangs directly downwards. Only during fast galloping does the wolf somewhat raise it, and carries it "outstretched" but not higher than the back level. In the live animal, the tail moves little and looks like a chunk of wood.

The German Shepherd in Figure 5.10 C exhibits a long hooked tail atypical of wolves.

Figure 5.10. The wolf's tail

A: The tail of a Finnish wolf (Photo by the author).

B: The tail of a Russian wolf (Photo by Gisela Möller).

C: The tail of a German Shepherd (Wikipedia Commons).

However, this type of tail has appeared in several wolf populations around Europe, suggesting some level of introgression. In Lüneburg, Germany, there are photos of wolves with curled tails (Internet A18).

Wolves that have migrated from Germany to Denmark exhibit typical traits inherited from dogs. A photo taken in Denmark reveals two "wolves" with white tail tips, slightly curled tails, and a color setting atypical of wolves (Internet A23).

The Head

The wolf's ears are relatively short, as described in Chapter 2, and they are placed apart from each other. Figure 5.11 shows the head of a dog and the head of a wolf. Notice the difference in the orbital angles (OA) A-B-C and D-E-F. In early studies, the angle for dogs was reported to be between 49 and 55 degrees, and wolves between 39 and 46 degrees. A recent Scandinavian study suggests that there is some overlap. Despite the overlap in observations, the study claims that angles greater than 60 degrees are certainly from dogs and angles under 35 degrees from wolves (Janssens et al. 2016). However, this study assumes the investigated canines were pure wolves, but Robert Wayne's research team found widespread introgression in the European wolf population (Wayne et al. 2018). This, in turn, suggests that there is ongoing genetic drift toward dogs in the European wolf populations, probably also affecting the values of the orbital angle.

Differences in the orbital angle can be observed at a distance. Even though differences between bare skulls are smaller, the wolf's large jaw muscles highlights the difference.

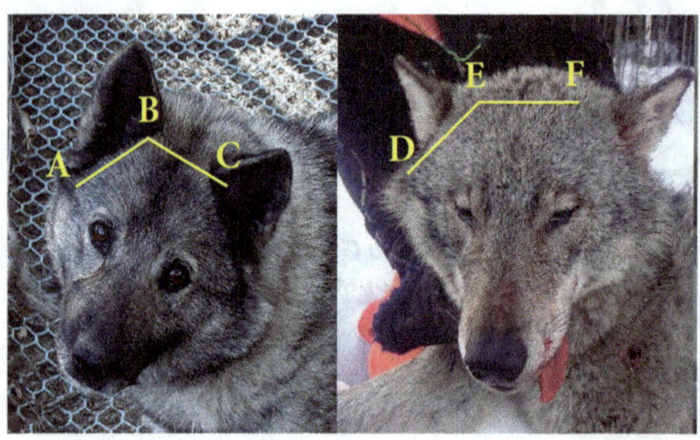

Figure 5.11. A dog and a wolf (photos by the author).

The Wolf's Posture

The wolf's appearance may vary during the year, and females, having nursed their pups, may exhibit an atypical appearance. However, some facts remain despite some loss in weight and fur. Figure 5.11A shows a Swedish wolf called Sjunda tiken or the Sjunda female, where Sjunda is the name of the wolf's territory.

This wolf needs a short evaluation. In our morphological studies, the relationship between the length of the thigh bone and the shank bone is on average 0.9, and the relation between the arm and the forearm is on average 0.9 as well. The wolf in Figure 5.12A seems to have both an unusually short arm and a short thigh bone. A wolf's head is typically some 30% larger than a dog's head, but this wolf seems to have an exceptionally small head, with long pointed ears.

From these photos, we notice that something does not match. The wolves in B and C both look like wolves should in their summer pelage. The wolf in A does not!

However, genetic tests carried out in Sweden "confirm" that this is a pure wolf.

Figure 5.12. A Swedish wolf (photo by Petter Rybäck).

Two Finnish wolves in their summer pelage (photo by the author).

Paw Prints Reveal Ancestry

Tracks, paws, and paw prints were discussed in Chapter 2. Adult wolves have huge paws with long, sharp claws (see Figure 5.13). The track of an adult gray wolf is approximately 10 - 15 cm long by 8 to 10 cm wide. However, track size can vary with age and by gender. Tracks smaller than this probably belong to dogs. The distance between the foremost fore paw print to the hindmost paw print is often more than 150 cm for wolves and less than 120 cm for dogs.

Don't worry, you will notice the difference! Once you stumble onto the impressive paw print of a large male gray wolf, you know it is a wolf!

Wolves' hind prints fall directly on the forefoot's paw print. Because wolves have a narrower chest than dogs, their paw prints line up. A dog leaves paw prints that do not align. Wolves' overall trail forms a straight line, while the trail of a dog tends to meander. Since dogs have proportionally wider chests than wolves, the width of a dog's stride is greater, especially for dogs with tracks as large as a wolf.

Wolves usually travel at a loping pace, and this gait can be maintained for hours at a pace of 8 to 9 km/h, allowing the wolves to cover great distances. When you are out in nature examining wolf tracks, look at the paw print. Figure 5.13 emphasizes the difference. Although many sources on the internet claim that 5.13D is the paw print of a pure wolf, it does not match the formal specifications.

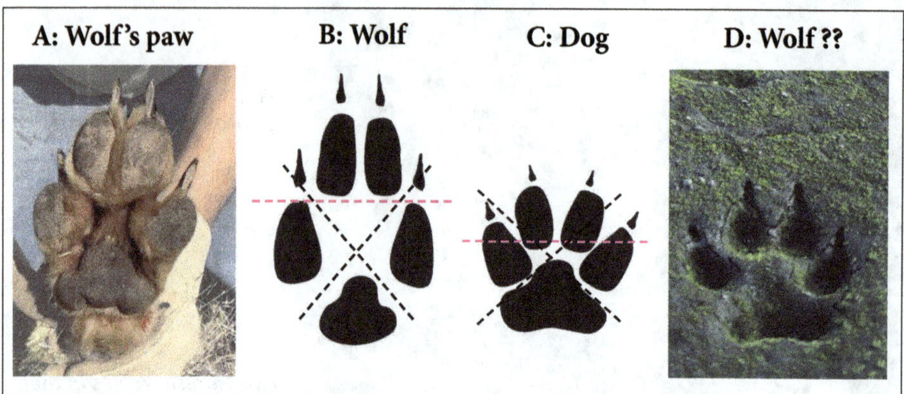

Figure 5.13. Wolves' and dogs' paw prints (drawings by Wernher Gerhards).

Professor Dmitry Bibikov presented a method for distinguishing wolf paw prints from dogs:

If a straw cannot be placed between the anterior part of the outer pads and the posterior part of the inner pads, then it is not a wolf's paw print. The same rules apply to the diagonal lines in 5.13B.

Figure 5.14. A golden jackal (photo Wikipedia Commons, Ilya Merlin).

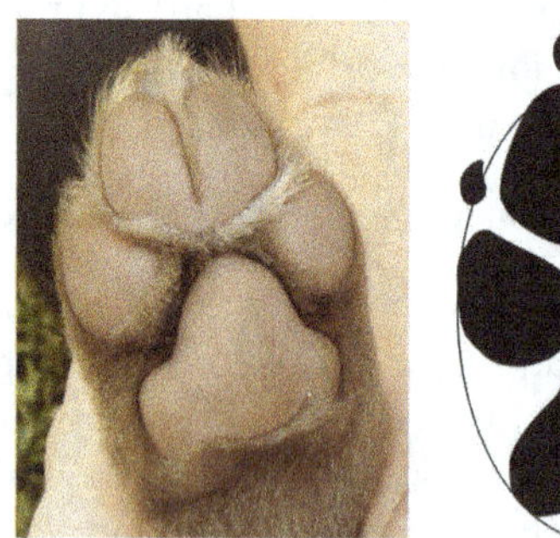

Figure 5.15. Paws of golden jackal (photo and drawings by Wernher Gerhards).

NEW SPECIES SHOWING UP

The Jackal

The golden jackal (*Canis aureus*) is rapidly spreading through Europe, and observations are reported from Central Europe to Estonia, Denmark, and the Netherlands. Recently, a jackal was caught on a game camera in France (Huisman 2018).

Because research results suggest the golden jackal has not been introduced to European countries by humans, it should not be treated as an alien species. For this reason the EU Commission has listed the golden jackal in Annex V of the Habitats Directive. This means that all European countries must ensure a favorable conservation status for the jackal.

The outcome will be another carnivore vulnerable to hybridization with wolves and dogs. I also expect conflicts between the North European red fox and the golden jackal, but who cares? To be perfect, Europe needs its own coyote as well.

A jackal–dog hybrid results from a mating between a dog and a golden jackal, and in 2015, hybridization between golden jackals and domestic dogs was confirmed when three hybrids were shot in Croatia. Genetic research has revealed wolf + jackal hybridization in Bulgaria and wolf like "jackals" have been observed in the Caucasus Mountains (Galov 2015).

The golden jackal's paw print is easily identified because of its connate pads on the medial digits of the forelimb. This feature may reveal hybrids with jackal ancestry (Figure 5.15).

The Coywolf

Coywolf is an informal name for a hybrid descended from coyotes, gray wolves, and dogs. Like all hybridization, the coyote–wolf hybrid adapts the behavior of three completely different species. Problems arise when urban coyotes residing in North American metropolitan areas interbreed with wild or habituated wolves and dogs. This, in turn, may result in a wolf-like animal thriving in human settlements rather than in the deep forests, where the wolf belongs. To fully understand the impact of these hybrids, we have to recall two biological principles:

1. Heterosis is the improved or increased function of any biological quality in a hybrid offspring. An offspring exhibits heterosis if its traits are enhanced as a result of mixing the genetic contributions of its parents.

2. Evolution allows the most suitable traits to survive.

When it comes to surviving in urban areas, a powerful coywolf may overcome the coyote, thus forming a completely new threat to human safety.

Figure 5.16. Coywolves (photo Wikipedia Commons; L. David Mech et al.).

Federal Border Guards

Russians were the first to make wolves serve people. However, experiments on inter-breeding dogs and wolves started long ago, and one experiment was carried out at the University of Cologne. They got over 200 puppies whose parents were wolves and dogs, but all of them demonstrated cautiousness and fear of humans, thus the experiment failed. At some point, researchers at Russia's **Perm Institute of Interior Forces** managed to establish an effective contact with the animals (Sudakov 2006).

The first ancestors of this unique Russian species were a pure female wolf named Naida and a male German Shepherd named Baron. From their offspring, a couple of stable puppies were selected for the experiment, and at the moment, several generations of wolf–dogs have been produced.

Russian experts have noticed that dogs and wolf–dogs employ different tactics for tracing criminals. Dogs chaotically run around the training hall and spend much time in studying the surrounding environment. Wolf–dogs circle the hall once, determine check points, and immediately trace hiding criminals, drugs, or explosives (Sudakov 2006).

The two wolf–dogs shown in Figure 5.17 are typical animals bred by the institute. Goy (the left) is from one of Naida and Baron's litters and thus is a wolf–dog with 50%

wolf and 50% German Shepherd. Lady, in front, is a descendant of Goy and a female wolf–dog called Dina. She is 68% wolf and 32% dog.

Figure 5.17. Russian wolf–dogs Goy (left) and Lady (right). This exclusive photo was taken by the Perm Institute of Interior Forces and used here with their permission.

Summary

The wolf populations in the United States and Europe are undergoing a dramatic revolution, while our genetic research is concentrated on the narrow genetic base of a tiny population. Less attention is paid to the fact that both wolves and hybrids are being reshaped by man-made changes to their natural environments. As a result, evolution will favor properties that help these animals live close to humans. The winners in this contest are the hybrids, and the authentic wolf will soon disappear.

My hope is for everyone participating in this debate to become able to recognize the major differences between hybrids and the gray wolf. Not everything that runs on four legs and feasts on carcasses is a wolf, even if a preponderance of our prominent nature photographers want to believe so. The differences between wolves and dogs are obvious, while the differences between wolves and hybrids can be subtle. In this situation, we should bear in mind a fundamental rule:

One doggish trait turns a wolf into a outlaw mongrel, whereas one wolf-like trait in a dog does not turn it into a wolf.

And—the biconditional truth remains: A canid is a wolf if and only if it looks like a wolf and behaves like a wolf.

Figure 5.18. A genetically "pure wolf" shot in November 2017 in Finland (photo by Sulo Suhonen).

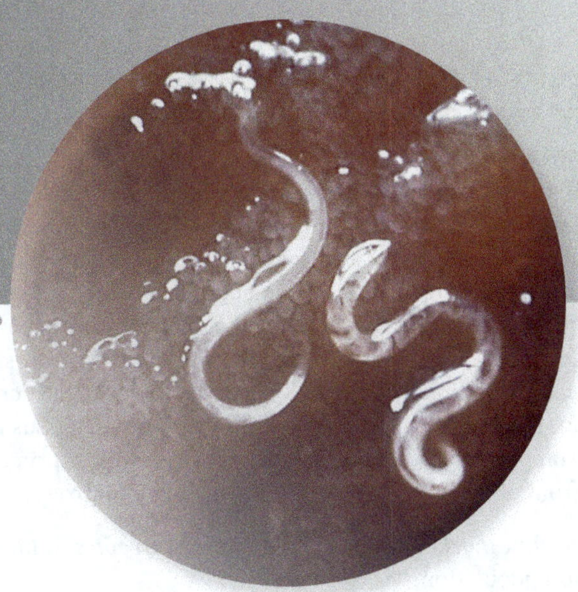

DISEASES AND PARASITES

Numerous infections and parasitic diseases have been reported for the gray wolf, including more than ten viral, bacterial, and mycotic diseases and more than seventy species of helminths and ectoparasites. However, wolf conservation has been the main issue in most Western countries, thus muting all information about their impact on human health and safety.

Although the risks imposed by diseases and parasites are known by the scientific society, less information about these is shared with the public.

WOLVES, DOGS, AND DISEASES

Infectious diseases spread by wolves pose a significant threat to livestock and human welfare. Wolves are susceptible to infections with numerous pathogenic organisms including dozens of viruses, bacteria, fungi and parasites, among others, more than seventy species of helminths and ectoparasites. An infection can affect wolf populations directly by causing mortality or indirectly by affecting reproduction, behavior, or social structure. In addition, wolves are hosts to infections that can affect prey species, thus affecting wolf populations indirectly by reducing prey abundance or increasing vulnerability to predation. Diseases such as *canine distemper* and infectious *canine hepatitis* are native to a wolf population, whereas *rabies* occurs in wolves primarily as a result of transmission from other species such as raccoon dogs and foxes.

Some pathogens, such as *canine morbillivirus*, and the parasite *sarcoptes scabiei* could even pose a threat to a wolf population.

Canine Parvovirus

Canine parvovirus type 2 (CPV2) is a virus mainly affecting dogs. It is extremely contagious and can be transmitted by any person, animal, or object that comes in contact with feces from an infected dog (or wolf). The virus is highly resistant, and can live in the environment for months, and may survive on objects such as food bowls, shoes, clothes, carpet and floors.

In dogs and wolves, this viral disease can produce a life-threatening disease. The virus attacks rapidly, dividing cells in the infected canine's body, most severely affecting the intestinal tract. When young animals are infected, the virus can damage the heart muscle and cause lifelong cardiac problems.

The disease spreads from one canine to another by direct or indirect contact with their feces, and if untreated, mortality can reach more than 90%. The virus is usually more lethal if the host is infected with worms or other intestinal parasites.

Canine Distemper

Canine distemper is a fever-causing disease of carnivores caused by a *parmyxovirus*. This virus is a worldwide problem in dogs, but reports in free-ranging wildlife are few. It affects several body systems, including the gastrointestinal and respiratory tracts and the spinal cord and brain. The mortality rate of the virus largely depends on the immune status of the infected wolves. Puppies experience the highest mortality rate.

The virus is spread by air or direct contact. Within a couple of days after exposure, the first signs appear. Signs include oral jaundice and ulceration, swollen feet, anorexia, loss of control of body movements, labored breathing, and neurological abnormalities.

In 2015, reports from Ethiopia indicated that an outbreak of canine distemper was causing fatalities among Ethiopian wolves in Bale Mountains National Park in southern Ethiopia. The disease had been transmitted to wild animals by domestic dogs living in human settlements inside and around the park area (Gordon et al. 2015).

The leader of the Bale Mountains Conservation Project said, "The death toll can be as high as 70%."

Sarcoptic Mange

Sarcoptic mange, a parasitic disease caused by the mite *Sarcoptes scabiei*, is regularly reported in wolves (Figure 6.1). *Sarcoptic mange* is a highly contagious infection of a burrowing mite that is able to infect cats, pigs, horses, sheep, and various other species. The mites dig into the skin, causing intense itching from an allergic reaction to the mite, and crusting that can quickly become infected. Hair loss and crusting frequently appear first on elbows and ears and skin damage can occur from the animal's intense scratching.

Figure 6.1. A young wolf after having died from sarcoptic mange (photo by Heikki Kulmala).

Sarcoptes scabiei mites are able to survive for up to three weeks off a host. Transmission normally occurs through close contact between wolves, thus when one wolf in the pack is infected, the mite will most likely be transmitted to the rest of the pack. Observations in Yellowstone National Park suggest that the spatiotemporal patterns of mite infection on wolves are related to distance from the next infected pack, indicating wolf-to-wolf transmission (Almberg et al. 2012).

The parasite may cause devastating mortality at the pack level, but in cases where wolves' territories do not overlap, transmission from one pack to another is less likely.

In areas where wolves hunt foxes, and raccoon dogs, these may transmit the mite to the wolves but usually not the other way around.

Threats to Humans

Zoonoses are infectious diseases that can be transmitted between animals and humans. Humans and animals coexist in a complex, relationship, and we depend on nature for our food and livelihoods. Thus, the interface between humans, animals, and the environment we share, is a source of diseases (zoonoses) impacting public health.

Some well-known zoonoses are, for instance, the Ebola virus and salmonellosis. HIV was originally a zoonotic disease transmitted to humans in the early part of the twentieth century that has evolved into a human-only disease.

Zoonoses can be caused by a range of disease pathogens such as viruses, bacteria, fungi, and parasites; of 1,415 pathogens known to infect humans, 61% are zoonotic. Most human diseases originate in animals; however, only diseases that routinely involve animal to human transmission, like rabies, are considered direct zoonoses (Wikipedia).

Some severe zoonoses can be transmitted to humans from canines, e.g. wolves, coyotes and dogs.

RABIES

Rabies is an infectious viral disease that is almost always fatal following the onset of clinical symptoms. The incubation period for human rabies is typically 2 to 3 months but may vary from 1 week to 1 year, depending on how fast the virus spreads to the central nervous system. Initial symptoms of rabies include fever with pain, and unusual or unexplained tingling at the site of exposure.

In up to 99% of all human cases, domestic dogs are the source of the rabies virus. The virus spreads to humans through bites or scratches, usually via saliva. Globally, children between the ages of 5 and 14 years are most commonly infected. Africa and Asia have the highest rates of rabies and account for 95% of rabies deaths worldwide (WHO).

Human vaccines and immunoglobulins exist for rabies, but the average cost of rabies post-exposure prophylaxis may be thirty to forty times the daily income of the infected person in areas where rabies is common.

When rabies enters its active phase, the following symptoms occur: violent movements, uncontrolled excitement, fear of water, an inability to move parts of the body, confusion, and loss of consciousness.

Once symptoms appear, the result is nearly always death.

Wolves and Rabies

It is common knowledge that in populations of wolves, as well as in populations of foxes and other canines, there are outbreaks of epizootic rabies. In the northern Kazakhstan regions the population of foxes was reduced by 16%, and the procurement of their pelts reduced by 20% (Graves 2007).

However, among wolves, such episodic outbreaks were not found anywhere—not in forests, mountains, tundra, nor in the steppes. At no time, past or present, have there been examples of wolf populations that were decimated by rabies.

Mikhail Pavlov believes there are more convincing explanations of why wolves escape decimation by diseases. It is thought that numerous cases of deaths of wolves, even from rabies, are impossible due to the great dispersal of wolf packs. It is quite possible that when a wolf feels the first symptom of indisposition, it leaves its pack or is dismissed. Thus, in any epizootic situation, the lifestyle of wolves helps save packs from extinction (Graves 2007). Also, the fear of being killed and eaten by its pack mates may contribute to this.

The incubation period of rabies in wolves is from 8 days to 3 weeks. Rabies causes a drastic change in wolf behavior. Rabid wolves become agitated; they desert their packs and run far away, traveling up to 80 kilometers per day. As they move, they attack livestock, poultry, and whatever else they meet, and they may even bite trees and branches.

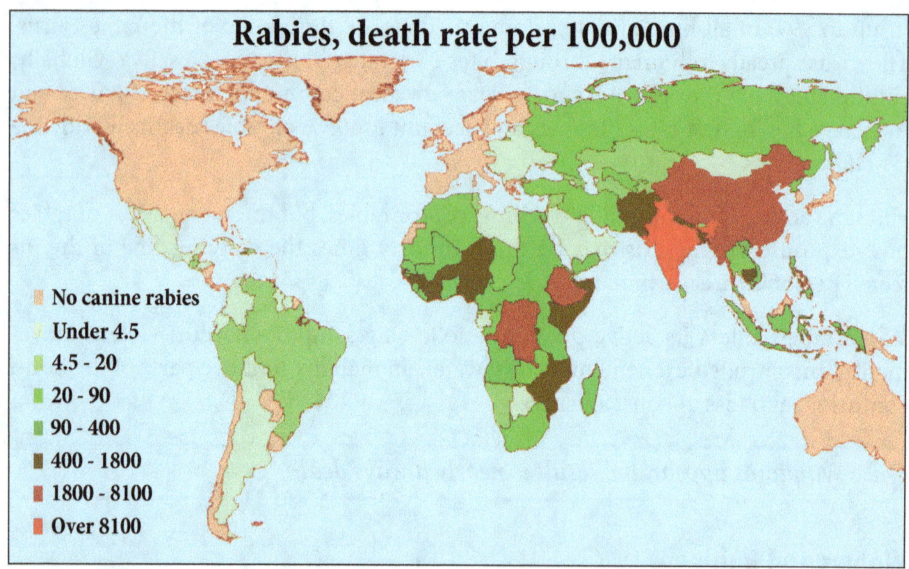

Figure 6.2. Canine rabies according to WHO.

In contrast to healthy wolves, rabid wolves do not avoid people and are attracted to any unusual noise. Rabid wolves violently attack people in villages and fields during daylight hours. Wolf bites are extremely dangerous to humans as they are wide, deep, and often multiple. Rabid wolves attacking humans typically aim for the head. Bites to the head, face, and neck are especially dangerous. A video showing a rabid wolf attacking people in a shopping center in Israel is available on YouTube (Internet A1).

Most often, wolves attack and bite people working in fields, herders of livestock, agricultural workers, children, and automobile transport workers. Attacks by wolves are particularly frequent during their winter migrations, when they hunt around human settlements.

Wild carnivores maintain the natural centers of rabies infection. The reservoir for the rabies virus and the main distributors of this disease are foxes and wolves. In 1997, rabies epizootic centers were discovered in thirty-four regions of the Russian Federation. There were 349 problematic points with wild rabid animals. From 1990 to 1997, there were seventy-six cases of human death from rabies in thirty administrative territories of the Russian Federation, and in 1998, 2,868 cases of rabies were registered (Graves 2007).

Other Sources of Transmission

An animal is usually infected following a bite or scratch from an animal carrying rabies. The major source of human infections is from dogs, but bat rabies is an emerging threat in Australia and Western Europe. Human deaths following exposure to infected foxes, raccoon dogs, jackals, and other wild carnivore are very rare, and bites from rodents are not known to transmit rabies.

Human-to-human transmission through bites is theoretically possible but has never been confirmed.

Post-Exposure Actions

Post-exposure prophylaxis (PEP) is the immediate treatment of a victim after rabies exposure. This prevents virus entry into the central nervous system, which results in imminent death (WHO 2014). PEP consists of the following

- First-aid and extensive washing and local treatment of the wound for a minimum of 15 minutes with soap and water, detergent, or any substance that will kill the rabies virus.

- A course of potent and effective rabies vaccine that meets WHO standards.

- The administration of rabies immunoglobulin (RIG), if indicated.

- Effective treatment soon after exposure to rabies can prevent the onset of symptoms and death.

Depending on the severity of the contact with a suspected rabid animal, administration of PEP is recommended as follows:

- Touching or feeding animals, and licks on intact skin do not require any action.

- Nibbling of uncovered skin, minor scratches or abrasions without bleeding, single or multiple bites or scratches, licks on broken skin, contamination of mucous membrane with saliva from licks, and contacts with bats requires immediate local treatment of the wound and PEP.

According to the WHO, the risk is increased if any of these apply

- The biting mammal is a known rabies reservoir or vector species.

- The exposure occurs in a geographical area where rabies is still present.

- The animal looks sick or displays abnormal behavior.

- A wound or mucous membrane was contaminated by the animal's saliva.

- The bite was unprovoked.

- The animal has not been vaccinated.

Why the Wolf?

Domestic dogs are the most common reservoir of the virus, with more than 99% of human deaths caused by dog-mediated rabies. Strict animal control and vaccination programs have decreased the risk of rabies from dogs in a number of regions of the world. As wolf populations keep growing and wolves habituating to humans in the United States and Europe they are likely to replace domestic dogs as a rabies reservoir.

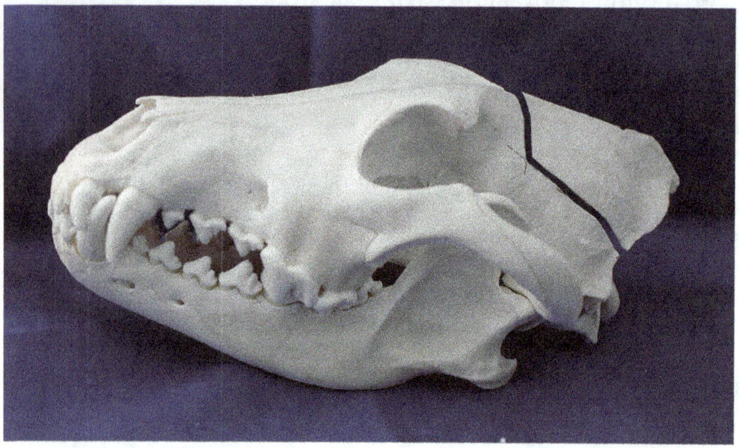

Figure 6.3. A wolf's braincase that was opened for rabies inspection (photo by the author).

ECHINOCOCCUS

The family of tapeworms that are of the most importance to human and carnivores is *Taeniidae*. This group of parasites includes the genera Taenia and Echinococcus. The genera are distinguished by the morphology of the adult tapeworm and the form of the immature worm in the intermediate host. There are currently two species, *E. granulosus* and *E. multilocularis* that are found worldwide and two species, *E. oligarthrus* and *E. vogeli* that are found in central and south America.

Human echinococcosis is a zoonotic parasitic infection caused by the larval stage of the genus *Echinococcus*, with the two most important species being *E. granulosis* and *E. multilocularis*. Infection is a result of direct or indirect infection from canid hosts, which are themselves infected by various domestic and wild mammals. Despite being a significant health burden to humans, it remains a neglected disease (WHO).

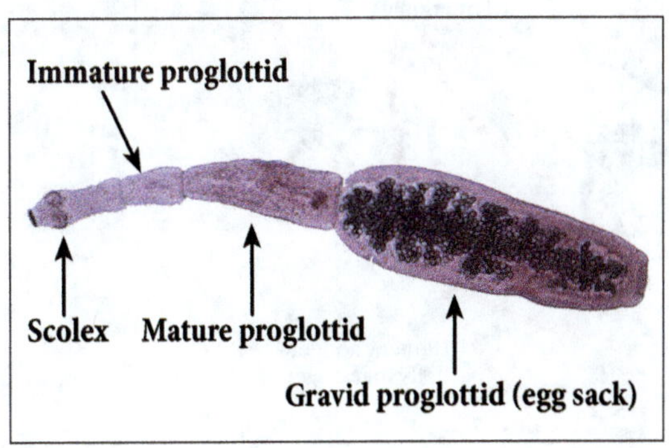

Figure 6.4. Proglottid (photo by CDC).

The most frequent clinical forms of echinococcosis, cystic echinococcosis (*E. granulosus*) and alveolar echinococcosis (*E. multilocularis*) are, according to the WHO, responsible for a substantial health and economic burden, particularly in low-income societies.

The distribution of *E. granulosus* makes it a worldwide threat, with only a few areas, such as Iceland, Ireland, and Greenland, believed to be free of *Cystic echinococcosis* (CE). However, CE is not evenly distributed geographically. For example, the United States has few cases in livestock, and most human cases are imported. The same is true for regions of western and central Europe. In many parts of the world, however, CE is considered an emerging disease.

In this chapter, we concentrate on the CE. The *alveolar echinococcosis* differs only in its impacts on the secondary host.

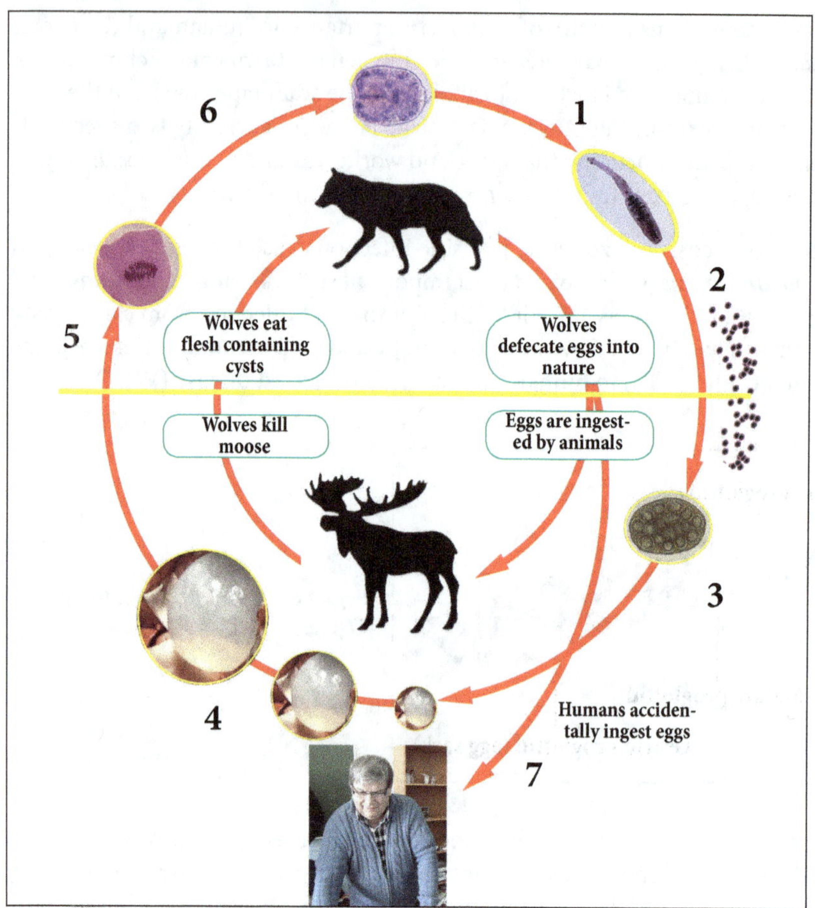

Figure 6.5. E. granulosus life cycle (Centers for Disease Control and Prevention).

Echinococcus Granulosus

To date, the species **E. granulosus** comprises eight genotypes (G1–G3, G6–G9 and G10) and two species, **E. equines** (G4) and **E. ortleppi** (G5) (Karamian et al. 2017). In this chapter, we use the common name **E. granulosus** for all genotypes.

E. granulosus is a parasitic tapeworm that uses two hosts, an intermediate host and a definitive host. In the definitive host, the tapeworm dwells in the small intestine of canids as a 3 to 6 mm long adult. The worm has four suckers on its head (*scolex*) with which it attaches to the walls of the small intestine. The adult also has three segments (*proglottids*) when intact—an immature proglottid, a mature proglottid, and a gravid proglottid (Figure 6.4). Each gravid proglottid may contain more than 1,000 eggs.

Echinococcus Granulosus Life Cycle

The life cycle involves dogs, wolves, and other wild canines as the definitive host for the adult tapeworm. Definitive hosts are the animals where parasites reach maturity and reproduce. Wild or domesticated ungulates, such as sheep, serve as an intermediate host. Figure 6.5 illustrates the life cycle of the parasite (CDC).

1. The definitive hosts (wolves or dogs) become infected when they ingest cysts (*metacestodes*) from the tissues of intermediate hosts. As the parasite is ingested, it attaches to the wolf's intestines, where it starts growing into the adult stages. The wolf's intestine can contain more than 10,000 *E. granulosus* worms (Table 6.1). Each worm has three segments, or proglottids, with each being in a different stage of development, and each worm releases a gravid *proglottid* containing eggs in the intestine. The *proglottids* are shed in the feces, and the eggs are immediately infective. *Echinococcus* eggs have a sticky coating that can adhere to the wolf's fur. Insects, such as flies and beetles, or birds, can also act as mechanical vectors (Internet A2).

2. As feces dries, the eggs are spread by the wind into the surrounding forest. Depending on the environment, the eggs land on tree branches and leaves or they may fall to the ground. The eggs can be scattered for up to 200 meters (656 feet) by the wind and attach to obstacles at heights of six feet. NOTE! Wolves mark their territory with feces and urine; thus, contaminated wolf scat is found all over the territory (Nygren 2008).

3. When eggs contaminate grass, leaves, or water, the intermediate host may ingest the parasite by grazing in the contaminated pasture. Humans can also get infected by eating contaminated berries or other plants collected in nature.

4. The ingested tapeworm's eggs hatch and develop into *oncospheres,* which will then burrow through the gut wall in order to access the organs or tissues of the intermediate host. Here, they continue the next stage of their development as *bladderworms.* The *bladderworm* is a cyst created by the oncosphere. The cysts are slow-growing but will, sooner or later, cause severe clinical symptoms in humans. It can take anywhere from two to twenty years before symptoms develop (Nygren 2008).

5. ***Echinococcus granulosus*** is transmitted from the intermediate host (moose, elk, or sheep) to wolves when they feed on the intermediate hosts. As the wolves fight for their share at a carcass, they devour whatever they can, including cysts. The cysts hold thousands of ***protoscolices*** (hydatid sand) that enter the intestine and attach to its walls. Survival time of protoscolex varies with temperature, where: −20°C takes 1 hour; −10°C, 4 hours; 1°C, 16 days; 10°C, 16 days; 20°C, 8 days; 30°C, 4 days; 40°C, 2 days, and 50°C, 2 hours. In general, protoscolices survive considerably better when stored in intact cysts (Andersen & Loveless 1978).

6. In the intestine, the protoscolex develops into a scolex within thirty-two to eighty days, and then starts to produce proglottids with fresh eggs to be shed into the environment. Although the parasites stop laying eggs after 6 to 10 months in wolves, the adult worms may survive for up to three years.

Date	Parasite found	Amount
June 18, 2011	*Echinococcus granulosus*	>2,000
	Taenia SPP	Several
July 13, 2011	*Echinococcus granulosus*	>10,000
	Taenia SPP	Several
July 13, 2011	*Echinococcus granulosus*	>200
	Taenia SPP	Several
July 28, 2011	*Echinococcus granulosus*	>10,000
	Taenia SPP	Several
Aug. 10, 2011	*Taenia SPP*	Several
	Uncinaria (Hookworms)	Several
Aug. 17, 2011	*Echinococcus granulosus*	>4,000
	Taenia & Uncinaria	Several

Table 6.1. Infections in wolves in Washington State (Internet A2).

This is the normal cycle. There is another branch that takes the worm to human settlements. Humans can ingest these eggs as well, but the sources are not necessarily the same. The dog is, like the wolf, a potential host of *E. granulosus*. Dogs get infected by scavenging on carrion left by wolves or guts left by hunters. An infected dog releases eggs in the yard, from where they can get transported into the house and, further, into another intermediate host–the human. Hopefully, the human is a ***dead end***.

Not all eggs follow the feces, but some (a lot) may adhere to the wolf's (or dog's) pelt. Figure 6.6 shows the area where *E. granulosus* eggs are most concentrated.

To prevent transmission to humans, dogs can be given anthelminthic treatment and deworming. However, it is important to note that deworming only kills adult worms, not the eggs in the proglottids.

Figure 6.6. Hazard area containing E. granulosus eggs (photo by the author).

Figure 6.7. Wolf scat–keep away from this! Dry wolf scat may release E. granulosus eggs (photo by the author).

Echinococcus Granulosus Eggs in Nature

The life expectancy of the parasite also plays a role in the rates of infection in an area. The most important factors are temperature and humidity, which both affect the survival of the eggs. Under normal conditions, the eggs remain viable for several weeks or even up to months in pastures or gardens. Only in dry conditions (humidity <25%) do they die within four days. They survive for months under moist conditions and in temperatures from +4°C to +15°C. Viable eggs have been found in water and damp sand for three weeks at 30°C, 225 days at 6°C, and 32 days at 10–21°C (Internet A2). Echinococcus eggs are inactivated by heat (hot water of 85°C or above is effective). They can also be killed by freezing at –80°C for 48 hours or –70°C for four days. Freezing of tissue or scat containing eggs is a normal procedure before studying them in laboratories.

Echinococcus Granulosus and Human Welfare

As already noted, humans act as an accidental intermediate hosts for *E. granulosus* and are infected when they ingest tapeworm eggs from a definitive host. The eggs may be ingested with food such as vegetables, fruits, or herbs, or ingested from contaminated water. They can also stick to the hands when a person pets an infected dog or handles a wild animal or its carcass. Dogs may carry the eggs on their fur if they get in contact with the feces of an infected hosts.

The incubation time varies from two years up to the following (Dethlefsen 2015).

1. Adults, 10 years (normally 72 % of cases)

2. Adults, 20 to 30 years or more (at times)

3. Children and toddlers 2 to 6 years

Approximately 60 to 70 % of *E. granulosus* cysts occur in the liver, and 20 to 25% in the lungs. The remaining cysts can be found almost anywhere in the body, including the bones, kidneys, spleen, muscles, and even behind the eye.

Percentage	Impact
2.2 %	Death due to, for instance, anaphylactic shock
2–5 %	Brain damage
1–5 %	Vision problems
2–5 %	Extremity paralysis
60–70 %	Degradation of vital organs
20–30 %	Respiratory problems (lungs)
5-10 %	Urogenital impacts

Table 6.2. Impacts of cystic echinococcosis worldwide (Dethlefsen 2015)

Treatment of Echinococcosis

In the past, surgery was the only treatment for CE. However, chemotherapy, cyst puncture, and puncture aspiration injection reaspiration (PAIR) are used to replace surgery, although surgery remains the most effective treatment for removal of the cyst and can lead to a complete cure.

PAIR is considered an alternative treatment for CE and is often indicated for patients who do not respond to surgery or benzimidazoles (Wikipedia). In general, the clinical approach depends on the World Health Organization (WHO) diagnostic classification (Brunetti et al. 2010). With cysts that have a single compartment, that are <5 cm may be treated with albendazole, a medication used for the treatment of a variety of parasitic worm infections, alone. In settings where albendazole treatment is not feasible, the use of PAIR is an alternative approach. Cysts that are >5 cm may be treated with albendazole in combination with PAIR. These cysts often have multiple compartments that require individual puncture, and therefore, management of these cysts requires surgery.

Physical and Medical Impacts

A study carried out in Tibet aimed to assess the effectiveness of cyclic albendazole treatment, and concurrently monitor the changes of serum specific antibody levels during treatment taking place from 2006 to 2008. A total of 196 cases were identified by ultrasound, of which thirty-seven (18.9%) showed evidence of spontaneous healing. Of forty-nine enrolled cases, 32.7% (sixteen) were considered to be cured after 6 to 30 months of regular albendazole treatment, 49.0% (twenty-four) were improved, 14.3% (seven) remained unchanged, and 4.1% (two) became aggravated (Li et al. 2011; Rajesh et al. 2013). Other impacts are listed in Table 6.2.

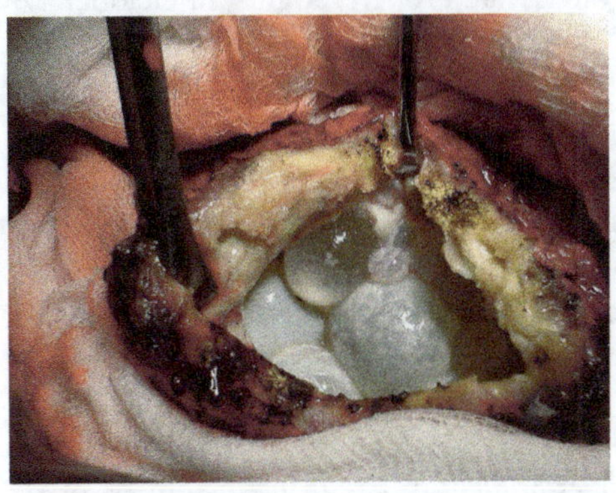

Figure 6.8. Cyst removal from human liver (photo by Dr. Luis Ruso Martinez).

Prevention—Know the Disease

It is difficult to completely prevent exposure to *Echinococcus* from wild animals. However, food safety precautions, combined with good hygiene, can be helpful. Fruits and vegetables picked in the wild, should be washed thoroughly or even cooked to remove or inactivate infective eggs. The hands should always be washed after handling pets, farming, gardening, or preparing food, and before eating (Internet A2).

In European countries where it is strictly forbidden to remove or scare wolves from yards, preventing exposure to *Echinococcus* is practically impossible.

Prevalence of Echinococcus Among Wolves

Foreyt et al. (2009) examined the small intestines of 123 gray wolves collected from Idaho, USA (n=63), and Montana, USA (n=60), between 2006 and 2008 for the tapeworm *E. granulosus*. The tapeworm was detected in thirty-nine of sixty-three wolves (62%) in Idaho, USA, and thirty-eight of sixty wolves (63%) in Montana, USA. The detection of thousands of tapeworms per wolf was a common finding.

Hydatid cysts were detected in elk, mule deer, and one mountain goat. In Montana, hydatid cysts were detected in elk, and it was assumed that the parasite was well established in wolves in those states (Foreyt et al. 2009). A later study was carried out by Cerda and Ballweber (2018) examining seven wolves, eleven coyotes, and three foxes. All wolves were infected with *Taenia* however, only four wolves were infected with *Echinococcus*. *E. granulosus* (*canadensis G10*) was identified in three wolves, with *canadensis G8* identified in the fourth. *Echinococcus* was not found in any of the coyote or fox samples, although three coyotes harbored *Taenia sp.*

Clayton Dethlefsen presented a paper about tests conducted by the WPCA at the Nineteenth Annual National Conference on Private Property Rights, in October 17, 2015. In his speech, he says

> *I was mentioning Dr. Evans and Tim Kemery, we grab some samples right around the populated area in Challis and we sent them off to the lab in Denver. They came back and they told us, "Oh, by the way, 100% of the samples that you sent us have the disease." Not 63, but 100%. You have to keep in mind this is sampling and there's all kinds of statistical ways that you can show whether it applies to the whole of the population or just part of it. What we found out was, in this, the G8 and G10 strains were dominant in these samples. Where did it come from? It came from Canada. What happened was that over the generations of the pups, the original ones brought it in. During the process of each generation of pups growing from a pup to an adult, the adult parents and the rest of the pack infect the offspring and so every one of the wolves that we tested was a new generation so it had to pick up the disease in our country area Montana. There's no other place they could have got it.*

In northern Europe, *E. granulosus* is shown to occur with wolves as the definitive host and domestic reindeer, elk, and wild forest reindeer as intermediate hosts. The parasite seems to be quite common in the Finnish wolf population, with a prevalence of approximately 30% in both intestinal and fecal samples. The results indicate that the parasite has not spread to dogs in reindeer herding areas (Hirvelä-Koski et al. 2003).

My study of four randomly selected Siberian wolves in the Yakutsk area in 2016 showed that three of four wolves carried the *E. granulosus* parasite. The genotype was not specified.

Torgersen reported findings in central Asia, where eight out of forty-one (20%) wolves were infected with *E. granulosus*, with a mean abundance of 1,275 parasites per wolf

Region	Date	Species	Number Infected	Total number	%
S. Kazakhstan	2001–2002	Sheep	732	2,152	34.0
Kazakhstan	2001–2002	Sheep	169	353	48.0
S. Kazakhstan	2001–2002	Cattle	31	431	7.2
Naryn, Kyrgystan	2006	Sheep	694	1,081	64.0
Central Tajikistan		Sheep & goat	401	3,400	11.8
Southern Tajikistan		Sheep & goat	N/A	N/A	36.2
Central Tajikistan		Cattle	N/A	N/A	2.5
Tajikistan		Cattle	N/A	N/A	7.9
Tajikistan		Pigs	33	1,601	2.1
Uzbekistan	1990–2002	Sheep	N/A	N/A	62.0
Uzbekistan	1990–2002	Goat	N/A	N/A	11.0
Uzbekistan	1990–2002	Cattle	N/A	N/A	46.0
Uzbekistan	1990–2002	Camels	N/A	N/A	35.0

Table 6.3. Livestock infections in central Asia (Torgersen 2013).

(Torgersen 2013). The same report estimates that 64% of foxes in Kyrgystan are infected with *E. multilocularis*, with a mean abundance of 8,669 parasites per fox.

True or not, we know that this disease is spreading simply because there is no mechanism to limit the number of infected hosts. Strict protection brings wolves closer to human settlements, thus increasing the risk of infecting humans.

Cystic Echinococcosis and Livestock

For livestock and horses, the development of hydatid cysts is mostly asymptomatic unless the cysts cause pressure on organ tissues. If parts of the tissue die, it may impair the affected organ. The major damage from hydatid disease in livestock arises from the downgrading of edible meat by-products because of hydatid cysts.

Diagnosis in livestock is usually made after slaughter. So far, there are no reliable biochemical tests for early detection.

Torgerson's summary of livestock prevalence and transmission dynamics reported from central Asia is shown in Table 6.3 (2013).

From Russia, we learned that 250,000 to 350,000 cases of CE in livestock per year. Cysts were found in 12% to 60% of sheep between 2005 and 2009. The sheep/dog strain of *E. granulosus* (G1) is expected to be the most significant pathogen for human infections locally (Konyaev et al. 2012).

A survey was conducted to investigate the role of cattle in the transmission chain of CE in the Campania region of southern Italy. Out of a total of 434 cattle examined,

Category	Loss in USD
Liver condemnation	$141,605,195
Decreased carcass weight	$241,525,979
Decreased hide value	$34,871,148
Decreased milk production	$378,722,717
Decreased fecundity	$453,141,617
Overall cost	$1,249,866,660

Table 6.4. Global annual CE-associated livestock production losses (Budke et al. 2006)

forty-five (10.4%) were found to be infected. A total of 363 cysts were collected from the infected animals: 239 in the liver and 124 in the lungs. The cysts were either sterile (42.7%) or calcified/caseous (57.3%); no fertile cysts were found. This observation suggests that cattle do not have any role in the persistence of this zoonosis but rather are indicators of infection (Rinaldi et al. 2008).

In Ethiopia hydatid cyst in cattle were found in sixty-six cases (17.6%, n=376). The number of cysts ranged from one per organ to as many as twenty per lung and two per liver. The total number of organs with one or more cysts was fifty-eight (78.38%) in the lungs, 14(18.92 %) in the liver, 1(0.8 %) in the spleen, and 1(0.8 %) in the heart (Taha and Hassen 2018).

Economic Losses Related to Wolves

Although it seems as if dogs are responsible for spreading CE among cattle, the impact of wolves cannot be underestimated. The wolf is able to spread CE to cattle as well, and in areas where wolves constantly inhabit pastures, these become sites for infections of echinococcus (Graves 2007).

In Russia, wolves are infected with more than fifty types of intestinal worms, and they cause noticeable damage to wild ungulates by carrying echinococcus, cysticercus, and coenurus, parasitic diseases that can also infect humans. In the St. Petersburg region,

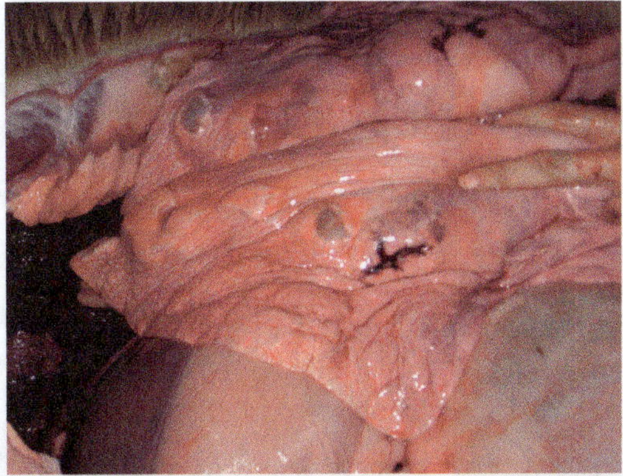

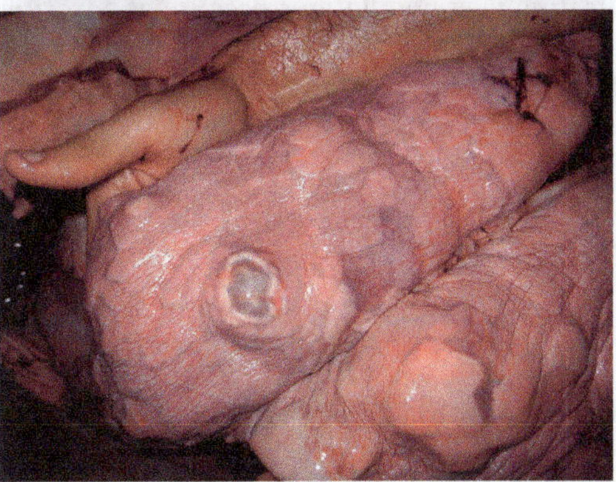

Figure 6.9. Hydatid cysts found in moose lungs (photo by Steve Alder).

when there was a serious outbreak of cysticercus, not one female moose observed had two calves. However, in the Murmansk region, where the infection rate was three times lower, all of the female moose had two calves. The same was observed in the Tambov Oblast (Graves 2007).

In Kazakhstan wolves are a serious problem for the agricultural economy, as they play a substantial role in maintaining a number of epizootic diseases, including rabies.

In Nenets Autonomous Okrug, all wolves examined were severely infected with tapeworms, including four out of five wolves with echinococcus. In Belovezhskij in 1957-1962 all eight scats of wolves examined were infected with intestinal tape worms. Nazarova noted that there is ample documentation of the negative role that wolves play in the biocoenosis by spreading various animal and human diseases. Sick animals killed by wolves may become the sources of diseases for healthy animals, which are then infected by wolves. This supports the conclusion that it is necessary to investigate the role of the wolf in epizootic diseases in the ecosystem and - conduct such research without unwarranted preconceptions (Nazarova 1978).

Summary

There is no politically correct way to cleanse a region of the *Echinococcus* parasite. In Finland, the parasite has spread into livestock populations twice. At first in the late 1960s, when it was spreading in the reindeer population, and a second time in the 1980s, when the parasite was observed in sheep in the area of Ilomantsi. In both cases, the local wolf population was eradicated and the epidemic was cut off.

Due to wolves' strict protection, eradicating wolf populations because of parasitic diseases is now most likely out of the question.

TAENIA

Taenia spp. are long, segmented, parasitic tapeworms belonging to the family *Taeniidae*, subclass *Cestoda*. These parasites have an indirect life cycle, cycling between a definitive and an intermediate host.

Taeniasis

Taeniasis is the disease of humans caused by the adult tapeworm of *Taenia saginata* or *Taenia solium*. Humans are the only definitive hosts for *T. saginata*, *T. solium*, and *T. asiatica*. Animals are the definitive hosts for *T. crassiceps*, *T. ovis*, *T. taeniaeformis*, *T. hydatigena*, *T. multiceps*, *T. serialis*, and *T. brauni*.

As definitive hosts, humans can become infected with *T. saginata* or *T. solium* when they consume infected beef or pig tissue, respectively, which has not been adequately cooked. However, the infection has no major impact on human health. Cysts are usually located in the striated muscles, but can be found in other organs as well.

Cattle are intermediate host for *T. saginata*, and pigs are intermediate host for *T. solium*, while humans are definitive hosts harboring the adult worms. *Taenia* is found globally and most prevalently where cattle are raised and beef is consumed. Humans are generally infected as a result of eating raw or undercooked beef or pork that contains the infective larvae.

Eggs or gravid proglottids are passed to the environment through feces.

Most *Taenia* species have an indirect life cycle, with dogs, wolves, and humans as final host, and livestock as intermediate hosts. We can follow the life cycle shown in Figure 6.10.

1. The final host sheds the eggs with the feces. A chain of gravid segments or single eggs are shed. The gravid segments are visible in the feces of the host or on the pelt around the anus. Individual eggs have a diameter of 31 μm to 43 μm, and thus invisible to the human eye without a microscope. Inside each egg is an *oncosphere* with six hooks. The eggs are directly infective for the intermediate hosts and can remain infective for months in a moist and cool environment but die quickly under dry and hot conditions.

2. The intermediate host (cattle or pig, shown in Figure 6.10) ingests the eggs with contaminated vegetation.

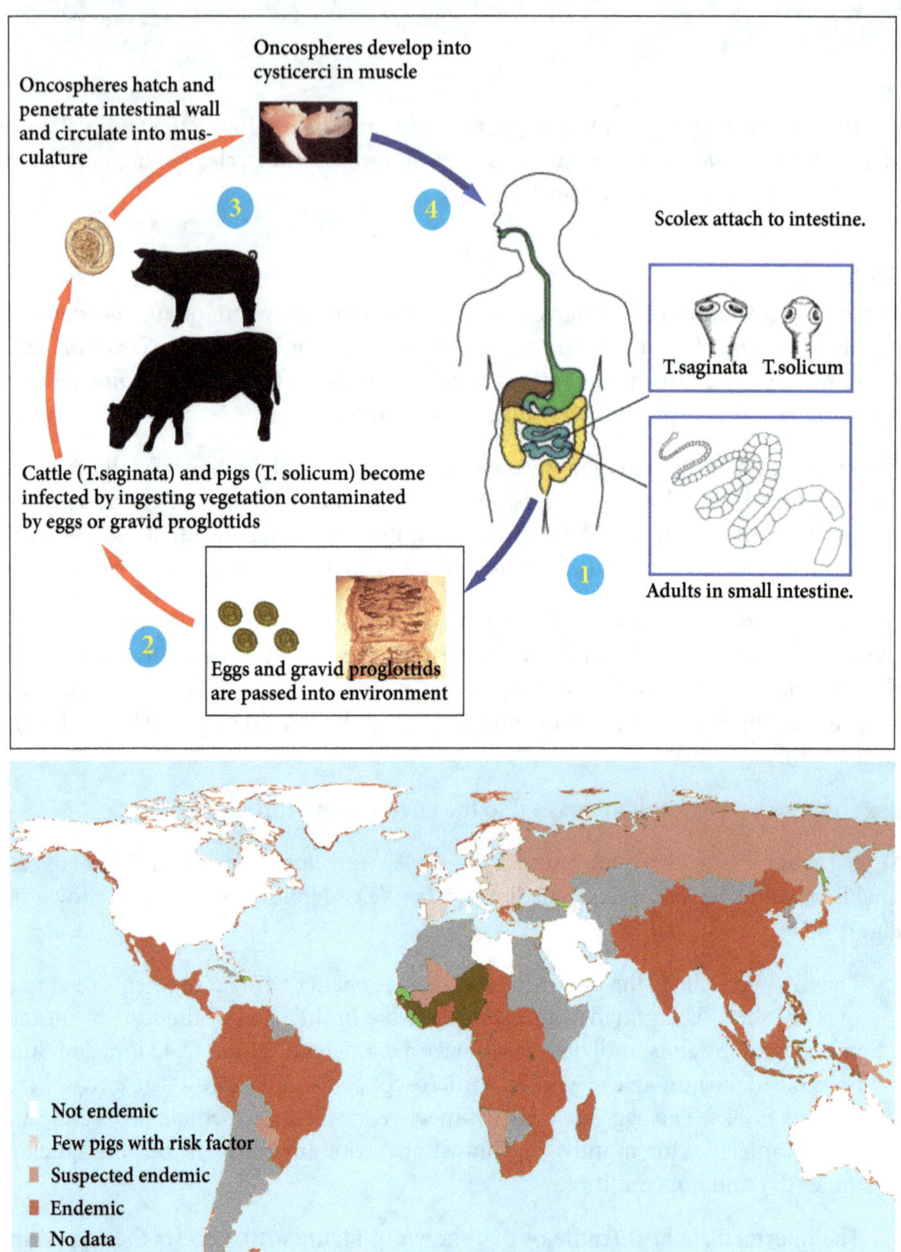

Figure 6.10 Taenia life cycle and distribution worldwide (parts from PHIL).

3. In the host's intestine, the oncospheres hatch and penetrate the intestinal wall, and then follow the bloodstream into muscles. After stopping, they develop into *cysticercoids*.

4. The final host becomes infected when it feeds on flesh contaminated with *cysticercoids*. In its intestine, the *cysticercoids* release *scolexes*, which attach to the intestinal wall and start producing *proglottids*. The *proglottid* has complete sets of both male and female reproductive parts.

The time between infection and shedding of the first eggs is from five to twelve weeks.

Definitive Host

Taenia saginata is the largest species in the genus *Taenia*. The gravid *proglottids* are at the posterior end, and an individual can have as many as 1,000 to 2,000 proglottids; *T. solium* adults have an average of 1,000 proglottids. *T. saginata* may produce up to 100,000 and *T. solium* may produce 50,000 eggs per proglottid (CDC).

The length of adult worms is usually 5 meters or less for *T. saginata* (however, it may reach up to 25 meters) and 2 to 7 meters for *T. solium*. The adults produce proglottids that mature, become gravid, detach from the tapeworm, and migrate to the anus or are passed in the stool (approximately six per day). *T. saginata* adults usually have 1,000 to 2,000 proglottids, while *T. solium* adults have an average of 1,000 proglottids. The eggs contained in the gravid proglottids are released after the proglottids are passed with the feces. *T. saginata* may produce up to 100,000 and *T. solium* may produce 50,000 eggs per proglottid (CDC).

Intermediate Host

Cattle acquire the embryonated eggs, the oncospheres, when they eat contaminated food. The larvae can move to all parts of the body the general circulatory system and settle in skeletal muscles within 70 days. Inside the tissue, they cast off their hooks and develop a cyst and become a fluid-filled *cysticerci*. The inner membrane of the *cysticercus* soon develops numerous small *scolices* that are attached to the inner surface. This parasite can be found where beef or pork is eaten, even in countries that have strict federal sanitation policies (Figure 6.10).

Cysticerosis

Infection with the larval form of *T. solium, T. saginata, T. crassiceps, T. ovis, T. taeniaeformis,* or *T. hydatigena* is called *cysticercosis*. The larvae of these organisms are called *cysticerci*. Humans can be intermediate hosts for *T. solium, T. crassiceps, T.*

ovis, T. taeniaeformis, and *T. hydatigena.* Of these five subspecies, *T. solium* is often found in humans; the other four species are very rare, and *T. solium* is the only *Taenia* species for which humans are both the definitive and intermediate host. Animals can be intermediate hosts for these five species as well as for *T. saginata* and *T. asiatica.*

Infestation with the larval forms of *T. multiceps, T. serialis,* or *T. brauni* is called *coenurosis.* The larval stage is called *coenurus.* Both humans and animals can be intermediate hosts for these three species.

Wolves and Taenia

Two species of *Taenia* tapeworms were found in Finnish and Swedish wolves: *T. hydatigena* and *T. krabbei* (Lavikainen et al. 2011). A study in Italy found *Taenia* subspecies in the local wolf population: *T. hydatigena* was identified in 19,6%, *T. krabbei* in 4.5%, and *T. ovis* in 2.2% of the samples (Gori et al. 2015). A team from Sweden reported that taenia specimens were found in wolves, of which 25 % belonged to *T. hydatigena* and 25% to *T. krabbei* (Al-Sabi et al. 2018).

Table 6.1 shows findings reported by Washington State University indicating that *Taenia spp* are carried by most wolves in the United States. Wolves carrying gastrointestinal tapeworms are usually in good body condition, suggesting that the parasite infection has no negative impact on wolves' general health (Al-Sabi et al. 2018).

From this discussion it is obvious that *T. hydatigena* spread by wolves poses a substantial threat to human health as the wolf population spreads toward human settlements.

Infection

Tapeworm infection due to *T. solium* are more prevalent in underdeveloped communities with poor sanitation and where people eat raw or undercooked pork. Higher rates of illness have been seen in people in Latin America, Eastern Europe, sub-Saharan Africa, India, and Asia. In the United States, *T. solium* is seen among Latin American immigrants. Infections due to *T. hydatigena* are relatively rare, but may increase in the future because the disease is spread by an increasing number of habituated wolves.

Taenia eggs may infect humans if they are ingested, causing infection with the larval parasite in the tissues which are called *human cysticercosis.* This infection can have devastating effects on human health. The larvae may develop in the muscles, skin, eyes, and central nervous system. When cysts develop in the brain, the condition is referred to as neurocysticercosis. Symptoms include severe headache, blindness, convulsions, and epileptic seizures, and it can be fatal. The total number of people suffering from *neurocysticercosis*, is estimated to be between 2.56 and 8.30 million (Internet A27).

A person gets cysticercosis by swallowing *T. solium* eggs found in the feces of a person who has an intestinal tapeworm. People living in the same household with someone who has a tapeworm have an extremely high risk of getting cysticercosis especially if their hygiene is poor.

Again! T. solium is the only Taenia species for which humans are both the definitive and an intermediate host!

Where animals are definitive *Taenia* hosts, humans can be intermediate hosts and infected as shown in Figure 6.11.

In the United States, *cysticercosis* is considered one of the neglected parasitic infections (NPIs), a group of five parasitic diseases that have been targeted by the CDC for public health action (Internet A28).

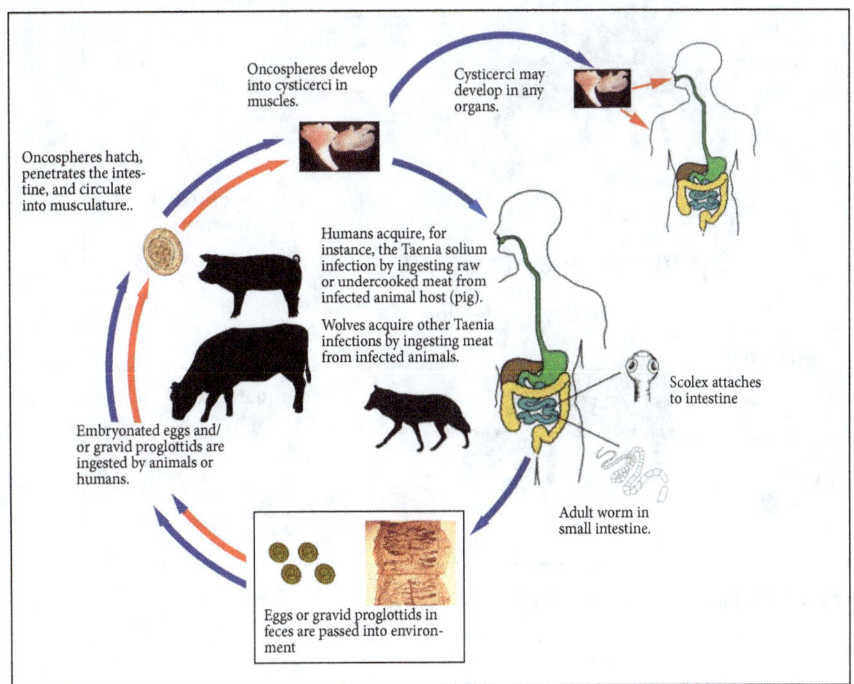

Figure 6.11. Cysticerosis (drawing by CDC).

Prevention

Infection can be effectively prevented through personal hygiene and sanitation. This includes cooking pork well, proper toilets, sanitary practices, and improved access to clean water. Adequate cooking at 56°C (133°F) for 5 minutes for beef destroys *cysticerci*. Refrigeration, freezing at −10°C (14°F) for 9 days, or long periods of salting are lethal to cysticerci (Wikipedia).

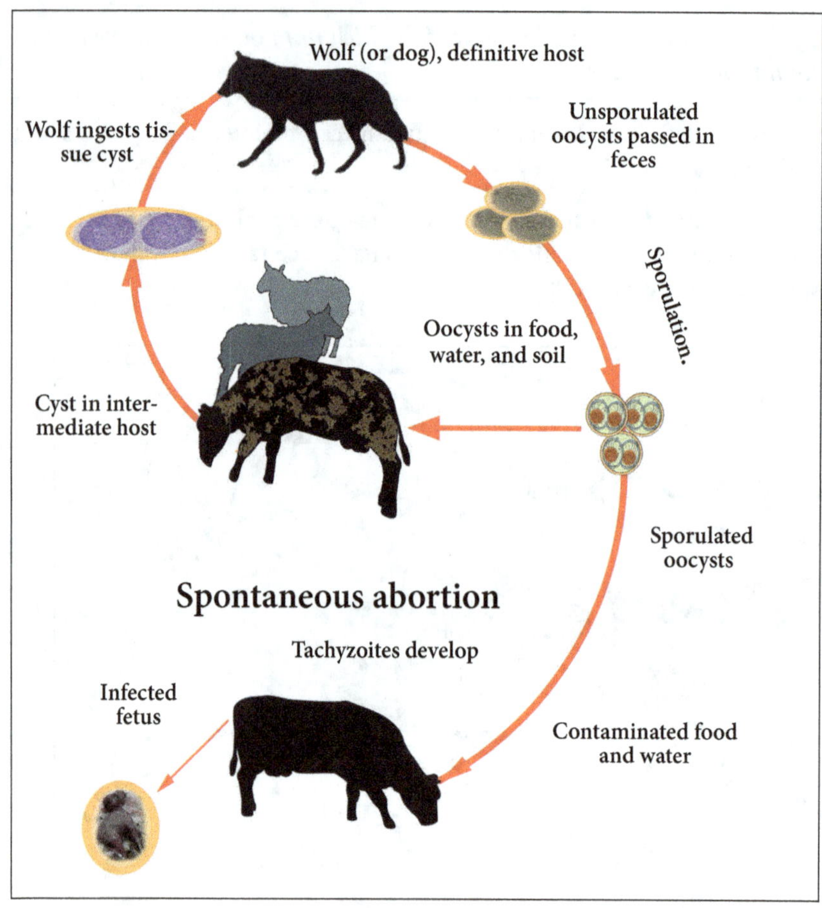

Figure 6.12. Neospora caninum cycle.

NEOSPORA CANINUM

Neospora caninum is a parasite that was identified in 1988. At the moment, *N. caninum* is recognized as the most common cause of repeated miscarriages and stillbirths in cattle, and infected herds have been reported in most parts of the world.

Zoonotic Aspects of N. caninum

Although antibodies to *N. caninum* have been reported, the parasite has not been detected in human tissues. In Denmark, serum samples from seventy-six women with a history of miscarriages were investigated for evidence of *N. caninum* infection. No antibodies to the parasite were detected (Petersen et al. 1999).

Host Range

In order to understand the epidemiology of *N. caninum*, it is important to identify its host range.

Viable *N. caninum* has been isolated from cattle, sheep, dogs, white-tailed deer, and water buffaloes. Isolation has been carried out by feeding infected tissues to dogs and then examining canine feces for oocysts (Dubey, Schares, & Ortega-Mora 2007). *N. caninum* has also been found in free-range chickens in the Henan Province of China (Feng et al. 2016).

Life Cycle and Transmission

The sexually reproductive stage of the *N. caninum* life cycle occurs in the intestine of a definitive host. Research has determined that dogs and canids such as coyotes (*Canis latrans*) and gray wolves (*Canis lupus lupus*) are definitive hosts (Gondim et al. 2004b; Dubey et al. 2011). The discovery that wolves and coyotes are definitive hosts may increase the risk of transmission of *N. caninum* to domestic livestock as well as to wild ruminants such as white-tailed deer (*Odocoileus virginianus*). Coyote ranges includes most of North and Central America.

It Starts with the Wolf, Coyote, or Dog

The environmentally resistant stage of the parasite, the oocyst, is excreted in the feces of dogs and coyotes. *Oocysts* sporulate outside the host in as few as 24 hours and oocysts can survive for months to years in the environment (Silva and Machado 2016).

Carnivores probably become infected by ingesting tissues containing *bradyzoites,* and herbivores probably become infected by ingesting food or drinking water contaminated by *N. caninum* sporulated *oocysts.* Transplacental infection can occur when *tachyzoites* are transmitted from an infected dam to her fetus during pregnancy.

Oocysts

Oocysts are a thick-walled free-living stage in the life cycle of *N. caninum.* This is the stage that is shed in the feces of wolves and dogs infected with the parasite. Oocysts are key in the epidemiology of the disease *neosporosis,* caused by infection with *N. caninum.* Wolves, coyotes, or dogs shed oocysts at the earliest five days after having ingested tissues from infected animals.

When shed, the **sporulation** process starts, when immature (noninfective) oocysts develop into the mature, infective form. Oocysts sporulate outside the host in as few as 24 hours.

Three infectious stages are identified: *tachyzoites, bradyzoites,* and *oocysts,* and all three stages can cause the transmission of the parasite.

The mature oocysts are ingested by an intermediate host, such as cattle. After ingestion of an oocyst, motile and rapidly dividing *tachyzoites* are released. These *tachyzoites* disseminate throughout the host, and in response to the host immune reaction, they differentiate into *bradyzoites,* which form cysts in muscle and tissue. Formation of these cysts results in chronic infection of the intermediate host. Ingestion of infected intermediate host tissue by the definitive host completes the life cycle (Dubey, Schares, and Ortega-Mora 2007).

There are two forms of vertical transmission. At first, when pregnant cattle ingest oocysts which can cause abortion. The other form is recrudescence of infection in a persistently infected cow during pregnancy and is the principle mechanism responsible for maintaining the parasite within cattle populations. Once infected, a cow remains infected for life and may pass infection to consecutive generations of offspring.

Bovine and N. caninum

The sporadic abortions associated with *N. caninum* in bovine herds may have an *epidemic* (a widespread occurrence of *N caninum* within a community at a particular time) or *endemic* (regularly found among particular herd or in a certain area) pattern. Spontaneous abortion outbreaks have been defined as epidemic if the abortion outbreak is temporary and if 15% of the cows at risk abort within 4 weeks, 12.5% of cows abort within 8 weeks, and 10% of the cows abort within 6 weeks (Dubey, Schares, and Ortega-Mora 2007). In contrast, an abortion problem is regarded as endemic if it persists in the herd for several months or years.

For beef cattle, there is yet no evidence that farm dogs or dogs kept in the surroundings of farms pose an infection risk. On the other hand, oocyst-contaminated pastures, fodder, and drinking water are regarded as potential sources for postnatal infection of cattle.

Diagnosis of Bovine Abortion

Serologic testing can be used to determine whether *neosporosis* is a major reproductive problem in a herd. Serum samples should be collected from aborting dams and from an equal number of matched herdmates with normal gestation. Sera should be tested and classified for *Neospora* antibodies. If most cows in the aborting group are seropositive and few are seropositive in the normal group, then *neosporosis* should be suspected as cause of abortion in the herd; this may be confirmed by statistical comparison. If most aborting cattle are seronegative, then *neosporosis* is unlikely to be a major problem (Internet A29).

Treatment and control

There is no approved treatment for *neosporosis* in cattle. Dogs are treated with prolonged administration of clindamycin or potentiated sulfa drugs. The prognosis is negatively associated with the severity of presenting clinical signs and with delayed treatment. The prognosis is poor in puppies if disease has progressed to muscular weakness in the hind-limbs (Internet A29).

In addition to being an important cause of cattle abortions, neosporosis is a significant disease in dogs throughout the world. Prevention requires an understanding of the transmission cycle, especially the connection between cattle and canids. Canids may pick up the parasite from eating infected material and spread the disease through contaminated feces.

One control method is to test for the disease and remove infected cattle from the herd. Another method of control is preventing canids from entering the cattle holding area.[

To reduce the risk of transmission of *N. caninum* in intensively farmed cattle, it is recommended to use fences and ensure careful disposal of dead stock (Gondim et al. 2004b).

SUMMARY

Biological interactions between wolves and parasites (an interspecific interaction) has created a win-win game, the result of which benefits both parts. This kind of relationship is called symbiosis. Parasites such as *E. granulosus* rely on the predator–prey relationship between the wolf as the definitive host and prey such as the moose, as an intermediate host, to complete the life cycle.

It seems as if heavy infection of parasites, such as *E. granulosus* may predispose moose to increased risk of predation by wolves. This increase in predation rate due to parasitic infection may influence the role of wolves in regulating moose populations.

From Dr. Paul R. Torgerson:

Thank you for your interest in our article. However I know little about wolves, other than there are lots of them in Kazakhstan. The primary interest was really in the parasites - especially Echinococcus granulosus. E. granulosus is a very serious zoonosis and in rural areas of Kazakhstan infects about 20% of dogs. It then transmits to people through close contact with dogs causing hydatid disease which is a large cystic lesion in your liver or lungs. The parasite naturally circulates between sheep and dogs. However the parasite almost certainly originated in wild life, probably circulating between wolves and wild ungulates. Man has been getting this disease ever since dogs were domesticated. I work with several scientists in Kazakhstan and the material for the manuscript was supplied by local hunters. In many areas wolves are considered a pest and a danger to livestock, especially as there are so many in Kazakhstan.

Dogs are the health risk to humans because of close contact. Dogs are infected through eating offal (usually sheep offal, but any infected mammal will do). Wolves are unlikely to directly transmit to humans because there is no close contact between wolves and humans.

There is no vaccine for dogs and Kazakh people do not deworm their dogs and consequently there are over 1,000 cases of human hydatid disease in Kazakhstan each year.

HUNTING WOLVES

There is only one country where wolves have been hunted since ancient times, and where wolf hunting is still going strong. That country is Russia. It is probably one of the few countries where professional wolf hunters can earn their living shooting or trapping wolves. The Russian hunting methods have been documented by scholars and writers since the early eighteenth century and most of the old methods are still in use. Only snowmobiles have changed wolf hunting from being a team endeavor to trapping and persecuting wolves.

Most of the hunting methods in this chapter are described in Will Graves's "Wolves in Russia" (Graves 2007) and Leonid Sabaneev's book "Hunting Animals" (Sabaneev 1876). Most of these methods are no longer allowed in Western countries, and the wolves in both United States and Europe are so habituated to humans that no sophisticated methods are required.

INTRODUCTION

Wolves have been actively hunted since 8,000 to 10,000 years ago, when they began to pose a threat to livestock vital for the survival of human communities. The threat wolves posed to both livestock and people was considered significant enough to warrant the conscription of whole villages under threat of punishment.

In this chapter, we shall study different methods of hunting wolves, most of which are no longer allowed.

Battue–Drive Hunting with Fladry

The most popular hunting method in Russia, Finland, and Scandinavia is hunting with flags (fladry). Hunters cut squares of cloth that are about 15 x 30 cm and attach these cloths, which are called flags, to a thin rope. The distance between flags is usually about 60 to 70 cm. The flags are most often red, but you may remember from Chapter 2 that wolves do not care because they don't see red light. The rope with the attached flags is wound on a spindle, and each spindle can carry up to three kilometers of flags.

Figure 7.1. A typical fladry (photo by the author).

The flags are mounted high enough to flap freely in the wind and they are dipped in a substance such as kerosene so that the odor will to scare off the wolves. The length of the fladry should be 10 to 15 kilometers, which is important because the exact location of the wolf pack is unknown and the distance from the fladry to the pack should be more than 1.5 kilometers.

If the wolves remain within the encircled area for longer than one day, the odor on the flags has to be masked with another smell!

The leader checks in advance whether the wolves are where they are supposed to be or whether they have moved to any neighboring terrain. Checking the nest should be done in either the evening or early morning of the appointed day. Verification is necessary because the success of round-up hunting depends on this information. Because a hunting plan is drawn up in advance, the leader has to decide the dimensions of the hunting area, the number of hounds, the length and direction of the beaters' and shooters' lines, where to use nets, and even the places where each hunter stands.

The leader should also take into consideration the weather, in particular, the direction of the wind. The line of shooters should always stand against the wind. In the case of an unfavorable wind, it is better to push the line farther from the wolves' lair. Otherwise, wolves will inevitably sense the hunters and break through the line of beaters, and all the labor and costs will be wasted.

At a distance of 2 kilometers from the nest, any noise or scream should stop. It is forbidden to even speak loudly. When the conditions of the terrain make it possible to place the shooters against the wind, then they are set up before the beaters. When it is necessary to put the shooters by the wind, then the beaters are put out first and the shooters as soon as possible.

The shooters' chain is usually placed on the circumference of the circle in a line forming a shallow arc that is concave toward the lair.

The hunt starts when the leader gives a signal, and the entire chain of beaters immediately starts shouting unanimously, knocking with sticks, pounding axes on the trunks of trees, and rattling ratchets.

Usually, at the beaters' first screams, the whole wolf pack will leave the shelter and run in the opposite direction of the beaters' sound, where no noise is heard, mostly toward strong places such as ridges between thick forests and shrubs. If possible, the wolves adhere to their path from their lair.

The best opportunities are when the wolves do not come out in a line, but gradually, one by one. However, this happens only in the beginning of autumn. Later, when the leaves have fallen, the forest is exposed and the corral is visible from a greater distance, and then the wolves do not hesitate and run out toward one of the hunters, often managing to break through the line of beaters or shooters. At that time, the wolves rely on their speed, which makes it much harder to shoot them.

This is one of the great inconveniences of late autumn hunts.

Immediately after World War II, this method of hunting was highly successful in controlling the number of wolves. However, as wolves became more accustomed to the smell of humans, this method of hunting became less successful, and the wolves began to cross under or over the line of flags.

Winter Hunting with Pskovites

The art of Pskov hunting originally comes from Lithuania, where it was used by peasants in a village on the Island of Porkhov, a district of the Pskov province. Here lived descendants of Luke and Peter, known under the name of Lukash and Petrovs. It was here that the word of Lukashi became known in the middle of the nineteenth century.

Hunting with the Pskovites derived its origin from the wolf's simple habit of following the same paths, especially in winter when the snow is deep. Even today, in many wooded and mountainous regions of Russia and Siberia, in the winter and sometimes even in the late fall, one or two trappers can circle around wolves and quietly, without hurrying, drive them toward a hidden shooter.

This method has been in use for time immemorial and has not been subject to any changes or improvements. The main drawback of this simple hunting method is that success is directly dependent on the direction of the wind. It is successful only when the wind blows away from the wolves and toward the shooter.

In order to make the wolf go in the desired direction, that is, downwind, they drive it quietly, almost without shouting, so that it proceeds a short distance from the beaters in the opposite direction, approximately to the edge of the forest or a glade, where it waits for the hunters. As the wolf calmly moves away from the beater's neighborhood, it has to watch for suspicious objects, and prefers to go where the terrain is free. When the wolves put their attention on the beater, they don't sense the hidden shooters, but approaches them at the closest distance.

This is still far from the real hunting in the Pskov way, where it is possible to say exactly where the wolf or fox will go, obeying the order as if it were tied to a leash.

Preparing for the Hunt

The use of carrion is much more important in winter hunting than it is at other times, and the benefits are significant. It saves a lot of time needed for reconnaissance, and the carrion keeps wolves in place for several days, giving time to collect beaters and hunters. Usually, the carrion is placed shortly before the onset of winter, meaning in early or mid- October, depending on the terrain. Thus, wolves learn to walk to carrion in advance. It is only necessary to put out a new carcass, and you can be almost certain that the wolves will come the next night. For wolves, horse or cow carcasses are used.

The carrion is always placed in open places like in a paddock or field, at some distance from bushes, marshes, islands, or detached small forests–in general a good place for the wolf and at the same time convenient for hunting. After eating, the wolf will probably rests somewhere in the nearby surroundings, usually less than a mile from the carrion.

Locating The Wolves

When fresh tracks have been found, the wolves have to be tracked to the place where they rest. As soon as the track reaches a solid place where it can be assumed that the wolves will lie down, the tracker begins to look for a detour; he must circle around the location to make sure there are no tracks leading out of it. While doing this, absolute silence must be observed in order to not frighten the wolves away.

The leader and most experienced beater places the shooters, while the others hang the nets—one on the right, another on the left, and along also the edge of the forest behind the place where the wolves lie.

Usually, the beaters are placed in such a way that the best shooters are in the middle of the chain and the other two are at a some distance from the middle.

The Beaters

The success of the hunt depends on the uniformity of screaming and the accuracy of the beaters' progress. The cry of all three beaters must be exactly the same in strength, as well as in intervals between cries, during which he listens to the voices of his comrades and conforms with them. Each gap should last approximately five seconds. The most convenient cry is a four-syllable one with an accent on the last syllable, almost like a rooster's singing. These monotonous and equivalent exclamations are called ordinary screams. But when the terrain demands that the voice of one of the beaters be heard more strongly, then the beater should be ordered to shout with a cry and clap.

Success depends on the vocalization of all three beaters, and if even one of them fails, there is no use in continuing the hunt.

The correct course is when all three beaters move forward at exactly the same speed so that the distance between the middle beater and both flanks remains entirely equal. Any slight deviation in either direction by the middle beater should be immediately corrected.

Hearing a cry, the wolf immediately rises, listens to the sound, and tries to go in the opposite direction. If he hits a flank, then after observing the nets, he takes a new direction and eventually runs straight toward the beaters' line. However, the reason for this is not its stupidity, but the fact that the wolf panics at being unable to figure out what is going on around him.

When all the rules are observed and the beaters master their craft, the wolf can be exposed to any one of the shooters if the chief beaters know where the shooters stand.

Figure 7.2. A wolf escaping through the fladry (photo composed by the author).

The Shooters

The optimal number of shooters is three or four. In deep snow, wolves go in a line, stepping in each other's paw prints, and consequently, they all exit in one direction. At the first shots, the rear wolves rush to where they do not see any nets, which means rushing toward the next shooter. Sometimes it happens that after the old wolves, who were mostly coming first in line, are killed, the young wolves run several times under gunfire or panic and run directly toward the shooters.

Hunting with Nets

The real wolf net should be knit from thick and strong twineso that the wolf could not tear the net or cut it. The mesh size should be large enough for a wolf to be able to put its entire head and neck up to the shoulders in the net.

The height should be at least 2 meters (7 feet) but not more than 3 meters (10 feet). The length of each net should be from 30 to 80 meters, and the net is made to be pulled on a thick rope. The more of these nets are available, the more space that can be covered by them and the more likely the hunt will be successful.

The best time for hunting with nets is late autumn and early winter, when the snow in the forest is not deeper than 60 cm (2 feet). This depth of snow does not prevent hunters from moving in the forest, but it will tire the wolves.

The nets are hung on a slack rope attached to tree branches or support, located 5 to 10 meters from each other and inclined toward the beaters, with the lower edge of the net lying half a yard on the ground and firmly attached to the ground with small pegs to prevent the wolves from slipping under it.

Figure 7.3. A typical configuration when hunting with nets (photo by the author).

When walking without hurry, the wolf always notices the net and follows it. If it does not find an outlet, it tries to raise the lower edge with its muzzle. But if the beaters pursue the wolf, then it rushes into the net and gets its head entangled, and in its efforts to keep moving forward, overturns itself, gets tangled with its paws, and finds itself in a poke.

Hunting With Carrion

The wolf's sense of taste is weakly developed. The best evidence of this is its extreme indiscrimination regarding food and sometimes the wolf even prefers rotten meat over fresh. This is because the wolf does not taste bitter flavors (Sabaneev 1876). However, in the summer, when the smell from carrion is much stronger, wolves go to it only in the absence of live prey. In winter, when the weather is cold, they only smell carrion at a close distance, and when looking for food, they most often follow the raven's scream or the crow's croak.

The choice of placement is extremely important, and it should not be placed too close to human settlements. Usually, a good location is at the edge of small forests, near the crossroads of low-traffic roads. A small hut should be built close to the carrion in early autumn before, the hunt is intended to start. The hut should be just large enough to hold a seated person which is about 1.5 meters (5 feet) in width and depth. A half-yard-high ledge is used as a seat. The floor should be covered with fresh horse manure. If the terrain allows, the hut should be placed on a steep slope descending toward the carrion (Figure 7.4)

Figure 7.4. A typical carcass and a hut. This hut is for photography, not for hunting, but the principle is the same (photo by Tapani Pääkkönen).

Early in the autumn, the carrion is placed on a pile of hay some 30 meters from the hut. When the wolves start to feed on the carrion, a new one should be brought without touching the bones of the previous carrion. The new carrion is dumped with its head or tail turned toward the hut. Otherwise, the wolves can hide behind the carcass as soon as they notice something. If the carcass is not put out in the autumn but out in the winter, it should be taken to the place with a so-called potato, which is a piece of roasted meat (preferably a roasted cat) attached to a rope and dragged along in the snow behind the sled. Having placed the carcass, the horse and sled should circle around the carrion in various directions to ensure that the wolves, after finding the trail, quickly locates the carrion.

How do wolves approach carrion? Elis Pålsson describes in his book (1984) how wolves reacted to small changes at a carrion.

Russian researchers placed a coat on a branch of a tree some 150 meters from the carrion. The next day wolves did not approach closer than 300 meters from the carrion but escaped. Three days later they came no closer than 200 meters from the carrion. One week later one wolf passed the carrion at a distance of 80 meters. Two weeks later two wolves came no closer than 30 meters from the carrion and three weeks later the wolves visited the carrion but did not eat anything from it. After four weeks the pack returned as normal and accepted the coat.

When reconnaissance shows that the carcass has been visited by wolves, the ambush may start. Approaching the hut is done with great precautions. Stopping at the door that faces toward the field, the hunter enters the hut from the sleigh without, touching the ground outside the hut. His partner continues in the same direction and makes his detour as large as possible. All this is done in order to not raise suspicions and to deceive the cautious and sensitive wolves. Despite taking every precaution the wolves may not come on a bright night.

The hunter's gun must be cleaned and loaded with large buckshots. Since there is rarely a possibility to fire more than one shot, there is no need for a double-barrel shotgun, and most convenient is the single-barrel of the largest caliber, from which, when a whole pack comes, several wolves can be killed or at least wounded. In general, one should wait until a number of wolves come to the site and they begin to bicker with each other.

Just in case one of the old wolves is killed, the young ones sometimes turn back to the carrion. Thus, it may pay off to not leave the hut after the first shot but, rather, wait for an hour or two. Wounded wolves can be traced the next morning.

Hunting with Eagles and Falcons

Hunting with eagles and falcons in Kazakhstan and parts of Mongolia dates back to 2000 BC. This is the only region in the world with such a long and unbroken tradition of this type of hunting. This heritage is threatened now, as presently, the number of eagle hunters has been reduced to just a few old men. The eagle hunter will walk, or if on horseback, trot, over the Kazakh Steppe with his right arm resting on a wooden fork called a baldak, which is attached to his saddle.

Perched on his right hand is a trained eagle, some of them weighing up to five kilograms. If the hunter spots any prey, he removes the leather hood, that covers the eagle's eyes. The bird immediately spots the prey, which could have been a wolf or a fox. An eagle can have a wingspan of almost 2 meters and can dive at a speed of 100 kilometers per hour. The eagle lands upon its prey and seizes the animal in its huge claws, then holds the prey until the hunter arrives.

It takes time to train an eagle to capture prey animals. A young eagle may be taken from a nest and trained, but the preferred method is to capture a wild bird that already knows how to hunt. The training takes months, but once the relationship is established between the eagle and its master, real hunting can begin. The eagle's eyesight is said to be eight times better than a human's. If the hunter sends his eagle after a wolf, the hunter must be close by, as a wolf can kill or wound an eagle if the eagle does not immediately grab the wolf by the neck or head.

The golden eagle is the symbol of an independent Kazakhstan and is on the national flag as well as on the tails of the jet airplanes of Kazakhstan Airlines.

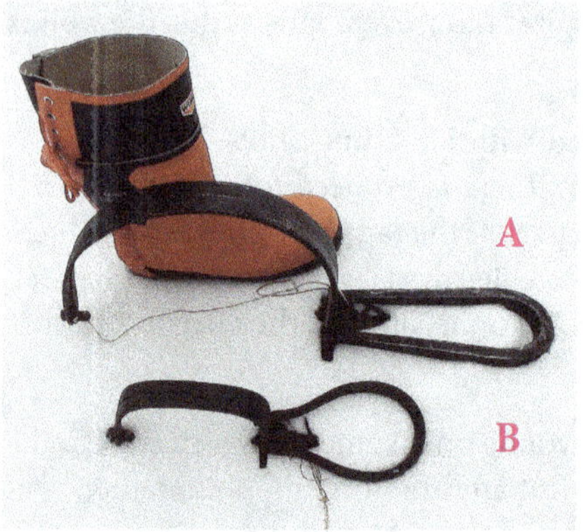

Figure 7.5. Homemade swan neck traps from the nineteenth century (photo by the author).

This ancient type of hunting with eagles is still wide spread in Kazakhastan. The hunters are called kusbegy and most of the hunting is for foxes, but saiga, roe deer, and rabbits are also hunted, and sometimes, a hunter will send his eagle, if it is a large one, to attack a wolf.

Hunting with eagles starts in October and usually stops when the snow melts.

Trapping Wolves

In its simplest form, the trap consists of two iron arcs connected by a hinge and one large spring. Such traps, called arc or swan neck, are used with a piece of bait placed in the trap, as shown in Figure 7.5. Their action is based on the fact that as soon as the beast pulls the bait attached to a rope or string and connected to the trigger of the lock located between the spring, the lock jumps out, releases the arcs, and the arcs then slam together. The trap catches the wolf by its neck. Modern wolf traps like the Alaskan wolf trap MB-750, catch wolves when they step on the trap, and they get caught by their foot.

Since the wolf has a very good sense of smell, and iron, especially rusted iron, has a rather strong smell that even humans can sense, one of the main conditions for the success with this method is that the trap has no odor. The traps should be boiled in water that contains pine clippings and pine boughs. After boiling, the traps must be dried in the air and not touched by humans unless special gloves are worn. Before activating the trap, it is dipped in hot wax and hung up to dry.

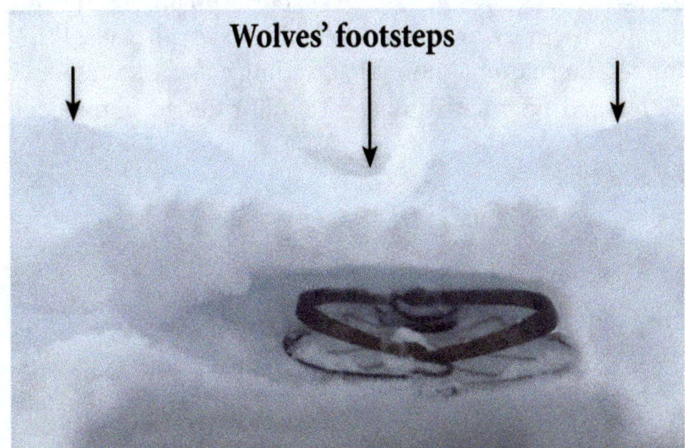

Figure 7.6. A wolf trap under the wolf's trail (Photo by the author).

The trapper must not smoke near the traps. There are special techniques for setting the traps, and only a highly skilled trapper will be able to catch a wolf, but Russian peasants who grew up in remote rural areas often developed the skills to trap wolves. Figure 7.6 shows how a trap is placed under a wolf's trail. Because the wolves use the same trail over and over, they also step in the old footsteps. Thus, placing a trap under the footstep grants a successful hunt.

Due to the fact that traps can only be placed under wolf tracks, it is more convenient to catch them in the winter than in the summer, and the trapper must make sure the wolf path is a permanent trail, not an accidental one.

Siberian wolf hunters have observed that the alpha female, instead of walking first in line, forces youngsters to act as minesweepers and sacrifices them rather than get caught in the traps herself. As a result, hunters using this method catch more youngsters with less valuable fur than they otherwise would.

Catching wolves with traps is the most popular method used by professional wolf hunters in Siberia. Because of the extremely cold Siberian climate, the traps do not collect wet snow, which would prevent them from firing at freezing temperatures.

Catching wolves with traps is allowed in Idaho and Montana, but both states require trappers to take a wolf-specific trapper education class. However, some states in the United States have banned leghold traps.

In Europe, the situation is similar. EU Council Regulation (EEC) No, 3254/91 prohibits the use of leghold traps in the European Union as well as the introduction into the EU of pelts and manufactured goods made from certain wild animal species originating in countries that catch them by means of leghold traps or that use trapping methods which do not meet international humane trapping standards. The EU Member States have each designated national competent authorities to implement this Regulation.

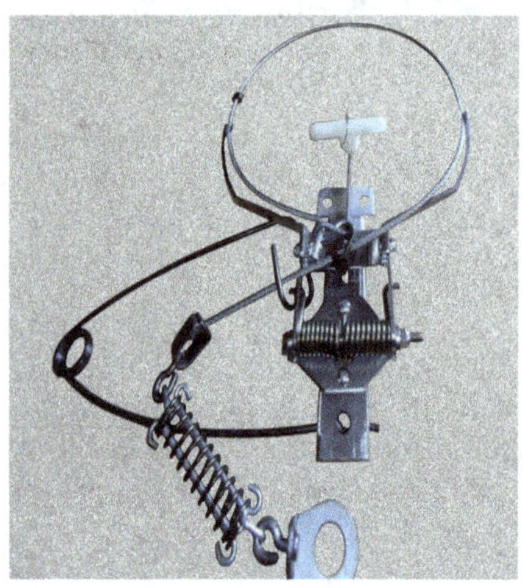

Figure 7.7. A Collarum™ trap (photo by the author).

The Collarum™ Trap.

A growing concern for animal welfare, combined with the need to capture and handle specific species for conservation, management, or recreational purposes has fueled the scientific evaluation of different capture methods.

The Collarum™ trap is a spring-loaded mechanism that throws a non-choking loop over the canine's head, which secures the animal as a tether keeps them in place. It is designed to capture canines only, and as the end of the capture loop is anchored in the ground, the canine is held like a dog on a leash.

The trigger mechanism is what makes it canine-specific, because it requires a pull action rather than the push mechanism normally employed by traps. The trap is also much safer to utilize in areas where people, pets, and other domestic animals could come in contact with it. Animals other than canines are very unlikely to be caught by this device even if they spring it, and captured domestic dogs can be released with no harm done.

Licensing of this trap in Europe is in process, and it can currently be used in UK and Spain.

Hunting with Wolfhounds

Russian landowners and Cossacks hunted wolves with Russian Wolfhounds prior to the Socialist Revolution in 1917. When hunting a wolf, the hunters stayed close to the hounds so they could kill the wolf quickly because they did not want their dogs to be mauled by a large wolf.

Beaters holding up to six scent dogs on leashes enter an area where wolves have been sighted. The hunters, on horseback, select a place in the open fields where the wolves may break out. Each hunter holds one or two Borzois, which are released when the wolf escapes out of the forest. Once the beater sights a wolf, he shouts "Wolf! Wolf! Wolf!" and releases the dogs. This method traps the wolf between the pursuing scent dogs and the hunters on horseback with their borzois outside the forest. Once the wolf is caught by the borzois, the foremost rider dismounts and quickly euthanizes the wolf with his knife.

The essence of this style of hunting lies in the fact that the hunters take the scent hounds to the wolf's track. These dogs drive the wolves out of the forest, swamp, or the ravine—in short, away from any kind of shelter and out to an open place where hunters with greyhounds or borzois wait for them. When the wolf approaches, the hunter closest to the wolf releases his pack of borzois, which stop the wolf and hold it with their teeth until the hunter euthanizes the wolf.

Winter hunting can only be successful with borzois. Often, in steppe areas, in the semi-desert, or desert regions of Kazakhstan, hunters on horseback searched for wolves while their wolfhounds rode in the sleds. When wolves were spotted, the borzois was released from the sleds, and the hunt began. It ended when the Borzois kept the wolf in place and the hunter arrived and quickly dispatches the wolf by stabbing it between the shoulder blades with a dagger.

This method was also used in France by the Royal Wolfcatchers (louvetere).

Hunting with Pigs

Hunting with a pig originated in Poland and Lithuania, and from there, it came to Russia, Finland, and Scandinavia. Experiments have shown that a dog's squeal is more attractive for wolves, and therefore, in places where there were very few or no pigs, a dog could be used instead of a pig.

The idea of hunting with a piglet arose from the facts that wolves attacked dogs with audacity in the winter, not only in forest and not only at night or at dusk, but even in broad daylight. So people concluded that a dog could be used to lure a wolf into a gunshot. Later, the dog was replaced by a more vociferous piglet, which wolves consider tastier and thus more attractive.

Figure 7.8. A wolf caught by greyhounds (painting by Alfred Kowalski).

Hunting with a piglet starts as several hunters with guns and a piglet ride to places where wolves usually roam, and when the wolves are attracted by the shriek of a pig they approach the shooter. For this reason, hunting is successful only when there are a lot of wolves and their hunger forces them to forget all caution. This is possible in winter and when predators are taking the town mongrels, catching all the hares in the neighborhood, and wandering along country roads because of the deep snow.

Based on the wolf way of life, hunting with a pig is best at the beginning of wolves' estrus season, when old wolves are running and young ones are left without experienced leaders.

The best bait is a half-year-old pig whose duty is to scream all night. The more noise, the better. A pig shrieks when it is taken by the ear, and pigs with erect ears are favored as they seem to be much more sensitive than pigs with floppy ears. A good pig should not squeal incessantly, but only as soon as it is taken by the ear.

Despite the most desperate scream of a pig, wolves do not approach hunters in a sled. So in order to stimulate the wolf's appetite, hay sewn into a bag, then tied with a thin rope no longer than 20 meters and pulled behind the sled to give the appearance of a pig running after the sled.

Hunting with a piglet is all the better on a quiet and moonlit night, because in windy weather, the squeal is heard only in one direction. The frantic squeal of a piglet on a quiet night is heard a mile away. Wolves attracted by this squeal run out on the trail or onto the road, and when they sense the smell of a pig, run after the sled (Figure 7.10).

Figure 7.9. Hunting with a pig (painting by Alfred Kowalski).

In order for the wolves to not notice the deception, and to further provoke them, the horses are driven at a fast trot. Wolves rush to the sled, and at that moment the driver stops the horse, and the hunters, having agreed in advance which direction each one shoots, open fire.

Scouting for Wolves and Finding Dens

Searching for and finding wolf dens is one of the traditional methods used in Russia to control wolves. When Russian hunters need to locate dens, they use some of the following techniques:

1. Watch for crow and magpie activity over a particular area. These birds often circle around or over a wolf den, waiting for scraps of food.

2. Watch for trails from water sources to the dens. Wolves often leave clear trails back and forth from water sources.

3. Watch for wolf tracks in early morning frost or dew, as these tracks are easy to follow.

4. Be alert for the smell of rotten meat, as a wolf den may be nearby.

5. In some situations, a well-trained dog may help, but the dog must be kept on a leash.

Howling is an old method of locating wolves' dens. At the beginning of summer, the wolves begin to howl at night, and the location of the brood are easily determined. As long as the cubs don't move around by themselves, the wolf's howl is almost inaudible because the old wolves are afraid of revealing the location of their defenseless offspring. Most of the early summer, howling is a kind of roll-call between pack members.

Figure 7.10. A wolf pit (photo by Georg Waß-muth).

The wolves howl starting before sunset, and at dawn, they go looking for prey. Hence, in quiet weather and with some skill, it is possible to count how many wolves there are in a lair and possibly even determine their age.

In order to find the den, an experienced scout takes one or two assistants with him to who listen to the howling from opposite sides. To avoid being revealed, the scouts need to find out when the old wolves have left the den. They do this with an imitation of a male wolf. If the old wolf is nearby, he will respond to the howling. If the cubs are hungry, they respond immediately. Experienced whining can even entice wicked wolves who take him for a lone intruder and rush toward the voice in order to drive the stranger out of their territory. It is even possible for the scout to go closer to the lair and howl early, when the old wolves are still at home, when the wolves will walk some ten to fifteen steps towards the scout and eventually get shot (Sabaneev 1876).

Late in the autumn, wolves very rarely respond to the voice of the hunter luring the wolf by imitating their howling.

Wolves protect the pets in the neighborhood of their lairs because they are afraid to expose the dens to humans, and when there is enough food, cattle may graze safely almost next to the wolf's den. This explains why the peasants in villages close to a den did not try to exterminate the young cubs and even tried to hide their location, thus making it difficult for hunters to find the dens.

Sabaneev describes how some peasants, in order to avoid having adult wolves attack livestock on pastures close to the den, would cripple the cubs and then kill them later that autumn. In such cases, the alpha pair continued to nurse the cubs without knowing that the cubs were unable to take care of themselves (1876).

On the first powder snow, the crippled wolves were localized and a caught with snares, and shot.

In some Russian provinces, extermination of wolves in this way was common.

Although this was done in order to avoid wolves' surplus killing of livestock in the autumn, it gives us a good view of how our relationship to animals has changed.

Hunting with Wolf Pits

Trapping pits are deep pits dug into the ground in order to trap animals. European rock drawings and cave paintings reveal that elk and moose were hunted since the stone age using trapping pits. In Northern Scandinavia, it is still possible to find remains of trapping pits. In central Finland, there are large areas with dozens of pits used to catch wild reindeer.

Wolf pits, which were camouflaged with branches and leaves and baited with carrion, had steep sides lined with masonry, making it impossible for the wolf to escape once it had fallen in. Figure 7.10 shows a typical wolf pit near Hohenwart, Bavaria, Germany.

Hunting with Poison

Historically, poisoning was very successful in reducing wolf populations, and strychnine was the most frequently used compound. Strychnine is a highly toxic, colorless, bitter crystalline alkaloid. When swallowed by wolves, strychnine poisoning results in muscular convulsions and death.

The poison was typically mixed in lard or tallow and spread on pieces of meat or placed within incisions on the bait. Though effective, the method had the disadvantage of greatly loosening the wolf's fur, so wolves killed by strychnine were typically skinned immediately after death in order to avoid the fur absorbing too much of the poison. The toxic and medicinal effects of Strychnos nux-vomica have been well known since ancient times, although the chemical compound itself was not identified and characterized until the nineteenth century.

In 1818, strychnine production begun and the extermination of wolves escalated to new dimensions. In 1818, in France, the Minister of the Interior, Lane, sent out a circular to the prefects requesting the mayors to order the hunting guard or field guard to manufacture strychnine poison and place the poison where it would be consumed by wolves (Sabaneev 1876).

Additionally, the notion that wolves in Russia could be eradicated, or their numbers significantly reduced, through the use of poison gained prominence with the 1876 publication of a seventy-page brochure entitled "On the Destruction of Domestic Livestock and Wild Game by Wolves and on the Eradication of Wolves." The author was V. M. Lazarevskii, who had been commissioned by the Russian government to investigate the "wolf problem," and his findings, based upon extensive analysis of statistics from the year 1873, were published as a supplement to the Government Bulletin.

Sabaneev writes in his book (1876):

> *With all these ways of hunting I had come to the conclusion that the only rational way of exterminating wolves is poisoning them.*

As we all know, Russia failed in their efforts to exterminate the wolf.

D. Plotnikov reported that from 1961 to 1963 in the Yakutskij ASSR, about 100,000 doses of barium (*floratsetata bariya*) were used to poison wolves. There were also three to five airplanes assigned to assist. The Council of Ministers of the Yakutskij ASSR recommended that collective and state farms award hunters with one colt or one reindeer for every male wolf killed and two reindeer for each female wolf with cubs. Approximately 24.6% of all the wolves killed in the RSFSR in 1963 were killed with poison (1,239 out of a total of 5,045 adult wolves).

Information in *The Book of the Hunter* describes how poison was used in Kazakhstan to control the number of wolves. Barium and carefully prepared phenobarbital were used.

Poisoning wolves has now been banned all over the world.

Hunting Wolves from Light Aircraft

In the former Soviet Union reports had begun to drift into state wildlife management and agricultural offices that pilots of small planes flying at relatively low altitudes were seeing numerous wolves from the air. Often, these pilots were sport hunters, and they had developed habits of looking for game animals when they were flying. These pilots suggested that light aircraft could be used to help control the number of wolves.

Around 1946, the Soviet Union started a campaign to exterminate wolves. The scope of this effort was huge. For example, in just one year, 1946, the Soviets culled 62,600 wolves. But over many years the Soviets gradually changed this policy from extermination of the wolf to control of wolf populations (Graves 2007).

The Chief Directorate of Civil Aviation took the first action in 1946. An organized effort to shoot wolves from aircraft was initiated based on the reports of the pilots. A few top shooters and aircraft were formed into a special expedition in order to determine if this new method would be successful and practical. It was not known at that time if pilots would be skillful enough to bring the shooters into good shooting range if the shooters would be able to hit the wolves with any consistency. The experiment was first tried in the Kalinin region. Although few funds and resources were available, it was discovered that shooting wolves from small planes was not only possible, but it was an excellent method of controlling the number of wolves (Graves 2007).

Members participating in the experiment came to the conclusion that the best type of plane available in the USSR at that time for shooting wolves was the Polikarpov PO-2 (Figure 7.11). The PO-2 may be fitted with skis (C model) or with wheels (A model). It was a single-engine biplane and was used in the USSR for passenger and cargo transport. The plane could take off and land in small, flat areas, which meant it could land almost anywhere in the steppe regions.

The PO-2 was designed to operate at low altitudes and has three open cockpits. The pilot sits in the first, the shooter in the second, and killed wolves were placed in the third. Sometimes, the dead wolves were tied to the fuselage or wings of the plane. The third or rear cockpit could hold four wolves. In addition to the four wolves in the last cockpit, two dead wolves could be put in the shooter's cockpit (if he sat on them). The plane was fully loaded when carrying two men and five full-grown wolves. This was in addition to carrying enough gas to last for six and a half hours' flying time.

The Soviets learned from experience that shooting wolves from a PO-2 was highly effective. Almost every wolf seen from this plane on the steppes or tundra was killed. It was also possible to land the PO-2 near the killed wolves in most cases.

The PO-2 was an old model, and in the 1960s it lost most of its duties to the new AN-2, which was built according to specifications ordered by the Soviet Ministry of Agriculture and Forestry.

Figure 7.11. A PO-2 A replica (photo by Alan Wilson).

The Hunt

The best time to hunt wolves from planes is during their mating season near the end of January and February. During this period, wolves stay in the open all day, making it easier to spot them from the air. Once the pack is spotted, it is most effective to try killing the alpha female first, because she often runs in front of the pack. If this is done, the other wolves do not tend to run off so fast or far, and it is often possible to kill every wolf in the pack. If the first shot kills the alpha male, then the female turns rapidly away for cover, and the other wolves then also flee.

The normal protocol when flying was that the pilot would look for wolves to the front, and the shooter would look to each side. This meant that 70% to 80% of the wolves would be seen by the pilot first.

The shooting was complicated due to the varying circumstances. At the moment when the plane overtook a wolf—about 30 to 45 meters away—usually the wolf would usually change its direction. Sometimes a wolf would throw itself at the plane. For all these reasons, accurate shooting from a plane is difficult, and different circumstances occurred on each and every flight. Most shooters preferred to shoot toward the rear and left of the plane as this angle is the most advantageous for the shooter; it is also the safest angle to shoot from the PO-2.

Some wolves learned to pretend they had been hit and would lie still and then suddenly come to life after the plane had landed. Occasionally, one would charge at the plane and have to be shot at close range. The pilots learned not to land close to a shot wolf, but to taxi toward it with the shooter prepared to shoot.

The shooter would watch the wolf's ears when approaching one that had been shot and is lying on the ground. If the ears were sticking up, the wolf was not capable of attacking, but if they were folded back and the wolf appeared to not be breathing, then the wolf would be shot again. The wolves often surprised the shooters with their toughness and ability to survive numerous hits from buckshot at close range.

Figure 7.12. An AN-2 (photo by Sergey Ryabtsev).

A wounded wolf is one of the most difficult targets because it would move away from the plane as the plane was being turned around, but when the plane approached, it would turn toward the plane, snarling. These circumstances resulted in the shooter having very little time to plan his shot.

Summary

Hunting was the primary means of survival for humans for many thousands of years, and then, step by step, hunting slowly became a sport. Sport hunting was first done only by the wealthy, but gradually, it became more available to the general public.

To many non-hunters, those who did hunt were the violators of nature. Hunters were accused of destroying game, which was considered by some to be damaging to nature, and those people wanted to stop sport hunting. Some newspapers and magazines attacked sport hunters and proposed banning many types of traps they used. Various reforms were proposed–ranging from limiting hunting methods, to outlawing every type of hunting.

To some nature protectors, there is a precise link between shots from a gun and the reduction of animals in the world. To them, every sport hunter falls into the category of enemy of all animals. Much time and effort needs to be made to convince people that most wild game is not being destroyed by hunters, but by bulldozers and land development.

Protecting nature does not mean that coexisting with nature, such as by banning all sport hunting. Protecting nature means using it intelligently–and using science to help develop conservation policy and wildlife management. An educated, conscientious hunter harvests game in a sustainable manner. When scientific studies done by professional wildlife managers conclude that there are too many predators of a certain type in a certain area, skilled hunters can be used to help control the predators in efforts to restore a balance.

One point sometimes made against hunting is that the killing of wild animals and birds is immoral. This is a strange accusation when every day, all over the world, millions and millions of domesticated animals and birds are killed to feed humans. How can one differentiate between the wild and domesticated animal? Harvesting wild game animals and birds produced a great deal of meat that was badly needed in the USSR. The annual production of game reported in 1981 was 60,000 to 70,000 moose; over 300,000 saiga antelopes; 50,000 to 55,000 roe deer; tens of thousands of wild boar, red deer, caribou, musk deer, wild goats, and sheep; and several million various types of rabbits. The harvest of wild game birds is about 25,000,000 to 30,000,000 each year. Together, this amounts to tens of thousands of tons of meat urgently required for human nutrition.

BEHIND THE BOOK

This last chapter is divided into four sections. The first one introduces some less known scholars referenced in this book. The second section contains literature cited and the third section Internet links referenced. The last section contains obsolete Russian units of measurement.

Section I – Scholars Behind the Curtain

Some information about Russian scientists and other well-known wolf experts that I have referred to in this book.

Korytin, Sergei Aleksandrovich

S.A. Korytin was born in 1922. In 1947, he enrolled in hunting studies at the Moscow Medical Academy, then continued with graduate school, and from 1956 until the end of the century, he worked as a professor at VNIIOZ (Research institute in Kirov). His pen produced more than three hundred works, including scientific articles, books, pamphlets, popular scientific works and naturalistic sketches beloved by the readers of the magazine *Hunting*.

Krushinsky, Leonid Viktorovich

Leonid V. Krushinsky (1911–1984) was a Russian biologist, corresponding member of the Russian Academy of Sciences, laureate of the Lenin Prize, and professor of the Lomonosov Moscow State University in the scientific fields of biology, ethology, and genetics.

Lazarevskij, Vasily Matveyevich

V.M. Lazarevskij was born on February 26, 1817 and died April 28,1890 in St. Petersburg. Lazarevskij was a great connoisseur of the animal world, an authority in the field of hunting and the author of a number of studies. He gained special fame in 1876 after the publication of his book *On the Destruction of the Wolf by Livestock and Game and On the Destruction of the Wolf.*

In his time, the wolf was a real scourge for the peasantry, and Lazarevskij got access to a large quantity of statistical material collected by the government and Zemstvos. His work was the first serious study of the "wolf question" in Russia and prompted numerous responses. Lazarevskij's book has never been reprinted.

Lindqvist, Bernt

Bernt Lindqvist was born on December 30, 1930, at Lerhaga estate outside Södertälje, Sweden. He had a long career as a lawyer specializing in hunting issues, and from 1975 to 2000, he worked as a specialist for the Swedish government shaping, among others, current Swedish hunting legislation. From 1982 to 2009, he worked as a consultant in hunting issues for the Russian government and the Russian Federal Game Administration. He has been decorated for his contributions to the Russian government by both President Yeltsin (2000) and President Putin (2003).

Nyholm, Erik S.

Erik S. Nyholm was born in 1929 and is considered one of the most prominent Finnish expert on large carnivores. He has a special interest in bears and wolves. Nyholm earned his doctorate degree in 1965 and spent his entire career as a researcher at the Finnish Fish & Game (RKTL). With a special relationship to animals and nature, he never used state-of-the-art technology to study wild animals but preferred to observe and track them by skiing or walking. He had his "own brown bear" that sometimes followed him in the forest–yes, a wild one. During his expeditions to Svalbard, he became famous when he hand-fed wild ice bears completely unarmed. In a phone conversation on December 19, 2018, he laughed and said to me, "Ice bears are not dangerous unless you don't show fear."

Pavlov, Mikhail Pavlovich

Mikhail Pavlovich Pavlov (1920–2009) was born in the village of Vereya, Ramensky district, near Moscow. As a well-known researcher of the ecology of acclimatized animal species, he was the inspirer and organizer of the rational reconstruction of hunting fauna at the hunting economy's present stage of development. He had a special interest in the wolf, and in 1982, the first edition of his famous book *The Wolf* was published. He was also a regular contributor to the magazine *Hunting and Hunting Economy*.

Sabaneev, Leonid Pavlovich

Leonid P. Sabaneev (1844–1898) was a Russian zoologist who made extensive contributions to the study of hunting in Russia. He set up *Hunter's Gazette* in 1888 and was the author of the enormously popular *Hunter's Calendar*, featuring valuable practical information. His work *Freshwater Fishes and Fishing in Russia* (1875) is considered a minor classic. He is also considered to be the first scientist to write about wolves in Russia. His well-researched book, published in 1876, contained detailed information about wolves and their damage to the Russian economy. It also dealt with wolf attacks on humans.

Bernt Lindqvist

Erik S. Nyholm

L.P. Sabaneev

Section II – References

A   **Adams J, Leonard J, Waits L.(2003).** Widespread occurrence of a domestic dog mitochondrial DNA haplotype in southeastern US coyotes. Molecular Ecology. 2003: 12:541–546.

Al-Sabi MNS, Rääf L, Osterman-Lind E, Uhlhorn H, Kapel CMO. (2018). Gastrointestinal helminths of gray wolves (Canis lupus lupus) from Sweden. Parasitol Res. 2018 Jun;117(6):1891–1898. doi: 10.1007/s00436-018-5881-z

Allen, Benjamin & Allen, Lee & Andrén, Henrik & Ballard, Guy & Boitani, Luigi & Engeman, Richard & Fleming, Peter & Ford, Adam & Haswell, Peter & Kowalczyk, Rafał & Linnell, John & David Mech, L & Parker, Daniel. (2017). Can we save large carnivores without losing large carnivore science?. Food Webs. 10.1016/j.fooweb.2017.02.008.

Allender Kent. The Siberian Husky. http://www.vargevass.com/websiberian/engels/breed/breedtypes.html.

Almberg, E. S., Cross, P. C., Dobson, A. P., Smith, D. W., & Hudson, P. J. (2012). Parasite invasion following host reintroduction: a case study of Yellowstone's wolves. Philosophical Transactions of the Royal Society B: Biological Sciences, 367(1604), 2840–2851. http://doi.org/10.1098/rstb.2011.0369

Andersen Ferron L. & Loveless Raymond M. (1978). Survival of Protoscolices of Echinococcus granulosus at Constant Temperatures. The Journal of Parasitology Vol. 64, No. 1 (Feb., 1978), pp. 78–82

Anderson, T. M., vonHoldt, B. M., Candille, S. I., Musiani, M., Greco, C., Stahler, D. R., Smith, D. W., Padhukasahasram, B., Randi, E., Leonard, J. A., Bustamante, C. D., Ostrander, E. A., Tang, H., Wayne, R. K., Barsh, G. S. (2009). Molecular and evolutionary history of melanism in North American gray wolves. Science (New York, N.Y.), 323(5919), 1339-43.

Axelsson Erik et al. (2013). The genomic signature of dog domestication reveals adaption to starch-rich diet. Nature vol 495 – 21 March 2013.

B   **Backeryd J. (2007).** Wolf attacks on dogs in Scandinavia 1995–2005. SLU, Uppsala 2007.

Baker, R. O. and R. M. Timm. (1998). Management of conflict between urban coyotes and humans in southern California. Pp. 229–312 in R. O. Baker and A. c. Crabb eds. Proc. 18th Vertebrate Pest Conference, University of California, Davis).

Ballard, W. B. et al. (1997). Ecology of wolves in relation to a migratory caribou herd in northwest Alaska. Wildl. Monogr. 135: 147.

Ballard, W. B. et al. (1998). Comparison of VHS and satellite telemetry for estimating sizes of wolf territories in northwest Alaska. Wildl. Soc. Bull. 26: 823829.

Barabash-Nikiforov, I.I. (1957). Zveri yugo-vostochnoi chastichernozemnovo tsentra [Animals in the southeastern part of Chernozem Center]. Voronezh.

Berryere Tom G., Kerns Julie A., Barsh Gregory S., Schmutz Sheila M. (2005). Association of an Agouti allele with fawn or sable coat color in domestic dogs. Mammalian Genome May 2005

Behdarvand Neda, Kaboli Mohammad, Ahmadi Mohsen, Nourani Elham, Salman Abdolrassoul Mahini, Aghbolaghi Marzieh Asadi . (2014). Spatial risk model and mitigation implications for wolf–human conflict in a highly modified agroecosystem in western Iran. Biological Conservation 177.

Behdarvand, Neda & Kaboli, Mohammad. (2015). Characteristics of Gray Wolf Attacks on Humans in an Altered Landscape in the West of Iran. Human Dimensions of Wildlife. 20. 1–11. 10.1080/10871209.2015.963747.

Berge Lars, (2018). Vargattacken (The wolf attack); Albert Bonniers Förlag; ISBN 978-91-0-016988-6

Berryere, Tom, Kerns, Julie, Barsh Gregory, Schmutz, Sheila. (2005). Association of an Agouti allele with fawn or sable coat color in domestic dogs. Mammalian genome : official journal of the International Mammalian Genome Society. 16. 262-72. 10.1007/s00335-004-2445-6.

Bibikov, Dimitry I. (1985). Волк Издательство "Наука" Москва 1985 (The Wolf).

Boren Zachary Davies. (2015), Coywolf: New coyote-wolf hybrid sees explosion in numbers. The Independent, Sunday 1 November 2015.<https://www.independent.co.uk/news/science/coywolf-new-coyote-wolf-hybrid-sees-explosion-in-numbers-a6717151.html> (visited: Nov. 20 2018).

Borg Karl. (1975). Viltsjukdomar; LTs förlag1975; ISBN 91-36-00595-9.

Brandshaw, Blackwell, Casy. (2009). Dominance in domestic dogs – useful construct or bad habit?

Brunetti Enrico, Kernb Peter, Vuittonc Dominique Angèle, Writing Panel for the WHO-IWGE. (2010). Expert consensus for the diagnosis and treatment of cystic and alveolar echinococcosis in humans. Acta Tropica, Volume 114, Issue 1, April 2010, Pages 1–16

Budke Christine M., Deplazes, Peter & Torgerson, Paul R. (2006). Global Socioeconomic Impact of Cystic Echinococcosis. *Emerging Infectious Diseases,* 12(2), 296–303. http://doi.org/10.3201/eid1202.050499

Budke, C. M., Carabin, H., Ndimubanzi, P. C., Nguyen, H., Rainwater, E., Dickey, M., ... Qian, M.-B. (2013). A Systematic Review of the Literature on Cystic Echinococcosis Frequency Worldwide and Its Associated Clinical Manifestations. The American Journal of Tropical Medicine and Hygiene, 88(6), 1011–1027. http://doi.org/10.4269/ajtmh.12-0692

C   **Cerda Jacey Roche and Ballweber Lora Rickard. (2018).** Confirmation of Echinococcus canadensis G8 and G10 in Idaho Gray Wolves (Canis lupus) and Cervids, Journal of Wildlife Diseases, 54(2), 2018.

Cherkasov, A. A. (1867). Zapiski okhotnika Vostochnoi Sibiri [Notes of a hunter in eastern Siberia]. Saint Petersburg.

Christiansen Per C., Wroe Stephen. (2007). Bite Forces and Evolutionary Adaptions to Feeding Echology in Carnivores. Ecology, 88(2), 347–358.

D   **Dale Miquelle, Stephens Philip, Smirnov E.N., Goodrich John, Zaumyslova O.Yu, Myslenkov, A.I.. (2005).** Tigers and Wolves in the Russian Far East: Competitive Exclusion, Functional Redundancy and Conservation Implications. 179–207.

de Menten B. (2010). Peisey-Nancroix : 593 moutons s'écrasent au pied d'une falaise <http://www.buvet-tedesalpages.be/2010/08/peisey-nancroix-593-moutons-s-ecrasent-au-pied-d-une-falaise.html> Accessed 11 Dec 2017.

de Vaca Cabeza. (1542). Adventures in the unknown interior of America. ISBN 978-0-8263-0656-2. Reprinted by The Cromwell-Collier Publishing Company in 1983.

Dethlefsen Clayton. (2015). Presentation at the wolf symposium in Wettringen, Germany. Western Predator Control Association.

Dethlefsen Clayton. (2016). Presentation at the open wolf symposium in Salo, Finland. Western Predator Control Association.

Dmitriev-Mamonov N.A. (1874). Hunting wolves and foxes with Pskovians. The Journal of Hunting, September 1874.

Dreger Dayna L. And Schmutz Sheila M. (2011). A Sine Insertion Causes the Blackand-Tan and Saddle Tan Phenotypes in Domestic Dogs. Journal of Heredity 2011:102(S1):S11–S18.

Dubey, J. P., Schares, G., & Ortega-Mora, L. M. (2007). Epidemiology and control of neosporosis and Neospora caninum. Clinical microbiology reviews, 20(2), 323–67.

Dubey JP; Jenkins MC; Rajendran C; Miska K; Ferreira LR; Martins J; Kwok OCH; Choudhary. (2011). "Gray Wolf (Canis lupus) is a natural definitive host for Neospora caninum". Veterinary Parasitology. 181 (2–4): 382–387.

E   **Eckert J, Deplazes P. (1999).** Alveolar echinococcosis in humans: The current situation in Central Europe and the need for countermeasures. Parasitol Today 1999;15:315–9.

Eklund Ann, Vicente López-Bao José, Tourani Mahdieh, Chapron Guillaume & Frank Jens. (2017). Limited evidence on the effectiveness of interventions to reduce livestock predation by large carnivores.

Scientific Reports,7: 2017. DOI:10.1038/s41598-017-02323-w

Engdal Vilde Arntzen. (2018). Phenotypic variation in past and present Scandinavian wolves (Canis lupus L.). Master Thesis, Ecology and evolution, Department of Biosciences. Faculty of Mathematics and Natural Sciences. University Of Oslo. December 2018.

European Union. (2014). Applying The Bern Convention On The Conservation Of European Wildlife And Natural Habitats To The Problem Of Hybridisation Between Wolves (Canis Lupus) And Domestic Dogs; Dec. 16. 2014.

EU Commission. (2007). Guidance document on the strict protection of animal species of Community interest under the Habitats Directive 92/43/EEC <http://ec.europa.eu/environment/nature/conservation/species/guidance/pdf/guidance_en.pdf>. Accessed 4 Dec 2017.

EU Commission (2014). Exploring Traditional Husbandry Methods to Reduce Wolf Predation on Free-Ranging Cattle in Portugal and Spain. <http://ec.europa.eu/environment/nature/conservation/species/carnivores/pdf/pa_iberia1_finalreport.pdf>. Accessed 3 Dec 2017.

EU Commission (2016). What is 'favourable conservation status' for species? Researchers clear up misinterpretations. 03 June 2016 Issue 457 <http://ec.europa.eu/environment/integration/research/newsalert/pdf/what_is_favourable_conservation_status_for_species_457na4_en.pdf>. Accessed 4 Dec 2017.

EVIRA. (2017). <https://www.evira.fi/elaimet/elainten-terveys-ja-elaintaudit/elaintaudit/luonnonvara-iset-elaimet/susien-kuolinsyyt/yhteenveto-eviraan-2001---2014-lahetettyjen-susien-kuolinsyista/>. Accessed 29 Dec 2017.

F   **Fanning Robert T Jr. (2007).** <https://www.skinnymoose.com/bbb/2010/03/10/panel-roundtable-canadian-gray-wolf-introduction-into-yellowstone/ (23.8.2018).

Feng Yongjie, Lu Yaoyao,Wang Yinghua,Liu Jing, Zhang Longxian, and Yang Yurong. (2016). Toxoplasma gondii and Neospora caninum in Free-Range Chickens in Henan Province of China. BioMed Research International, Volume 2016, Article ID 8290536, 5 pages. http://dx.doi.org/10.1155/2016/8290536

Flemming, H. F. von (1749). Der Vollkommene Teutsche Jäger. – Leipzig, Germany

Foreyt William J., Drew Mark L., Atkinson Mark , McCauley Deborah. (2009). Echinococcus granulosus in Gray Wolves and Ungulates in Idaho and Montana, USA. Journal of Wildlife Diseases, 45(4):1208-1212.

Frank Harry. (1980). Evolution of Canine Information Processing under Conditions of Natural and Artifical Processing; Z. Tierpsychology 53, 389–399.

Frank Harry. (1987). Man and Wolf. ISBN 90-6193-614-4.

Fritts, S. H. et al. (2003). "Wolves and humans", in Wolves: Behavior, ecology and conservation, eds. L. D. Mech, and L. Boitani, pp. 289–316, Chicago, Illinois: University of Chicago Press, Chicago.

Fuchs, B., Zimmermann, B., Wabakken, P., Bornstein, S., Månsson, J., Evans, A. L., ... Arnemo, J. M. (2016). Sarcoptic mange in the Scandinavian wolf Canis lupus population. BMC Veterinary Research, 12, 156. http://doi.org/10.1186/s12917-016-0780-y

Fuller, T. K. (1989). Population dynamics of wolves in northcentral Minnesota. Wildl. Monogr. 105: 141.

Fuller, T. K., L. D. Mech, and J. Fitts-Cochran. (2003). Wolf population dynamics. Pages 161–191. Wolves: behavior, ecology, and conservation. University of Chicago Press, Chicago, Illinois, USA

Fuoco, L. W., & C. Harlan. (2006). Wolf dogs kill owner, autopsy determines. Pittsburgh Post-Gazette, July 19 2006. Pittsburgh, PA.

G   **Galov, A., Fabbri, E., Caniglia, R., Arbanasić, H., Lapalombella, S., Florijančič, T., Bošković, I., Galaverni, M., & Randi, E. (2015).** First evidence of hybridization between golden jackal (Canis aureus) and domestic dog (Canis familiaris) as revealed by genetic markers. Royal Society Open Science DOI: 10.1098/rsos.150450.

Gasaway, W. (1989). Management of complex predator-prey systems in Alaska. In Wolf-prey dynamics and management. pp. 124–135. Wildlife Branch, British Columbia Ministry of Environment, Victoria.

Wildlife Working Report WR-40.

Geist,Valerius. (2007). When do wolves become dangerous to humans. Publication available at www. wolfeducationinternational.com

Geist,Valerius. *(2008).* Death by Wolves and the power of Myths: the Kenton Carnegie Tragedy. Fair Chase Vol. 23, No. 4. pp. 29–33.Winter issue.

Geist Valerius. (2016). Habituation, Taming, Social Dominance Assertions, and Habituation, and "Freedom of the Woods". Proc. 27th Vertebr. Pest Conf. Published at Univ. of Calif., Davis. 2016. pp. 38–43.

Geist Valerius. (2016b). A Brief History of Human-Predator Conflicts and Potent Lessons. Proc. 27th Vetebr, Pest. Conf. (R. M. Timm and R. A. Baldwin , Eds.) Published at U. Of California, Davis. pp. 3-12.

Geist Valerius. (2018). Speech: Big Game Forever Banquet and Wolf Symposium Grand Junction, Colorado August 11th 2018. <www.wolfeducationinternational.com>

Gillman Ollie. (2014). Horrific wolf attack in Chinese village leaves six people disfigured and one missing an ear after pack of five 'starving mad' beasts surrounded small farming community. MailOnline, published: 12:22 GMT, 13 August 2014. < https://www.dailymail.co.uk/news/article-2723818/Wolf-pack-attacks-Chinese-villagers-tearing-victim-s-ear-leaving-two-seriously-injured.html>Accessed Nov 20, 2018.

Gondim Louis F. P., McAllister M. M., Mateus-Pinilla N. E., Pitt W. C., Mech L. D., and Nelson M. E. (2004a). Transmission of Neospora caninum between wild and domestic animals. Journal of Parasitology: December 2004, Vol. 90, No. 6, pp. 1361–1365.

Gondim Louis F. P., McAllister Milton M., William CPittb William C., Zemlickac Doris E. (2004b). Coyotes (Canis latrans) are definitive hosts of Neospora caninum.   International Journal for Parasitology. Volume 34, Issue 2, February 2004, Pages 159–161.

Gondim Louis F. P. (2006). Neospora caninum in wildlife. Trends in Parasitology Volume 22, Issue 6, June 2006, Pages 247–252

Gordon, C. H., Banyard, A. C., Hussein, A., Laurenson, M. K., Malcolm, J. R., Marino, J., … Sillero-Zubiri, C. (2015). Canine Distemper in Endangered Ethiopian Wolves. Emerging Infectious Diseases, 21(5), 824–832. http://doi.org/10.3201/eid2105.141920

Gori Francesca, Armua-Fernandez Maria Teresa, Milanesi Pietro, Serafini Matteo, Mági Marta, Deplazes Peter, Macchioni Fabio. (2015). The occurrence of taeniids of wolves in Liguria (northern Italy). International Journal for Parasitology: Parasites and Wildlife 4 (2015) 252–255

Granlund Kaj. (2015); Das Europa der Wölfe, ISBN 978-952-93-6322-3.

Granlund Kaj. (2016); Steuert Der Mensch Auf Einen Konflikt Mit Wölfen Zu; Beiträge zur Jagd- und Wildforschung. Bd. 41.

Graves Will N. (2007). Wolves in Russia, Anxiety through Ages; ISBN 978-1-55059-332-7.

Graves Will N. & Lyon Ted B. (2018). The real wolf, Science, Politics, and Economics of Co-Existing with Wolves in Modern Times; ISBN 978-1-5107-1961-3.

H   **Hedrick PW (2009).** Wolf of a different color; Heredity 103, 435–436.

Heptner V.G. & Naumov N.P. (1967). Mammals of the Soviet Union, Volume II, Part la- Sirenia and carnivora (Sea Cows; Wolves and Bears); Smithsonian Insitution Libraries and The National Science Foundation, Washington, D.C.

Herré W. & Rohrs M. (1973). Haustiere – zoologisch gesehen; Gustav Fischer Verlag, Stuttgart.

Hindrikson Maris. Männil Peep, Ozolins Janis, Krzywinski Andrzej, Saarma Urvas. (2012). Bucking the Trend in Wolf-Dog Hybridization: First Evidence from Europe of Hybridization between Female Dogs and Male Wolves. October 3, 2012. https://doi.org/10.1371/journal.pone.0046465

Hirvelä-Koski Varpu, Haukisalmi Voitto, Kilpelä Seija-Sisko, Nylund Minna, Koski Perttu. (2003). Echinococcus granulosus in Finland. Veterinary Parasitology 111 (2003) 175–192

Hoensbroech Lothar Graf. (1952). Abseits vom Larm. Bayerischer Landwirtschafts Verlag, Munich, p 84.

Holmström C. (2017). 44 vargar hittades i vargräkning. (44 wolves was found) Vasabladet 22.12.2017

Huisman Nick. (2018). Another golden jackal in south-eastern Austria. European Wilderness Society, February 14, 2018. < https://wilderness-society.org/another-golden-jackal-in-south-eastern-austria/> Accessed Nov. 20, 2018.

Hämäläinen S, Kantele A, Arvonen M, Hakala T, Karhukorpi J, Heikkinen J, Berg E, Vanamo K, Tyrväinen E, Heiskanen-Kosma T, Oksanen A, Lavikainen A. An autochthonous case of cystic echinococcosis in Finland. (2015). Euro Surveill. 2015;20(42):pii=30043. DOI: http://dx.doi.org/10.2807/1560-7917. ES.2015.20.42.30043.

I **Iljin N. A. (1941).** Wolf-dog genetics. Genetics. 42. 359–414. 10.1007/BF02982879.

J **Janssens Luc, Spanoghe Inge, Miller Rebecca, Van Dongen Stefan. (2016).** Can orbital angle morphology distinguish dogs from wolves? Zoomorphology (2016) 135:149–158

Jarva Hanna, Lavikainen Antti, Henttonen Heikki, Meri Seppo. (2002). Uhkaavatko ekinokokit meitä? Duodecim, 118(20), 2083–2090.

Jedrzejewski Wlodzimierz, Schmidt Krzysztof, Theuerkauf Jorn, Jedrzejewska Bogumil and Kowalczyk Rafal. (2007). Territory size of wolves *Canis lupus*: linking local (Bialowieza Primeval Forest, Poland) and Holarctic-scale patterns. Ecography 30: 66–76, 2007

Jensen C., Pagh S., Vik Stronen A. (2017). Ulvehegn der virker (a wolf fence that works). University of Aaborg. Aktuel naturvidenskab nr. 4.

Jhala, Y.V. and D.K. Sharma. (1997). Child-lifting by wolves in eastern Uttar Pradesh, India. Journal of Wildlife Research 2(2):94–101.

Johnson, S. (2003). Fear in the brain. Discover Magazine, Mar. 1, 2003 issue, pp. 33–39.

Joly DO, Messier F. (2004). The distribution of Echinococcus granulosus in moose: evidence for parasite-induced vulnerability to predation by wolves? Oecologia August 2004, Volume 140, Issue 4, pp 586–590

K **Karamian M, Haghighi F, Hemmati M. (2017).** Genotyping of Cystic Hydatidosis Agents in Birjand, Eastern Iran, Mod Care J. 2017 ; 14(3):e64531. doi: 10.5812/modernc.64531.

Kaverznev V. (1933). The extermination of wolf. M., KOIZ, 1933. 107 s.

Kay Charles E. (1993). Wolves In The West. What the government does not want you to know about wolf recovery. Hunting Magazine, vol 42 1993.

Kay Charles E. (1995). An Alternative Interpretation of the Historical Evidence Relating to the Abundance of Wolves in the Yellowstone Ecosystem

Kay Charles E. (2009). Two Views of the Serengeti: One True, One Myth. Conservation and Society 7(2): 145–147, 2009

Kay Charles E. (2012). Do predators always kill substandard individuals. Muleycrazy.com, August 2012.

Kay Charles E. (2013). Keystone Predation And Tropic Cascades. Muleycrazy.com, December 2013.

Kay Charles E. (2015). Wolves and livestock. The Never Ending Battle. Muleycrazy.com, June 2015.

Klein, R. G. (1973). Ice-Age hunters of the Ukraine. Chicago. University of Chicago Press. 140 pp

Khosravi, Rasool & Kaboli, Mohammad & Imani, Jalil & Nourani, Elham. (2012). Morphometric variations of the skull in the Gray Wolf (Canis lupus) in Iran. Acta theriologica. 57. 10.1007/s13364-012-0089-6.

Khudyakov, P. I. (1937). Bor'ba s voikami v Vostochnoi Sibiri [Wolf control in East Siberia]. Irkutsk.

Klinghammer Erich & Patricia Ann Goodmann; Socialization and management of wolves in captivity.

Konyaev Sergey V., Yanagida Tetsuya, Ingovatova Galina M., Shoikhet Yakov N., Nakao Minoru, Sako Yasuhito, Bondarev Alexandr Y., Ito Akira. (2012). Molecular identification of human echinococcosis in the Altai region of Russia. Parasitology International 61 (2012) 711–714.

Kopaliani Natia et al. (2014). Gene Flow Between Wolf and Shepherd Dog Populations in Georgia (Caucasus); Journal of Heredity, 2014.

Korytin Sergei. (1990). Lehti "Ohota i ohotnitshje hozjaistvo" (Metsästys ja riistatalous) N:o 6, 1990, ss. 6–7 sekä N:o 7, 1990, ss. 12–14.

Kozlov V. (1966). Vargen pä Sibiriens skogsstäpper och dess utrotning. Krasnojarsk, 1966.

Krusjinskij L. (1977). Det biologiska underlaget för djurens förståndsverksamhet. Izd-vo MGU, 1977. 272 s.

Krushinski, L. V. (1980). Behavior of wolves. Behavior of the wolf. Pages 129–134 in Krushinski — his scientific works. Academy of Sciences, Moscow

Kudaktin A. (1977). The wolf in Western Caucasus. "Ochota i ochotn. chozjajstvo", Nr 9.

Kudaktin A. (1978). "Food Specialization of the Wolf, Hunting and Game Management Aug. 1978: 9–10.

Kutjerenko S., Zubkov Ju. (1980). Wolves in the southern parts of the Far East. Ochota i ochotn. chozj., 1980:1, s. 20–23.

L   **Laitinen Marianna. (2012);** They are a family - A female and its four pups. Wild animals presented in BBC's programs. Master's thesis, University of Tampere, Finland. (Original Finnish text: He ovat perhe - Emo ja neljä pentua. Eläinten representaatiot BBC:n luontodokumentissa).

Landry J-M., Millischer G., Borelli J-L., Lyon G. (2014). Studying internal and external factors that may influence livestock guarding dogs' efficiency. Carnivore Damage Prevention, issue 10, spring 2014.

Lappalainen Antti. (2005). Suden jäljet", The Tracks of the Wolf, ISBN 952-5118-79-7.

Larter Nicholas C., Nagy John A., Bartareu Tad M. (2012). Growth in Skull Length and Width of the Arctic Wolf: Comparison of Models and Ontogeny of Sexual Size Dimorphism Arctioc VOL. 65, NO. 2 (JUNE 2012) P. 207 – 213.

Lavikainen Antti, Laaksonen Sauli, Beckmen Kimberlee, Oksanen Antti, Isomursu Marja, Meri Seppo. (2011). Molecular identification of Taenia spp. in wolves (Canis lupus), brown bears (Ursus arctos) and cervids from North Europe and Alaska. Parasitology International, Volume 60, Issue 3, September 2011, Pages 289–295.

Lazarevski, V.M. (1876). "On the destruction of the wolf by livestock and game and the destruction of the wolf", St. Petersburg, 1876. Ministry of Internal affairs of the Russian Empire (archives). 71 pages.

Le Monde des Pyrenees. (2016). Prédations et dégâts des loups en 2016 <https://www.pyrenees-pireneus.com/Faune/Loups/Europe/France/Predations-Degats-Indemnisation/2016/Predation-degats-Loups-2016.php>. Accessed 9 Jan 2018.

Li Tiaoying, Ito Akira, Pengcuo Renqing, Sako Yasuhito, Chen Xingwang, Qiu Dongchuan, Xiao Ning, Craig Philip S. (2011). Post-Treatment Follow-Up Study of Abdominal Cystic Echinococcosis in Tibetan Communities of Northwest Sichuan Province, China. PLOS, Published: October 25, 2011.

Liberg O., Chapron G., Wabakken P., Pedersen H.C., Hobbs N.T. & Sand H. (2012). Shoot, shovel and shut up: cryptic poaching slows restoration of a large carnivore in Europe. Proceedings of the Royal Society of London B, 279,910-915. DOI: 10.1098/rspb.2011.1275. Published 25 January 2012

Lindqvist Bernt. (2008a). Varg och vargjakt. Available only from the author.

Lindqvist Bernt. (2008b). Rovdjur och biologisk mångfald, En konsekvensanalys. Available only from the author.

Lucius R, Bilger B. (1995). Echinococcus multilocularis in German: Increased awareness or spreading of a parasite? Parasitol Today 1995;11: 430–4.

M   **Makridin, V.P. (1959).** Materialy po biologii volka v tundrakhNenetskovo Natsional'novo Okruga [Materials on the biology of the wolf in the tundras of the Nenets National Region]. Zool. Zhurn., 38, No. 2.

Moscow.

Makridin V. (1960). Vargen i nordområdena och dess bekämpning. Krasnojarsk, 1960. 74 p.

McFarland David. (1982). Oxford Companion to Animal Behavior – May 6, 1982

McKinney Michael L. (2006). Urbanization as a major cause of biotic homogenization; January 2006.

McNay Mark E. (2002). A Case History Of Wolf-Human Encounters In Alaska and Canada. Alaska Department of Fish and Game Wildlife Technical Bulletin 13 2002

Marvin, N.Ya. (1959). Mlekopitayushchie Karelii [Mammals of Karelia]. Petrozavodsk.

Mech David. (1977). Wolf-pack buffer zones as prey reservoirs. "Science", 198:4314, pp. 320–321.

Mech David & Boitani Luigi. (2001). Wolves: Behaviour, Ecology and Conservation. p. 448. ISBN 0-226-51696-2.

Mech David L. et al. (2011). Use of cranial characters in taxonomy of the Minnesota wolf (Canis sp.); Published by NRC Research Press.

Mech David L. (2012). Is science in danger of sanctifying the wolf? Biological Conservation 150 (2012) 143–149.

Mech David L. (2017). Where can wolves live and how can we live with them? Biological Conservation, volume 210, Part A, June 2017, Pages 310-317.

Miklósi A, Kubinyi E, Topál J, Gácsi M, Virányi Z, Csányi V. (2003). A simple reason for a big difference: wolves do not look back at humans, but dogs do. Department of Ethology, Eötvös University, Budapest.

Milenkovic M. et al. (2006). Cases of spontaneous interbreeding of wolf and domestic dog in the region of southeast Banat (Serbia); Arch. Biol. Sci., Belgrade, 58 (4), 225–231.

Montana official state website. <https://mhs.mt.gov/research/collections/newspapers/extra/wolves>. Accessed 18 Aug 2018.

Monzon J. et al. (2014). Assessment of coyote-wolf-dog admixture using ancestry-informative diagnostic SNPs. Mol.Ecol.23(1):182–197.

Moriceau Jean-Marc. (2007). Histoire du méchant loup : 3 000 attaques sur l'homme en France (XVe-XXe siècle) Broché – 6 June 2007. ISBN 978-2213628806

Moriceau Jean-Marc. (2014). The Wolf Threat in France from the Middle Ages to the Twentieth Century. 2014. <hal-01011915>

Moura,A.E. et al. (2013). Unregulated hunting and genetic recovery from a severe population decline: the cautionary case of Bulgarian wolves. Conservation Genetics 15(2):405–417.DOI: 10.1007/s10592-013-0547-y.

N   **Nazarova N. (1978).** The Wolf and the Spreading of Diseases. Hunting and Game Management Nov. 1978: 24-25.

Neda Behdarvand et al. (2014). Spatial risk model and mitigation implications for wolf–human conflict in a highly modified agroecosystem in western Iran: Biological Conservation 177 156–164.

Nickel R. et al. (1977). Lehrbuch der Anatomie der Haustiere, Band I; Verlag Paul Parey, 1977.

Nygren Kaarlo. (2008). Suden kääntöpuoli; Advectis 2008.

O   **Okarma Henryk & Buchalczyk, Tadeuz. (1993).** Craniometrical characteristics of wolves Canis lupus from Poland. Acta Theriologica 38 (3): 253–262.

Oriani A., and M. Comincini. (2002). Living with death in the 1700s. Paper presented at the Seminar Living Death Settecento, organized by the Italian Society of Studies on Century XVIII, Santa Margherita Ligure, 30 Sept - 2 Oct 2002. <http://www.storiadellafauna.it/scaffale/testi/oriani/oria_comi.htm>

Osipov. (1989). Susien jälkien ja polkujen tunnistaminen: Metsästys ja riistatalous, maaliskuu 1989: 6–10.

P   **Pavlov Mikhail P. (1982).** The Wolf in Game Management. First edition 1982. Agropromizdat, Moscow,

Peacher Amanda. (2016). Wolf Population Booming In Oregon 5 Years After OR-7 Began His Journey, Oregon Public Broadcasting, Nov. 3. 2016 (http://www.opb.org/news/article/oregon-wolf-7-population-boom/).

Petersen, E., Lebech, M., Jensen, L., Lind, P., Rask, M., Bagger, P., Uggla, A. (1999). Neospora caninum Infection and Repeated Abortions in Humans. Emerging Infectious Diseases, 5(2), 278–280. https://dx.doi.org/10.3201/eid0502.990215.

Phys.Org (2017). Wolves to the slaughter: France approves cull to save sheep. <https://phys.org/news/2017-07-wolves-slaughter-france-cull-sheep.html>. Accessed 28 Jan 2018.

Pulliainen Erkki, (1965). Studies on the wolf (Canis lupus L.) in Finland. Doctoral thesis, University of Helsinki, 1965.

Pålsson Elis. (1984). Bibikov: Поведение волк сборник научных трудов (Wolves behavior, collection of scientific papers). Translated into Swedish.

Pålsson Elis. (1987). Pattedyrene På Kola; Vadsö, Miljövernavdelingen Kirkenes, Sör-Varanger Museum, 1987.

Pålsson Elis. (2003). Vargens näringssök och människan, ISBN 01-631-3651-1 (reports from Michail Pavlov's wolf translated into Swedish).

R   **Radinger Elli. H.** Wieviel Wolf steckt noch in unseren Hunden? Autorenhaus Verlag ISBN 978-3-86671-107-5.

Rajesh, R., Dalip, D. S., Anupam, J., & Jaisiram, A. (2013). Effectiveness of Puncture-Aspiration-Injection-Reaspiration in the Treatment of Hepatic Hydatid Cysts. Iranian Journal of Radiology, 10(2), 68–73. http://doi.org/10.5812/iranjradiol.7370

Rajpurohit, K.S. (1999). Child lifting: Wolves in Hazaribagh, India. Ambio 28(2):162–166.

Randi E, Hulva P, Fabbri E, Galaverni M, Galov A, Kusak J, et al. (2014) Multilocus Detection of Wolf x Dog Hybridization in Italy, and Guidelines for Marker Selection. PLoS ONE 9(1): e86409. https://doi.org/10.1371/journal.pone.0086409

Rejón R (2016). La situación en Catalunya (the Situation in Catalonia) <http://www.eldiario.es/sociedad/ataques-ganado-suponen-cabana-espanola_0_541045973.html>. Accessed 28 Jan 2018.

Remington Thomas K. Wolf: What's to misunderstand; ISBN 978-1-50539-709-3.

Rinaldi L, Maurelli MP, Veneziano V, Capuano F, Perugini AG, Cringoli S. (2008). The role of cattle in the epidemiology of Echinococcus granulosus in an endemic area of southern Italy. Parasitol Res. 2008 Jun;103(1):175-9.

Rozell Ned. (2014). Solving the mystery of the South Fork wolf Article Number: 2,210 March 6, 2014, University of Alaska, Fairbanks; <http://www.gi.alaska.edu/alaska-science-forum/solving-mystery-south-fork-wolf>. Accessed 24 Aug 2018.

Rudnev, G.P. (1950). Zoonoses. Moscow.

Rutledge L. Y., Devillard S., Boone J. Q., Hohenlohe P. A., White B. N. (2015). "RAD sequencing and genomic simulations resolve hybrid origins within North American Canis". Biology Letters. 11: 1–4. doi:10.1098/rsbl.2015.0303. PMC 4528444. PMID 26156129.

S   **Sabaneev, Leonid Pavlovich. (1876).** Predatory animals. (Охотничьи звери). Republished by Physiculture and sports, 1988, 480 pages.

Satunin, K.A. (1915). Mammals of the Caucasian region. Tiflis.

Schenkel, Rudolf. (1947). Ausdrucks-Studien an Wölfen. Behaviour 1: 81–129.

Schenkel, Rudolf. (1967). Submission: Its Features and Function in the Wolf and Dog. Zoologist, 7:319–329.

Schmutz Sheila M., Berryere T. G., Ellinwood N. M., Kerns J. A., and Barsh G. S. (2003). MC1R Studies in Dogs With Melanistic Mask or Brindle Patterns.

Schmutz Sheila M., Berryere Thomas G., Barta Jodi L., Reddick Kimberley D., and Schmutz Josef K. (2007). Agouti Sequence Polymorphisms in Coyotes, Wolves and Dogs Suggest Hybridization. Journal of Heredity 2007:98(4):351–355

Schubel A.(1954) Ein Beitrag zur Morphologie des Wolfsschädels: Wissenschaftliche Zeitschrift der Universität Greifswald, Jahrgang III 1953/54.

Semenov, B.T. (1954). Volki Arkhangel'skoi oblasti i ikh istreblenie (Wolves of Arkhangel'sk district and their destruction). Arkhangel'sk.

Sikku Olov J. & Torp Eivind. Vargen är värst, traditionell samisk kunskap om rovdjur ISBN 978-91-7948-216-9.

Silva Rodrigo & Machado Gustavo. (2016). Canine neosporosis: perspectives on pathogenesis and management. Veterinary Medicine: Research and Reports. 26. April 2016.

Silver JR, (2007). Spinal injuries resulting from horse riding accidents. Spinal Cord (2002) 40, 264 ± 27.

Sinclair, A.R.E., C. Packer, S.A.R. Mduma and J.M. Fryxell (eds.). (2008). Serengeti III: Human Impacts on Ecosystem Dynamics. Chicago: University of Chicago Press. 2008. x+522 pp. (Hardcover). ISBN 978-0- 226-760339. (Paperback). ISBN 978-0-226-76034-6.

Stahl Earl. (2016). Wolves At Your Door. ISBN 978-1532823299.

Stewart Will. (2016). The world's toughest school run: Children forced to arm themselves with axes to fend off WOLVES and BEARS in Russia. MailOnline published: 16:02 GMT, 8 November 2016. <https://www.dailymail.co.uk/news/article-3917044/The-world-s-toughest-school-run-Children-forced-arm-axes-fend-WOLVES-BEARS-Russia.html>Accessed Nov 20, 2018.

St. John F. A. V., Keane A. M., Edwards-Jones G., Jones L., Yarnell R. W., and Jones J. P. (2012). Identifying indicators of illegal behavior: carnivore killing in human-managed landscapes. Proceedings of the Royal Society B-Biological Sciences, 279, 804–812.

Stronen Astrid V. & Paquet Paul C. (2013). Perspectives on the conservation of wild hybrids; Biological Conservation 167 (2013) 390–395.

Sudakov Dmitry. (2006). Russian police employ wolves for service. Pravda, 25 April 2006. <http://www.pravdareport.com/society/stories/25-04-2006/79498-wolf-0/>

Sundqvist Anna-Karin, (2008). Conservation Genetics of Wolves and their Relationship with Dogs; ISBN 978-91-554-7064-7.

Suutarinen J., Kojola I. (2017). Poaching regulates the legally hunted wolf population in Finland. Biological Conservation. 215. 11-18. 10.1016/j.biocon.2017.08.031.

T   **Taha Biniamin and Hassen Anwar. (2018).** The Prevalence of Cystic Echinococcosis in Cattle Slaughtered in Sebeta Municipal Abattoir, Central Ethiopia. Haramaya University, College of Veterinary Medicine, Haramaya, Ethiopia.

Temple Stanley A. (1987). Do Predators Always Capture Substandard Individuals Disproportionately From Prey Populations? Ecology, Volume 68, Issue 3, June 1987, Pages 669–674

Teperi Jouko. (1977). Sudet Suomen rintamaiden ihmisten uhkana 1800-luvulla. Suomen historiallinen seura. ISBN 951-9254-10-2.

Theberge, J. B. & M. T. Theberge (2004). The wolves of Algonquin Park, a 12 Year Ecological Study, Department of Geography, Publication Series Number 56, University of Waterloo, Ontario

Torgerson P. R. (2013). The emergence of echinococcosis in central Asia. Section of Epidemiology, Vetsuisse Faculty, University of Zurich.

Toverud Lars. (2018). Nationen <http://www.nationen.no/debatt/hva-foregar-i-julussa-reviret/>. Accessed 14 Sep. 2018.

V   **von Holdt Bridgett M. (2013).** Identification of recent hybridization between gray wolves and domesticated dogs by SNP genotyping; Mammal Genome (2013) 24:80–88.

W   **Walton, L. R. et al. (2001).** Movement patterns of barrenground wolves in the central Canadian Arctic. J. Mammal. 82: 867876.

Warfield D. (1973). The study of hearing in animals. In: W Gay, ed., Methods of Animal Experimentation, IV. Academic Press, London, pp 43-143.

Wayne Robert K., Bridgett M. von Holdt, James A. Cahill, Zhenxin Fan, Ilan Gronau, Jacqueline Robinson, John P. Pollinger, Beth Shapiro, Jeff Wall. (2016). Whole-genome sequence analysis shows that two endemic species of North American wolf are admixtures of the coyote and gray wolf; Science Advances 27 Jul 2016: Vol. 2, no. 7, e1501714 DOI: 10.1126/sciadv.1501714.

Wayne Robert K., Małgorzata Pilot, Claudia Greco, Bridgett M. vonHoldt, Ettore Randi, Elaine A. Ostrander. (2018). Widespread, long-term admixture between Grey wolves and domestic dogs across Eurasia and its implications for the conservation status of hybrids; Evolutionary Applications published by John Wiley & Sons Ltd; DOI: 10.1111/eva.12595; 2018.

WHO. (2014). Rabies Fact Sheet N°99, http://www.who.int/mediacentre/factsheets/fs099/en/ (2015.2.28).

Williams C.K., G. Ericsson and T.A. Heberlein. (2002). A Quantitative Summary of Attitudes toward Wolves and Their Reintroduction (1972-2000). Wildlife Society Bulletin, 30(2): 575–584.

Z   **Zhenxin Fan et al. (2016).** Worldwide patterns of genomic variation and admixture in gray wolves. Genome Research 26: 163–173, Advance December 17,2015, DOI:10.1101/gr.197517.115.

Zimen E. (1976). Verhaltens-Modell im Ökosystem Wölfe. "Bild. wiss.", 13:1, 36–45.

Section III – Internet links

A1   < https://www.youtube.com/watch?v=8w0lzWZYzAk> (Oct. 16.2018). Visited Nov. 21, 2018.

A2   <http://www.cfsph.iastate.edu/DiseaseInfo/disease.php?name=echinococcosis&lang=en> Visited Nov. 21, 2018.

A3   <http://www.buvettedesalpages.be/2010/08/peisey-nancroix-593-moutons-s-ecrasent-au-pied-d-une-falaise.html> Visited Nov. 28, 2018.

A4   <http://www.vargfakta.se/nyheter/52-lamm-och-far-vargdodade-tyskland/> Visited Nov. 29, 2018.

A5   < https://news.nationalgeographic.com/2016/03/160325-wolf-pack-kills-19-wolves-surplus-killing-wyoming/> Visited Nov. 29, 2018.

A6   <https://www.luke.fi/en/natural-resources/game-and-hunting/finnish-forest-reindeer/>

A7   <https://www.theguardian.com/world/2017/feb/25/europe-wolf-population-finland-culling-protection> Accessed 17 Sep 2018.

A8   <http://www.unicaen.fr/homme_et_loup/detail.php?id=2562> Accessed 30 Nov 2018.

A9   <http://www.unicaen.fr/homme_et_loup/_en/index.php> Accessed 30 Nov 2018.

A10   <https://www.expressen.se/nyheter/har-biter-vargarna-flickan-pa-kolmarden/> Accessed 30 Nov 2018.

A11   <http://www.capitalpress.com/Oregon/20180928/wolves-kill-guard-dog-at-sw-oregon-ranch> Accessed 30 Nov 2018.

A12   <https://www.jaktojagare.se/kategorier/aktuellt/bjallror-pa-hundar-och-lapptyg-vid-hagar-inget-skydd-mot-varg-20051209/> Accessed 10 Nov 2018.

A13   <http://riistahavainnot.fi/suurpedot/suurpetotutkimus/pannoitetut> Accessed 10 Nov 2018.

A14   <https://www.theguardian.com/cities/2014/feb/25/city-stress-mental-health-rural-kind> Accessed 30 Nov 2018.

A15   < https://www.thenewamerican.com/print-magazine/item/30138-ranchers-face-wolves-at-the-gate> Accessed 30 Nov 2018.

A16   <https://www.nps.gov/yell/learn/ys-24-1-yellowstone-wolf-facts.htm> Accessed 30 Nov 2018.

A17 < http://www.macroevolution.net/wolf-dog-hybrids.html> Accessed 30 Nov 2018.

A18 <http://www.nanomatic.fi/allwolf/US/de01.jpg> Accessed 30 Nov 2018.

A19 <http://www.lehtiluukku.fi/lehti/metsastaja/2-2013/37136.html> Accessed 29 Nov 2018.

A20 <https://www.google.fi/maps/@61.6932191,24.8697324,7z/data=!4m2!6m1!1szSWfSrrqpJXA.k190SD-l8ah2Y?hl=en> Accessed 12 Dec 2018.

A21 <https://youtu.be/qy6Pca3ihuw> Accessed 15 Dec 2018.

A22 < https://www.skinnymoose.com/bbb/files/2011/09/WashingtonStatewolfnecropsy.pdf> Accessed 3 Dec 2018.

A23 <http://www.nanomatic.fi/allwolf/US/danes.jpg>Accessed 12 Dec 2018.

A24 < http://idahoforwildlife.com/files/pdf/Do_predators_always_kill_substandard_Individuals_2-2013.pdf> Accessed 24 Dec 2018.

A25 < https://www.svt.se/nyheter/lokalt/varmland/jagare-hotade-efter-vargavlivning> Accessed Dec 21, 2018.

A26< http://www.tunturisusi.com/laumaelain.htm> Accessed 5 Jan 2019.

A27< https://www.who.int/features/factfiles/neurocysticercosis/en/> Accessed 12 Jan 2019.

A28< https://www.cdc.gov/parasites/cysticercosis/index.html> Accessed 12 Jan 2019.

A29< https://www.msdvetmanual.com/generalized-conditions/neosporosis/overview-of-neosporosis>

Section IV – Obsolete Russian Units of Measurement

Cyrillic	Transliteration	Translation	Metric	English value
тоучка	tochka	point	0.254 mm	$^1/_{100}$ inch
линия	liniya	line	2.54 mm	$^1/_{10}$ inch
дюйм	dyuim	inch	2.54 cm	1 inch
вершок	vershok	tip, top	4.445 cm	$1\,^3/_4$ inch
пядь, четверть	piad, chetvert	palm, quarter	17.78 cm	7 inch
фут	fut	foot	30.48 cm	1 ft
аршин	arshin	yard	71.12 cm	$2\,^1/_3$ ft
сажень	sazhen	fathom	2.1336 m	7 ft
верста	versta	turn (of plough)	1.0668 km	3,500 ft
миля	milya	mile	7.4676 km	24,500 ft

9 789529 413522